Stories of Predation

60 Years of Watching Wildlife

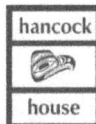

hancock

house

hancock

house

ISBN-13: 978-0-88839-438-5 [trade hardback]
ISBN-13: 978-0-88839-435-4 [trade paperback]
ISBN-13: 978-0-88839-313-5 [epub]
Copyright © 2021 Dick Dekker

Library and Archives Canada Cataloguing in Publication

Title: Stories of predation : sixty years of watching wildlife / Dick Dekker.

Other titles: Sixty years of watching wildlife | 60 years of watching wildlife

Names: Dekker, Dick, author.

Description: Includes bibliographical references and index.

Identifiers: Canadiana (print) 20200344978 | Canadiana (ebook) 20200345133 | ISBN 9780888394354 (trade paperback) | ISBN 9780888393135 (epub)

Subjects: LCSH: Dekker, Dick. | LCSH: Naturalists—Canada—Biography. | LCSH: Predation (Biology)— Canada. | LCSH: Wildlife watching—Canada. | LCSH: Animals—Canada. | LCGFT: Autobiographies. Classification: LCC QH31.D45 A3 2020 | DDC 508.092—dc23

Cover Design: Paul Ditters

Editing & photographs by the author unless otherwise stated

Printed in the USA

We acknowledge the financial support of the Government of Canada through the Canada Book Fund and the Canada Council for the Arts, and of the Province of British Columbia through the British Columbia Arts Council and the Book Publishing Tax Credit.

Hancock House gratefully acknowledges the Halkomelem Speaking Peoples whose unceded traditional territories our offices reside upon.

HANCOCK HOUSE PUBLISHERS LTD.
19313 Zero Avenue, Surrey, B.C. Canada V3Z 9R9
#104-4550 Birch Bay-Lynden Rd, Blaine, WA, U.S.A. 98230-9436
(800) 938-1114   Fax (800) 983-2262
www.hancockhouse.com   info@hancockhouse.com

Stories of Predation

60 Years of Watching Wildlife

DICK DEKKER

Table of Contents

The Fear Factor

The view from the hillside overlooking Jasper Park's lower Athabasca Valley is magnificent. The west-facing slopes of Roche Miette are glowing in the late March sun. On the uneven mountain meadow below the hill there are some thirty elk, grazing peacefully. Suddenly they become alert, ears pricked up like antennae, all eyes looking intently to the edge of the woods. Mesmerized, I focus my binoculars in the hope of discovering the cause of their disturbance. Have they become aware of the approach of a predator? Moments later, the herd takes fright and flees, bunching together. But they do not go far, and come to a hesitant halt. Looking back at the woods, their heads turn in unison as if they are following a chase hidden from view in the trees. Presently, the elk relax and resume grazing as if nothing had happened.

Disappointed not to have seen what I was hoping to see—a pack of wolves streaking after their prey—I wait another twenty minutes before descending the hill and following my usual trail to the cabin in the woods below.

An hour or so later, I return to the lookout and sit down on a makeshift seat. Through binoculars, I carefully scan the flats and the ice-bound Snake Indian River. The elk have gone. When the squawking of a raven draws my attention to the far side of the meadow, I discover two of the black rascals perched in the trees. Is there something going on there? Mindful of the elk's alarm earlier that evening, I recall that all of them were looking into that same direction. Presently, another scavenger arrives, an adult bald eagle that alights on a spruce top, its white head contrasting brightly with the evergreen background. The eagle probably saw the ravens gather from afar and has come up to share in a kill they might have discovered.

My curiosity piqued, I go downhill and quietly walk across the meadow to the edge of the woods. Nothing moves, not even a raven, and the eagle has already departed. But then, I catch the telltale white-and-black flash of a magpie. Near the spot where it flushes, behind some bushes, I behold a sight that makes me catch my breath: the bloody ribcage of an animal, like a wet, crimson tent protruding from the dry grass. It is the carcass of a just-killed mule deer, the skin torn off, the innards and some muscle already removed.

Where are the killers? There are no tracks to tell the story, for the winter's snow is practically gone. Drops and streaks of blood stain the still-frozen ground. In the immediate surroundings, there are a few remnant patches of crusty drifts. One of them holds the signature of *Canis lupus*, a single paw print, red on white.

For the remainder of the evening, I wait on the lookout hill. Winged scavengers fly off and on. And at dusk, I catch a glimpse of two wolves trotting across the meadow. Presently, I try a howl, just a brief and tentative imitation, but there is no answer. Wolves seldom vocalize when they are on a kill.

The next morning, I check out the carcass. All edible matter is gone, and the bones are scattered. There is no sign of the wolves. Although the entire chase and kill sequence had been hidden from my eyes, the above observation is one of the very few times that a successful hunt took place in my immediate vicinity, at least as far I am aware. No doubt, other kills may have been made when my back was turned or in a matter of minutes before or after my arrival on the lookout hill.

One stormy winter morning, while Peter DeMulder and I were walking in the lee of a wooded gully, we surprised a black wolf at close range, dashing away between the trees. Following its tracks, we found a dead deer, a white-tailed doe still warm to the touch, lying a little lower on the slope. The body appeared to be untouched except for a light scratch where the predator's fangs might have grazed the skin. The victim was a fawn, barely half a year old. Following the flagging tail of its mother and upon emerging from the woods, the fleeing fawn had been rudely intercepted. The cause of death may well have been shock, arresting its racing heart, snuffing out its tender life like a candle in a gust of wind.

As related elsewhere in these chapters, I have, on a few occasions, been in the way of a hunt, involuntarily causing a wolf to abort the chase, thus saving a deer from capture. Passing me by at arm's length, after a moment's hesitation, these deer continued their headlong flight, their intense fear frozen in glassy, unseeing eyes. One day I shared their fear, a deeply moving experience.

The timing of that memorable event was again a late March evening, when I was sitting on my usual spot overlooking the Snake Indian River flats. Two or three hundred metres away, a deer came running out of the shore woods, raced across the frozen river and, after a moment of hesitation, entered an open water hole, to drop out of sight.

Seconds later, on the trail of the deer, two black wolves burst out of the trees. Leaping over the snow-covered ice, they came to an abrupt halt at the water hole. The pair were followed by eleven other wolves, strung out as if they had been engaged in a long chase. All of them were black and belonged to the local pack of thirteen. Black is a common colour of the Jasper wolves, but this happened to be the largest group of blacks I had ever seen in the park. Some of them gingerly stepped down to the water's edge, while one of them hurried on downriver to another water hole, as if he expected the deer to emerge there. Other wolves spread out over the expanse of frozen river, describing a wide circle, nose to the snow, searching for fresh scent. After a few minutes, all wolves returned to the same stretch of shoreline woods from where they had come and disappeared from view.

Twice within the next hour or so, the wolves reappeared on the river. Some of them reinvestigated the waterhole, others ran in a semi-circle over the ice, downriver, nose to the snow. By the time the pack had once more retreated into the woods, the brief winter day was drawing to a close, leaving me with the burning question of what could have happened to the deer.

Watching from the lookout, I continued to scan the braided river channels through binoculars. Since I had not seen the deer leave the water hole, could it still be there? Eager to know and investigate before it got too dark, I descended the hillside and briskly set out across the frozen river that had expanded well beyond its summertime channel. Extreme cold during the past winter months had frozen the river to the bottom, forcing the water upwards through cracks in the thick ice. The overflow had repeatedly inundated the riverbanks, pushing the sheet of surface ice into the shoreline woods. For extra support while crossing slippery sections, I picked up a long pole and dragged it along with me, by way of security in case the ice gave way. Gingerly stepping across the uneven surface, I noticed that the river's main channel had caved in, forming a shallow depression, portions of which had opened up. The hole in which the deer has disappeared turned out to be no bigger than about eight metres long and half as wide. The snow along the edge was packed with wolf tracks, but there was no sign of the deer. On the downstream side of the hole, part of the sloping ice shelf had broken away, leaving an airspace over swiftly flowing water. Was the deer still hiding in that cave? Or had it already been swept away towards its death under the overhanging ice? I shall never know.

Just after I turned to leave, I caught a glimpse of two shadowy figures running away and vanishing between the trunks of trees encased in the ice. The wolves! They must have heard my footsteps and had come to investigate. What if they had mistaken me for easy prey? The image of the big pack stayed on my mind; thirteen black predators eager to make a kill.

In the woods, a wolf began to howl and bark. Was it to warn their own kind or a threat meant for me? Breaking out in cold sweat, I forced myself to slow down, to stop worrying unduly and pretend to be confident and at ease. Suddenly, I halted, with a shock of paralyzing fear. In the snow ahead, on the edge of the woods, I perceived four black silhouettes, like wolves watching and waiting. My myopic eyes have poor night vision. In the deepening dusk, I groped for the binoculars. A quick glance revealed that I was looking at the broken stumps of trees protruding from the ice.

With immense relief, I finally reached the shore from where I had started out on the river and clambered onto the open bank, well on the way to the warm cabin. Was my fear justified? Fact is that wolf attacks on people are extremely rare, but they do happen and could become more common in parks where wolves have been habituated to human visitors. In my case, the local pack of all-blacks had met me before and probably realized that I was harmless.

Safely back at the cabin I could afford to set all fear and risk aside. Was my deeply felt terror a throwback to our atavistic, stone-age past when humans were prey as well as hunters? Not necessarily. We don't have to go back that far at all. The travelogues of the first Europeans who canoed the rivers of northwestern Canada in the late 1700s and early 1800s had much to say about the insecurities of the Indigenous people who accompanied them on their journeys into the unknown. Both Alexander Mackenzie and Samuel Hearne had problems overcoming the visceral fears of their native guides, hesitant to enter enemy country. Tribes they met along the way were hostile and defensive, aiming their bows and holding their spears at the ready, while their women and children fled into the woods. Mackenzie needed all his diplomatic skills to secure their trust and cooperation. The north woods of Canada were certainly not a no-man's land. The sub-arctic reaches of the Mackenzie and Coppermine rivers were inhabited by Indigenous groups, some of which had never seen a white man.

Fear of aggressive or abusive strangers is still typical for modern-day city people, who tend to stay away from certain neighbourhoods, especially after dark. There is a parallel here between the attitude of humans and animals such as elk. During my long-term observations in the lower Snake Indian Valley, I noted that wintering elk avoided certain parts of the flats although the forage there was rich and untouched. These meadows were typically small, not much more than a hundred metres wide but hemmed in by evergreen woods. Afraid of being surprised at close range, the herd of cow elk and their calves also avoided a meadow at the base of a hillside trail that was part of the wolves' regular circuit. The elk's risk-based habitat choices made sense to me. In recognition of this same phenomenon, a professional field biologist has coined the term 'landscape of fear.'

Like deer, elk that are under direct attack from wolves commonly take refuge in water. During winter, when lakes and rivers are frozen, elk cows, yearlings, and calves draw together for protection, following the principle that there is safety in numbers and that two sets of eyes see more than one. To reduce the risk of ambush, the herd frequents open country, where their ancient nemesis can be spotted in good time. At the approach of wolves, the herd flees and heads for a steep ridge or escarpment, where the scared animals make a stand. Turning their vulnerable back side toward the edge of the precipice, they are ready to defend themselves with their sharp front hooves.

By contrast, moose seek solitude. Travelling as little as possible so as to leave a minimum of tracks, the lone moose beds down upwind, on a spot from where it can watch its back trail and see as well as smell possible pursuers.

Quite unlike the moose, mountain sheep have excellent eyesight. Afraid of being ambushed by predators, bighorn rams and ewes spend all year in open country, but they tend to remain near rocky terrain to which they can escape, where wolves would have trouble finding footing. By the same token, to avoid predators, woodland caribou withdraw to alpine tundra or snowy muskegs, where wolves are scarce. Quite apart from such collective antipredator strategies, the maternal instinct of pregnant herbivores is to isolate themselves and hide.

To survive in the wild, all animals—including the predators—are subject to and guided by their instinctive fears. Decades of detailed research in Alaska have shown that the most common mortality factor in wolf populations is intraspecific fighting. Territorial wolves often wound or kill trespassing conspecifics. Pack hierarchy is based on the threat of violence. Tail between their legs, low-status wolves cringe in abject submission, in the hope of inhibiting aggression from dominant family members.

How do sensitive people react to seeing the bloody evidence of predation? Like beauty, cruelty may be in the eye of the beholder. The phrase that *nature is red in tooth and claw* is usually attributed to Shakespeare, but that notion actually predates the famous bard by more than a century, and the matter is as true today as it was then. The famous Canadian naturalist Ernest Thompson Seton (1860-1946), who played an important role in nature appreciation in all of North America, wrote that the lives of wild animals always end tragically. Nevertheless, in my view, the more powerful a predator, the more merciful it seems to be. For instance, a park visitor who was fortunate enough to actually witness a wolf catching a deer said that all it took was one bite to the head. I for one am always happy to see a deer outrun a wolf, or a buck make a courageous stand, ready to defend himself with his dagger-like antlers. A case of a mule deer actually goring an attacking wolf is described elsewhere in this book. But what are a deer's chances if it is pursued by thirteen wolves? At least death may come quickly, quite unlike the fate of deer that are caught by smaller predators.

In regions where wolves are absent, coyotes take over as the dominant hunters of deer. Their kills can be messy and easily arouse compassion for the victim. I once watched a mule deer doe keep a coyote away from a river island on which she had hidden her newborn. Her attempts were probably futile, especially if the coyote should return with its mate. And one winter day, I spotted a doe standing on a stony islet in a turbulent stream. The binoculars revealed a bloody wound in her rump. As it so happened, I had just flushed a crouching coyote from the opposite shore, about 50 metres across from the islet. On the agricultural fields around Alberta's Beaverhills Lake, I once watched a coyote hunt a doe with a fawn. Time and again, the pair outran the coyote. Once safely ahead, the doe waited to see what the coyote would do. But their pursuer proved to be persistent and kept on tracking the deer. Eventually the chase went out of sight.

The only time I actually watched a hoofed mammal being killed by a predator involved a coyote that grabbed a bighorn lamb of about its own size. This happened at Cold Sulphur Springs along the Yellowhead Highway in Jasper Park. Seizing its fleeing victim by the rump and causing a large bloody wound, the coyote changed its grip to the lamb's throat when it fell. Holding on for many minutes, the coyote let go when a young woman, shocked by the violence of the scene, shouted and approached. Abandoning its victim, the coyote crossed the road and hunted down a second lamb, pursuing it into the cover of bushes.

I am not sorry to see that Jasper's coyote population, formerly ubiquitous, has steeply declined, at least in the backcountry, although they continue to thrive along the main traffic corridor, where they scavenge on road casualties as well as on the remains of wolf kills. Packs that take down large herbivores such as elk and moose, which are too big for one meal, usually benefit a range of scavengers, birds as well as mammals. In contrast to cougars and bears, which usually guard or bury their kills, wolves with full bellies leave their leftovers in the open and retire for a snooze some distance away. Because of this casual, not to say generous, attitude, wolves serve a crucial double function in the ecological dynamics of Jasper's main valley. Apart from supplying carrion to a host of smaller carnivores, they function as keystone managers of the herbivore community, keeping their numbers down and helping to prevent overgrazing of the winter range. That crucial aspect of the wolf equation is what has fascinated me over sixty years of observation. In 1959, the wolves of Jasper Park and adjacent provincial forests had been exterminated by six years of wide-scale poison campaigns. From the mid 1960s onward, though, I was fortunate to witness their big comeback. Four decades later, the pendulum has swung the other way again. In recent years, not only have the wolves of Jasper declined to a remnant of past numbers, but also the elk population, which has suffered a parallel and even greater downturn. The chronology of these dramatic fluctuations, as well as their causes, are detailed in the concluding chapters of this book.

My story of predation is not exclusively about wolves, but also, and very specifically, about the fastest predators on the planet, the eagles and falcons. The aerial contest between a raptor and its almost equally speedy prey makes for a riveting spectacle that was once the time-honoured sport of kings and emperors. For modern-day birdwatchers, the sight of a peregrine in action may represent the highlight of a day's excursion. For me, it has become a lifetime passion.

Over sixty years of field observations in half a dozen different habitats, varying from lakes and rivers to ocean coasts, I have seen wild peregrines capture hundreds of prey. The falcon's hunting methods and kill rates are described and detailed in a range of scientific publications, but my most intriguing questions concerned the behaviour of the prey species. For instance, how do defenceless sandpipers cope with a feathered bolt from the blue that is ten or twenty times their size? Whether the sandpipers flee or hide depends on the predator and the setting. Here, too, fear is the deciding factor. A fascinating and unprecedented discovery was that huge flocks of sandpipers wintering along the Pacific coast near Vancouver took to the sky and stayed on the wing, well offshore, for the duration of the high-tide period when the coastal mudflats were flooded. My explanation is that these sandpipers were afraid of being surprised by a falcon if they were to roost on the shoreline and sat out the high-tide interval until the waters began to ebb again. The term I coined for the sandpipers' aerial escape behaviour is *over-ocean flocking*.

Like the saga of the wolf, the population recovery of the peregrine has gone from near-total collapse to abundance, which constitutes one of the greatest conservation victories of our time. I feel privileged to have been a witness to their recovery. This book has been written in celebration of the return of the wolf and the peregrine, and I am dedicating these chapters to those who made it happen.

CHAPTER 1
High Hopes

Looking west from Calgary, the jagged skyline of the Rocky Mountains is farther away than it may seem on a clear day. It takes about an hour on the Trans-Canada Highway, sweeping through magnificent foothill prairies, to reach the gap in the abrupt wall of rock where the tempestuous Bow River breaks through the front ranges to force its way downstream to Calgary. On my first free weekend after arriving in that city in July 1959, as a new immigrant from Holland, I took the bus to Banff, the administrative centre of Canada's first and now internationally famous national park.

In those days, tourist traffic to Banff National Park was a fraction of what it is today, and the highway in the narrow Bow River valley was just a two-lane road, not the hectic, twinned and fenced transportation corridor it has become. A sightseeing tourist could stop anywhere for a photo or a picnic. Camping was free, and one did not have to register and pay for a permit to overnight in a pup tent in the park's backcountry.

Anyone who has seen the mountains of Europe will agree that the Canadian Rockies are awe-inspiring by comparison, although some tourists like the Alps better, because in Europe, at the end of a long arduous climb, one can count on finding a tea house or alpine hut. Simple-minded naturalists like me tend to prefer the opposite, the less development the better. Yet, just having arrived from the other side of the globe, and feeling dwarfed by the forested heights on either side of the highway, I was subconsciously looking for the familiar. Later I remembered reading a sentiment expressed by an Italian immigrant to America, who, in a letter to his parents, wrote that he was very happy now, for he had found a region that looked just like home. The Rocky Mountains definitely did not look like home to me.

Although exploring new country is always fascinating, it was reassuring to know that Canada's boreal forests were not all that different from those in northern Europe. The dominant trees were conifers, spruce, and pine, and the deciduous species included poplar, birch, and willow. Also the variety of indigenous wildlife was basically the same. For a start, the most eye-catching and noisy bird I saw that first day in Banff was the magpie, which is equally common in the Netherlands. Interestingly, its tail was substantially longer than the tail of its Dutch cousin, and its querulous squawk was more high-pitched. Also, the crows, ubiquitous on both sides of the pond, had a slightly different accent. Heard from a distance, I thought that they sounded like ravens, which made my heart skip a beat, for the raven was one of the birds I had hoped to find here.

Other prominent representatives of the avian fauna that I wanted to see in particular were eagles, both the golden and the bald eagle. And tops on my wish list of mammals was the wolf. Even the red fox would make me happy, because that interesting member of the canid tribe, abundant across the entire northern hemisphere, had been exterminated in the Dutch coastal provinces where I used to live. As it turned out, during my two years in Calgary from 1959 to 1961, while I spent all of my free days roaming the countryside, I observed plenty of eagles but not a single raven, nor did I see a wolf or a fox. The reason for their absence was a shocking fact that emerged soon enough.

During my second visit to Banff National Park, driving a just-acquired used car, I stopped to watch an animal that looked like a fox to me. But a man who had also stopped for a look at the animal told me that it was a coyote, a new species for me. In those days, books and films about nature were scarce and the informative internet did not yet exist.

This coyote had obviously been hurt and was limping. Halting shyly, it looked back at us when a third vehicle stopped, a park warden's truck. One of its two occupants, carrying a rifle, stepped out and barked an order: "Stand aside, please." He then shot the coyote, walked up to the carcass, dragged it to the road and threw it, like a sack of dirt, into the back of the truck. Aghast, I asked the warden for an explanation and he curtly said that they were doing coyote control in the park to protect the public. "This animal must have picked up one of our cyanide guns," he said. Cyanide guns are poison cartridges that are set up near a bait. If a coyote or other scavenger, attracted to the carrion, uses its teeth to pull up a cartridge, the lethal device explodes in its mouth.

Subsequent visits produced more bad news. Driving to higher altitudes near Banff's border with Jasper National Park, I passed by Hector Lake, glittering far below in the valley bottom, hemmed in by glacier-capped peaks. In those days, there was no hiking trail to that lake. So I just parked the car by the edge of the road and entered the virgin woods, a new and somewhat worrying experience. A grouse that exploded from the ground at my feet, with a burst of wing beats, gave me a bad start. It perched on a branch above my head, allowing me to admire the details of its beautiful plumage and fanning its star-spangled black tail. Later, I learned that this was a Franklin's grouse, the western subspecies of the spruce grouse. Along the way, I noted a cavity high up in the massive trunk of a conifer at the moment when a pine marten stuck its head out and looked down at me in perfect equanimity, showing no fear. This was the spirit of the wild I had hoped to find!

Finding my way back to the car and driving farther west, I stopped by a log house sign-posted as the district's warden station. The officer was at home and not in the least surprised to see a breathless young man at his door, nor by my first question: "Are there any wolves around here?"

"Wolves around here? None that I can remember. They were poisoned out of existence, you know, a few years back. By the province."

"Also in the national park?" I asked incredulously. "Yes, at least for a while."

When I told him where I had been that day, he shook his head. "If you continue to go to places like Hector Lake by yourself, one day you'll meet a grizzly that will knock the head off your body."

Meeting an aggressive bear in the mountain parks was indeed a real worry, a subject often discussed in the campgrounds by tourists and residents alike. It made a walk in the woods a tense experience, especially if you were alone. Carrying a gun was strictly prohibited, and the defensive pepper spray can had not yet been invented. Worry about bears did not keep me out of the woods, though, and I secretly hoped to see one. Black bears were actually quite common in Banff. And when I saw a sow with four small cubs crossing the highway, I parked the car and followed them into the woods, just to watch and observe their behaviour. Thinking back of that decision, I shudder to think of the risk I was taking. Fortunately, when mother bear sent her cubs up a tree and waited, ready to charge me if I came one step closer, I had the good sense to retreat.

A meeting with my first grizzly also ended well, more by sheer luck than wisdom. Hiking back over open alpine slopes from Banff's remote Egypt Lake, where a friend and I had gone fishing, we had to cross a deep draw. Looking up the narrow gulch, we spotted a grizzly with three cubs, about 200 metres farther upslope. They had not seen us, and we considered ourselves very lucky to have crossed the draw a safe distance from the bears, instead of unwittingly coming down on top of them. On the drive back, we stopped by the district warden to report our sighting. At the warden's request, we described the pelt colour of the bear, and he shook his head. "That bear, her three cubs in tow, recently chased a man on horseback and forced two other fishermen to climb a tree."

As the summer merged with a brilliant fall season, I continued my weekend drives to the mountains. Both the four-lane highway from Calgary to Banff and the older two-lane coach road follow the turbulent Bow River, on either side of the scenic valley. Ahead, the foothills sweep up to higher, partly wooded elevations. It is here that two major landscape forms meet, the thousand-kilometre-wide prairies and the three-kilometre-high Rocky Mountains.

Some distance west of the hamlet of Cochrane, I parked the car by the gate of an abandoned farmhouse and grabbed my treasured 10-by-50 Zeiss binoculars, thinking that the abrupt front ranges on the horizon formed a natural guiding line for the southward migration of hawks and eagles. In this spectacular setting, I had high hopes of watching raptors on the hunt, and the number of golden eagles I ended up seeing here during my two years of residence in Calgary exceeded all expectations.

In 1970 and again in 1985, I published a paper on the eagle migrations, which alerted other birders, who ended up forming the Rocky Mountain Eagle Research Foundation. From 1992 onward they monitored the seasonal passage of birds of prey in Kananaskis Provincial Park, some distance south of my former stamping grounds. In the fall of 2017, their tally of golden eagles was 3,233, plus 190 bald eagles.

During their daily watches, both in spring and fall, these enthusiasts focussed their binoculars and telescopes on the peaks of Mount Lorette, although the vast number of eagles counted stayed very high and were little more than mere specks to the naked eye. Instead, my hope was to watch eagles up close and in action. If I saw a distant eagle over the foothills, I waited anxiously for it to come closer and begin hunting.

The eagle's common prey was locally called a gopher. Its official name was Richardson's ground squirrel. By October, most of these summer-loving rodents had already begun their eight-month long hibernation, but some individuals, perhaps those that had not yet amassed sufficient fat reserves for the long sleep, stayed active well into autumn.

Spotting its prey from afar, the eagle's strategy was to take the gophers by surprise. Hugging the hill's profile at wind-hissing speeds, wings furled, the eagle skidded to a sudden stop if it was successful. If the target was missed, the eagle continued its low course across the slope or spread its wings into the wind and sailed back up, in preparation for another long-range attack elsewhere.

The ground squirrels were hunted by a host of other predators, including red-tailed and Swainson's hawks, goshawks and harriers, but the most impressive raptor was the prairie falcon. If I picked one up in the glasses, soaring high over a distant hill, I waited for its spectacular stoop. Descending like a meteor, the last phase of the falcon's trajectory was low over the grass, and its objective was similar to the eagle's: to catch the prey by surprise just before it had a chance to escape underground.

In addition to their winged enemies, the gophers were stalked by hungry quadrupeds. Coyotes commonly patrolled the hills during the daytime. One of them had teamed up with a badger. When this low-slung predator started digging, sending the sod flying, the coyote waited for gophers to emerge from nearby exit tunnels. A rare sighting featured a lynx that emerged from a belt of trees and padded down a grassy slope until it suddenly sprang at something in the grass ahead. With a gopher hanging limp in its jaws, the lynx returned to the woods.

My usual observation method was to sit down on a spot that afforded a wide view of a range of hills and the valley below. Frequently scanning through binoculars, I picked up a number of rare interactions between eagles and coyotes. Sailing down and hanging just above a coyote, the huge bird remained suspended on the strong wind, dwarfing the mammal, which reacted by confronting the threat. Some coyotes even jumped up defensively, forcing the eagle to pull up a little and stay out of reach of the coyote's snapping jaws. An even more memorable interaction occurred when a playful eagle planed down to a steer grazing on a hillside. Lowering its feet, the eagle actually landed on the bovine's broad back. Looking up in surprise or shock, the steer then ran down the hillside with the eagle trying to keep its balance, long wings flapping against the bovine's flanks. Near the base of the hill, the eagle lifted off to repeat its performance with another cow or steer.

When I met the local rancher and told him about my observation, he said that eagles had killed at least one of his young calves. While skinning the fresh carcass, he had found numerous small holes in its hide that looked like they had been inflicted by talons. In the published literature on eagles, there are indeed a few records of their riding down deer and antelope to their death.

At any time in September or early October, the Alberta foothills may receive an early snowfall, just a few centimetres or more. The white blanket will melt again in a day or two if the wind turns west. "If you don't like Calgary's weather, just wait an hour," is a standard joke of Calgarians, who tend to boast about their famous Chinook. And they point you to the Chinook Arc, a band of cloud that crowns the western skyline as a sign that the weather is changing. When the Chinook winds start to blow, the temperature may indeed rise from twenty below to well above freezing in a matter of hours. The Chinook brings moist air from the Pacific Ocean. As it rises over the Rockies, the moisture condenses as rain or snow, but on the east side of the mountain chain, the air is dry and relatively warmer through compression. Native tribes used to call this gusty west wind the 'snow eater.'

As the season progressed and winter began in earnest, I stopped my weekend excursions to the foothills and instead explored the agricultural plains and the Bow River valley, east of the city's outskirts.

CHAPTER 2
Falls, Failures, and Beginner's Luck

Early European immigrants probably had personal and nostalgic reasons for attaching the Scottish name Calgary to this modern, ever-expanding metropolis. But the obvious explanation for their settlement choice seems a natural one. Imagine, in the late 1800s, horse-mounted travellers leading a column of covered wagons and looking for a sheltered rest stop after a journey of hundreds of miles across hot, open plains. Shaded by huge poplar trees, the banks of the Bow River must have looked like an ideal place for a long rest stop, with a year-round source of cool water at the doorstep.

Today, Calgary has spilled hugely over its riparian cradle, and the Great Plains to the east, in their once unbelievable vastness, have been turned into farmland. The virgin grasslands were broken and divided into blocks of one square mile each. Gravelled county roads now run straight east-west or north-south, and each block has been further divided into four equal quarters, with barbed-wire fences in between. One could leave the city and drive east for hundreds of kilometres without much of a change in scenery, except for a small slough or marshy pond here and there. The cross-hatched symmetry made sense for early settlers, who couldn't get lost, unless one became disoriented in a snowstorm.

After I had stopped making weekend trips to the foothills and set aside my initial disappointment in the boring and unnatural aspects of the prairies east of the city, I gave it another try, because a Calgary birdwatcher had reported the first snowy owls of the season there.

One fateful Saturday in early November, with a strong north wind blowing, I was shocked by the severe drop in temperature. Knowing what I know now, I would not have ventured out, but with nothing better to do, I brushed the snow off the car and was happy to get it started. After the night's blizzard, the sky had cleared, and the immaculate snow had turned the barren fields into a wonderland. The gravelled county roads were mostly blown free of snow, but there were deep drifts that seemed fun to drive through, until the car got stuck and the engine died.

No cell phones in those days, no other traffic to be seen, and not a single vehicle track on the road. After some time sitting around and beginning to get very cold, this ignorant greenhorn, underdressed for the weather, headed out on foot to a distant farmhouse. It was a life-threatening experience. Fortunately, somebody was at home and kindly phoned a garage in the nearest town. It took a while for the tow truck to arrive. When the village mechanic looked at my car, he noted that the cap of the gas tank was missing. That morning I had stopped at a service station and not kept an eye on what the attendant was doing (in those days, all gas stations were full service). While I sent the car ploughing through the drifts, flying snow had entered the tank and resulted in frozen gas lines, or an iced carburetor.

A beautiful area for winter walks around Calgary is the river valley, downstream from the city. There, bald eagles are a common and welcome sight. In the hope of seeing them in action, catching a duck or a fish, I spent a lot of time in observation. I even built a blind from driftwood and laid out road-killed hares or other carrion in a vain attempt to lure eagles in front of the camera. But my only customers were magpies.

When the snow deepened, I thought that skis would be the answer for ease of travel. At the time, lightweight cross-country equipment was locally unavailable, so I purchased a regular downhill type with bear-claw bindings. The skis were cumbersome but safe on level ground. On a brilliant, sunny day when the snow was crusted, I became overconfident and raced downhill until I slammed face-down into the hard snow. My skis had broken through the crust into a knee-deep drift that stopped me cold. Fortunately, I did not get hurt, for there was no one who knew where this crazy Dutchman had gone that very cold day.

Stumbling along on skis where I should not have gone alone, I suffered another awkward fall in Banff National Park. On a Saturday in early December I had stopped by a warden station for information on wolves. Scratching his head, the district warden seemed to remember that someone had seen a wolf track in the Panther River valley last winter. He kindly gave me permission to go there and check things out. He even lent me the key to the off-limits warden trail that had recently been graded.

In the woods, the snow was a metre or more deep. Upon spotting two moose on an open crest, I approached for a closer look. My skis seemed to work satisfactorily, but on the steepest part of the slope I lost my balance and keeled over sideways, ending up with my head and shoulders lower than my feet, a very awkward angle for struggling back up in the deep powder snow. The moose must have laughed their antlers off. Fact was that the two bulls had indeed lost their head gear, which, as I found out later, was quite normal for the species. Whereas elk bulls keep their antlers until well into March, moose drop theirs already in early winter, which makes sense since these top-heavy male ornaments are only of value during the fall rutting season.

Having learned my lesson about the dangers of skiing in hill country, my next plan was to stay on level ground and follow a river. The bindings of my skis had been adjusted so that I now could lift my heel for easier walking. Bill MacKay, a fellow naturalist with bush experience, had lent me his kids' toboggan, which I loaded up with camping gear and some food for an overnight hike up the frozen North Saskatchewan River. The trip began with a three-hour drive to Rocky Mountain House. Beyond there, the bush road was snow-covered but passable. By the time I had found a spot within view of the river, it was already mid-afternoon. Parking the car on the road shoulder, I unloaded my gear and set off down the four-metre-high bank. The virgin expanse and the snow-dusted Christmas trees took my breath away. It was the incarnation of my wilderness dream. Having read the narratives of north-country bush travellers, I felt confident that I could survive the long night, with a good fire keeping me company into the evening and a long sleep in my double sleeping bag on a springy mattress of spruce bows. Hanging a metal billycan over the flames to melt snow for tea and roasting a sandwich on sticks over the coals already was routine for me.

I had a surprise coming, though, and all too soon. The going proved to be very much harder than expected. The snow was about a half-metre deep, soft and fluffy. My skis cut a furrow right down to the ice. Pulling the loaded toboggan was also very tough. After less than thirty minutes, with frequent stops, I realized that I would not get far. Exhausted and sweating, I sat down on a tree stump for a while and decided to return to the car on my own trail. By the time I had unloaded the toboggan and started the car engine, it was near sundown, too late for the 300 km drive back to the city. Looking for a sheltered spot to park under some big trees and sleep in the car, I drove farther along the narrow bush road, not knowing where it might lead.

After a while I passed a pedestrian, a First Nations man, who had a rifle strapped over his shoulder. When he raised his thumb for a lift, I waved and drove on. Farther on, where the road widened a bit, I turned around and headed back the same way I had come. I was not surprised to again meet the pedestrian, until he stuck up his thumb for a ride, but now into the opposite direction. I again thought better of stopping, for I was planning to overnight soon on the spot where I had begun my aborted ski tour.

By the time dusk began to descend between the trees, the interior of the car had cooled considerably. Bundled up in my sleeping bag, I curled up on the back seat, prepared for a long night, watching the moon rise and listening for the sounds of the wilds. Except for the hooting of a great-horned owl, there was total silence. But sometime in the middle of the night, I was startled by a small explosion, followed by a hissing sound that I could not place at first. It turned out to be a bottle of pop that had frozen and cracked.

Some time after I had returned to the city and dropped off the toboggan at Bill's residence, he called to say that the Calgary Herald ran a headline of interest that day: "Foothill forests overrun with wolves." The article reported that a pilot employed by an oil exploration company had sighted a pack of wolves west of Rocky Mountain House, and from the air he had spotted the apparent remains of several wolf kills on the frozen Brazeau River. The local hunting association had already approached the government to demand control of the predators.

Bill had told me an interesting story of his past having to do with wolves. When he was working on an oil rig in the wilds, he had suffered a serious accident. To recuperate, he had accepted an invitation from a friend to join him for the winter, trapping furbearers along the upper Athabasca River. To get there, they had chartered an aircraft and brought just a few extras along for Christmas time. The cabin had already been well stocked with bulk foods on an earlier visit. After waving their goodbyes to the pilot, Bill and his friend walked to the cabin and were horrified to discover that the place had been ransacked by a bear. Most of the supplies had been destroyed. As it was too late to recall the pilot, they decided to make the best of things and live on bush meat. However, after several weeks, they had failed to shoot a moose and were barely surviving on snared squirrels. Forced to give up, and unable to contact the outside world, they decided to walk out and follow the frozen river to the nearest settlement, a matter of several days of snowshoeing. "We were going to travel light," Bill said. "We carried just one rifle, one axe, and one sleeping bag. Taking turns during the night, one guy stayed awake and kept the fire burning." Their hardship increased after they stepped through overflow ice and got their feet wet. They managed to get out, though. The part of the story that was of special fascination to me was Bill's remark that they had come across the remains of a moose that had been killed by wolves.

The following Friday afternoon, Bill and I set out on a three-day camping trip to the foothill forests west of Rocky Mountain House. On a large-scale map we had figured out the best route to the Brazeau River once we got past the town. To check with the authorities, we stopped by the regional Forestry office and talked with a man named Williams. "Wolves overrunning this country?" he asked. "I haven't seen a track in years." In the same breath he told us that he had personally poisoned 67 of them in his district. That was sometime during the mid-1950s, when the Alberta government had unleashed the most intense poisoning campaign ever, to exterminate all canids in the southern half of the province. "At that time we were worried about rabies," Williams said. "I have nothing against wolves. Are you kidding? In fact, I like them better than people." What a weird thing to say, I thought.

Government concern about rabies had indeed been the explanation for the infamous carnivore eradication program of the 1950s, and the catalyst had been a report that one or more northern foxes had been tested and found to be infected by the feared disease. To halt its southward spread, Alberta wildlife managers decided to protect settled regions of the province with an 8,000-km-wide ring of poison, to be maintained by 170 hired trappers. Poison was also distributed to private landowners, free of charge. The number of units, as documented in official reports, is truly mind-boggling: 39,960 cyanide guns, 106,000 cyanide cartridges, and 628,000 strychnine pellets. Extremely toxic 10-80 bait stations increased from 25 in 1953 to 800 in 1956.

Official figures for animals found dead: 55,000 foxes, 171,000 coyotes, 5,200 wolves, 9,850 lynxes, 3,440 bears, and 64 cougars. No figures are available for wolverines, martens, otters, mink, and weasels. The number of scavengers that might have scurried off into the woods before dying is also unknown. The list of mortalities does not include birds, either. A native trapper who had been there during the poison campaign told me that the bush around beaver ponds where baits had been dropped was littered with dead ravens and chickadees.

Who knows how many eagles and other birds of prey died, for no defensible reason? Compared with Alberta's over-the-top reaction to the rabies scare, neighbouring provinces and northern states had kept their predator controls at very much lower levels. Today, the mildest criticism from responsible wildlife biologists is that the Alberta poison campaign had been continued for too long.

"Who are you guys with?" Williams had asked us. We explained that we were independent naturalists. We were here in the hope of finding some evidence that a few wolves had survived in western Alberta. Wolves were now all the more precious, we argued, because they played an important role in the ecological balance of the north woods. Williams wished us luck and added: "Let me know what you guys find."

Back in the car, Bill suggested that we should first go for a beer and a bite to eat. It was close to sundown and I wanted to get out of town before dark. We settled for a piece of pie and a coffee in a roadside restaurant. And by the time we had found our way to the bush road, it had begun to snow. The surface had been ploughed but the hills were very slippery. My car's headlights illuminated a winding corridor of dark spruce trees, mile after mile. We had no idea where we were going to spend the night.

After an hour or so, the falling snow and the overcast sky were illuminated by the lights of a working oil rig. "Let's stop here and ask these guys if they have seen any wolves," Bill suggested. And he added: "We shouldn't tell them that all we want is to see them, though, or find their tracks. Let's say that we are hunting wolves. Otherwise they might think that we are just a couple of sissies." The foreman was in his office trailer and he had time for a chat. "Wolves? Nothing here, as far as I know. You guys should go up to the Peace River country. Last winter I worked the rigs out there and we saw plenty of wolves. They like to follow ploughed roads, you know, and they hesitate to jump across the snow ridges along the ditch. We run them down any chance we get. Fearsome critters, they are. One of them tried to bite me when I approached to despatch him, lying on the road after my truck had crushed his hind quarters."

Keeping my mouth shut, I was happy to let Bill do the talking. Always ready with a smile and a positive word, Bill said that he too had worked the rigs and was now recuperating from a bad accident. He then casually added: "You wouldn't have a place for us to spend the night, would you?" "Sure thing," the foreman responded. And he directed us to one of the parked trailers, which we had all to ourselves. The following morning, we joined the short lineup to the kitchen trailer and sat down to the richest and most varied breakfast I had ever eaten in my life.

What a relief to step outside, well rested and with a full stomach. The snow had stopped falling and the sky was clear, although the temperature had dropped significantly. As long as the car started, I refused to worry. We were getting closer to our goal. The river could not be far once the road turned sharply east. Upon reaching that point, we parked the car, unloaded the toboggan, which was already packed with our camping gear, and embarked on a hike along an unploughed cut line that ran in a northerly direction, eventually ending at the Brazeau River. The snow was almost knee deep, but after we descended the steep riverbank, the going on the snow-covered ice proved to be a lot easier.

There was no wind, the sun was bright in a cloudless sky, and we were walking towards the shining mountains. Taking turns dragging the toboggan, we covered about ten kilometres and enjoyed one of the most glorious days I had ever experienced. The wilderness could not be more beautiful! We saw no animals and found no fresh tracks.

Well before the sun had completed its low circuit, we began looking for a place to set up camp. Oddly, a level spot was hard to find, and in the end we just made do under some tall poplars and small spruces. While one of us cut firewood, the other collected armloads of spruce bows for bedding. We dragged a log to serve as a seat and, before long, we were basking in the glow of a good fire. Chatting until deep dusk, we crawled into our sleeping bags early and fell asleep soon, being woken often by the cold air on our faces. As we bundled up again, our ears stayed attuned to the sounds of the night. The silence was emphasized by the muffled hooting of a distant owl, but the hoped-for call of wolves was missing. The river ice kept rumbling and cracking. Occasionally, the bark of some trees contracted and split in the cold with the sound of rifle shots.

Dawn was the greatest spectacle on earth. Ever so slowly but surely, the sun rose over the distant rim of trees. Later, upon our return to civilization, we heard that the local night temperature had dropped to minus 30 degrees Celsius.

The first order of business was to get a fire going again. Yesterday before dark I had collected an extra supply of dry spruce twigs that ignited with one match. Bill was bemused that the slab of beacon he had brought for breakfast was frozen solid and had to be cut with his axe.

The walk back on our own trail was again uneventful, no animal sightings and no fresh tracks, but the weather was magnificent. By early afternoon we were back at the car and the engine started fine. The snow that had fallen the previous day had created a perfect medium for fresh tracks, and when we came across something of interest we slowed down for a closer look. Besides one moose and a deer, the road had been crossed by a lynx. After several kilometres, just when we accelerated to normal driving speed, we came to a section of road that looked more interesting. There were several sets of large tracks, and one of the animals had left a yellow stain on the snow banked along the ploughed road. Getting out of the car for a closer look, we slowly came to the exciting conclusion that these tracks had indeed been made by wolves. After a careful count, we assumed that there were at least five or six members in this pack.

We got to Rocky Mountain House before dark, and although I wanted to hit the highway without delay, Bill thought that we should drop by the Forestry office to tell Williams about our find. "Otherwise he might think that we are just a couple of amateurs." Though it was a Sunday, we found Williams in his office. We were quite excited to tell him what we had found. In turn, he said that he had already been contacted by the Department of Agriculture. They had a crew doing coyote control around town, and their plans were to charter a helicopter in the next few days to set wolf baits on the upper Brazeau River. "These guys are from Agriculture and they came here to do their work in a Forestry jurisdiction," He said scathingly: "That's politics for you."

Williams asked detailed questions as to the location of the wolf tracks. He seemed to know the exact place when we mentioned a creek culvert under the forestry road. "Thanks for the information," he said when we left his office.

Two weeks later, I went back to the area where we had found the tracks. Snow conditions were not good for finding fresh tracks, but the one thing that hit my eye at once were yellow signs nailed to roadside trees. "Warning! In the interest of protecting livestock, poison baits have been placed in the area. Keep dogs on leash." Beneath the warning were the words: The Alberta Department of Agriculture.

Following the creek bed, I came to a small, snow-covered lake. Attached to a stake driven into the ground was another yellow warning sign. Nearby lay the bait, the head and neck of a horse. Later I inquired and learned that compound 10-80 (sodium fluoroacetate) is injected into a living horse. The toxin spreads throughout the animal's bloodstream so that all of the body parts become lethal to scavengers. Deeply saddened, I drove back to Calgary that same evening. When I phoned Bill, he said: "That Williams is a rat."

The bitter disappointment of trying to find wolves in western Alberta reinforced my tentative plans to go farther north. Searching the local library for literature about wildlife in the boreal forest, I picked up a narrative from an American ex-Marine, who had given up his rat-race existence in California during the economic downturn of the 1930s to try his luck trapping furbearers in the wilds of Canada. In those days the value of a silver fox skin could be more than several months of salary for a working stiff. He and his friend had set their mind on exploring the east arm of Great Slave Lake by canoe. His travelogue painted a realistic picture of battling huge waves and included lively details of several meetings with native tribes at places with colourful names such as Snowdrift and Artillery Lakes. Once they had selected a place to spend the winter, somewhere in the Northwest Territories, they had set to work building a log cabin. Their winter food supply consisted of a pile of frozen carcasses of caribou they had shot when the huge barrenland herds passed by on their seasonal trek to protective forest farther south. In addition, they had nets set under the ice to catch fish.

A map of northern Alberta showed that the east arm of Great Slave Lake splits into a labyrinth of narrow channels that looked intriguing, and slowly a plan ripened in my mind to go there myself. But I needed a companion for such an adventure.

Hard to believe as it may seem in the age of the internet, in those days the standard medium for publicity was the local newspaper. Explaining my quest in a few words, I placed a personal ad in the Calgary Herald. Next day a lady journalist wanted to know whether I was looking for a man or a woman. My mumbled answer was undecided. The Herald then printed a story about a naturalist from Holland who wanted to canoe down the Athabasca River to Great Slave Lake and beyond.

The story resulted in two telephone reactions from people who knew what they were talking about. The first to phone was a guy who asked what kind of canoe I had. A freighter canoe? When I replied that I was thinking of acquiring a sixteen-foot craft, he chuckled derisively and hung up. Later I learned that the standard freighter canoe is several metres longer and a lot wider than any recreational type I had ever seen. They are designed with a flat stern suitable for hanging an outboard engine. Even then, on huge Great Slave Lake, a freighter canoe would look like a matchstick in a swimming pool.

The second person to phone was a retired civil servant who had worked in the north, building fire towers, all of his professional life. He invited me to come to his house for a chat, which I gladly accepted. About my plans for Great Slave Lake, he warmed me about the hazards and discouraged me from going there. Why didn't I just drive up the Alaska Highway to the Yukon Territory? Beautiful mountain scenery and good fishing. And, talking about canoes, he offered to lend me his twelve-foot craft, easy to handle and light-weight. It did not take me long to accept his kind offer and advice.

In the spring of 1961, I loaded the little canoe on the roof of the old Pontiac, filled the trunk with dry foods, and left Calgary for an undetermined time. Starting at Dawson Creek on the province's eastern border with British Columbia, the Alaska Highway was just a ribbon of gravel that American army engineers had bulldozed through the wilderness during the war years in the 1940s. Today all of it is paved, but in 1961 it was still extremely dusty during dry periods and awfully muddy on wet days. The distance from Dawson Creek to Whitehorse, the capital of the Yukon Territory, was about 1,500 kilometres.

The farther north I got, and the more river valleys I crossed, the more I longed to get away from the road. At the only gas station in the Yukon hamlet of Teslin I asked the proprietor: "Are any of these rivers safe enough for a small canoe?" His answer was encouraging: "All of them, in fact. The drop in elevation is very gradual. Not much in the way of rapids." He then added: "Why don't you contact the local priest. He is the canoe expert around here."

This casual advice proved to be just what I needed. The priest was a young man from Ireland. Not at all surprised by my desire to see something of the backcountry, he was quick with more good advice. "Why don't you hire one of the local boys as your guide and go down the Nisutlin, a river that flows into Teslin Lake, right here. Ask Frank Peters. You can pay him five bucks a day, and I charge you the same for the use of my canoe." His canoe was a new 19-foot boat that barely fitted on the roof of my car.

One day later we were on our way. Frank's cousin came along to drive my car back to the village after he had dropped Frank and me off some 150 kilometres up the bush roads. Getting our canoe and camping gear to the river bank involved carrying them several hundred meters down a steep, forested slope.

Our planned Nisutlin trip took us four days of drifting downstream and camping in the woods along the way. The lazy current seldom speeded up to more than six or seven kilometres per hour. The water level was high, so that there were few muddy or sandy points where we could stop to look for animal tracks. The shore was heavily wooded and the forest buzzed with millions of mosquitoes and flies. Despite my high hopes of seeing wildlife, except for some waterfowl and the odd bald eagle, we saw nothing. Frank's unspoken intent had been to shoot a moose and bring the meat home, but we encountered none, although he made two short side trips to inland marshes where he felt sure to find moose.

Chatting with Frank was fascinating. Later that summer and fall, he expected to be hired as a guide by outfitters who were contracted to take well-paying foreign hunters out into the Yukon wilds to shoot trophy bears, caribou, or moose. As to Frank's close family, his only surviving sibling was a younger sister. Nine of his brothers had died after contracting diseases brought in by the American Army during the construction of the Alaska Highway. Asked about our chances of seeing wolves, lynxes, or otters, his standard answer was: "Lots. We'll see lots." Later, when I wrote a book about my Yukon trips, I titled the Nisutlin chapter 'The River of Lots'. Hilariously, as mentioned above, we saw nothing.

Nevertheless, the lack of wildlife sightings did not discourage me, and I kept my hopes up during the following three months of my planned stay in the Yukon. Exploring small lakes and creeks, I made several trips in the 12-foot canoe I had brought. In addition, I embarked on longer journeys in bigger canoes lent to me by people I met along the way. The most ambitious trip was the last, on the Big Salmon River, which had been recommended by an old, retired trapper. "Lots of grizzly bears there, and wolves," he said. "But watch out for log jams and sweepers." What that term meant I learned the hard way, when it was too late.

In the meantime, I had teamed up with a young tourist from Winnipeg, who had brought a new 16-foot Prospector made by Chestnut, a famous name in the world of canoes. Our trip was postponed because it rained and snowed for a week. The weather was still stormy on the day of departure, and on the second day, when the rain and wind had finally stopped, we hit a sweeper, a tall spruce growing on the riverbank which had been undercut by the stream and fallen into the water, partly blocking our passage. The strong current pushed us sideways against the tree, forcing the canoe to slowly turn over, spilling its contents and us into the deep water. I swam to shore, but Wayne did not dare to let go of the tree because his hip waders had filled with water. To rescue him, I crawled along the horizontal trunk and managed to pull him up and get us back to the riverbank.

Fortunately, the canoe had remained stuck in the tree branches. We pulled it free and recovered the paddles that were floating some distance downstream. Unfortunately, all our food and gear had sunk, except the sleeping bags and my empty packsack, which had remained caught in the upturned canoe. As luck would have it, the car keys and my passport were safely in a side pocket.

After drying out the next day, we worked our way upstream and eventually reached my parked car. Later, talking with members of the Whitehorse canoe club, we learned that the Big Salmon was the most difficult local river they knew about. A group of their members, all experienced canoeists, had made the same trip the previous year. One canoe was totally lost and none of the others came through without damage. We could consider ourselves lucky to have had the accident so early into the trip. If the spill had occurred farther downstream, we would have had a lot more trouble to struggle our way back up, if at all possible. It was beginner's luck that we had escaped a fate that has taken the lives of much more experienced canoeists in the past.

After three days of driving, I arrived in Calgary, returned the canoe to my benefactor, sold the car, packed up my few possessions and flew back to Holland to see my parents and brothers , who hadn't heard from me for quite a long time.

CHAPTER 3
Canoeing the Wilds

After my temporary return to Holland, it took until 1964 before I found someone who wanted to emigrate to Canada with me. "Do you think that she is going to make wilderness trips with you?" asked the Canadian consul, a skeptical smile on his face and looking askance at my wife and future life's companion. Ten years younger than I, Irma seemed the quintessential city girl; well dressed, her friendly face carefully made up.

Soon after we met at an advertising agency in Holland, I had told her that I intended to go back to Canada and that the winters there were very cold. As in other important matters, her reaction was spontaneous and positive: "I like snow!" she said.

To obtain the necessary immigration permits, Irma and I applied for an appointment with the Canadian embassy in The Hague. As a returning resident, the formalities for me were simple, whereas Irma underwent a detailed interview and a physical checkup, similar to my first visit in 1959. Once approved, she received a small amount of money to cover the cost of travel and a few days of subsistence upon arrival in her new country. Instead of flying, we booked passage on the Holland-America Line. My Volkswagen was hoisted aboard the same vessel we boarded for Montréal. From there we drove the Beetle to Alberta.

This time, instead of Calgary, I chose to settle in Edmonton, Alberta's provincial capital, 300 kilometres straight north of Calgary, because that's where my brother Marius was sent when he emigrated to Canada. Ironically, a year or so later, Marius moved to Vancouver, which had been my initial preference in 1959. In retrospect, for two important reasons Edmonton turned out to be a fine location for a naturalist. For one thing, famous Beaverhills Lake was less than an hour's drive east of Edmonton, and I ended up spending half of my life there to watch migrating peregrines and study their hunting tactics on ducks and shorebirds. Secondly, Edmonton was on the Trans-Canada

Highway to fabulous Jasper National Park, which became the location for my long-term observations of wolves and their prey species.

Less than a year after our arrival, we bought a canoe, the highly rated 16-foot Prospector made by Chestnut. Irma came to love our outings, starting with tryouts in Elk Island National Park and day trips on the McLeod and North Saskatchewan rivers. For our first backcountry adventure, we drove to Prince Albert National Park in Saskatchewan. North of there, we explored the interconnected canoe routes of the Churchill River watershed, which involved carrying our craft and equipment across portages from one lake to the other. We battled metre-high whitecaps that scared us to death, and we often ended up wind-bound for a day or more on a sheltered point. We ended up crossing some huge lakes at night after the winds had finally died.

In the way of hoped-for wildlife, we saw little. Except for iconic birds such as loons and bald eagles, the 'great lone land'—as wilderness writer Sigurd Olson labeled his canoe country—proved to be practically devoid of large mammals. In all of our time there, we did not see a single moose or deer, nor any wolves or bears. The explanation had to do with the thickly wooded shorelines and the high water levels. Most riparian habitat was flooded, and there were no open sand banks nor mud flats for finding tracks and spotting wildlife.

The Saskatchewan lake country, with its ancient network of portage trails, is part of the great Canadian Shield that has been the bedrock home for aboriginal groups over thousands of years. Their year-round hunting pressure, superimposed on natural predation from wolves and bears, tends to keep the moose population down to one animal per four square kilometres, or even lower in some regions. As I kept telling Irma, *ad infinitum*, our opportunities for seeing wildlife would be much better in the Yukon. There, along open riverbanks, the chance of spotting a moose, bear or wolf would add much to the enjoyment of canoeing a northern river.

In July of 1966, Irma and I were ready for our journey to the Yukon. At a point where the Alaska Highway crosses the Teslin River, a locality called Johnson's Crossing, we visited with a British fishing guide, named Leslie, whom I had met during my previous Yukon holiday. Leslie kindly kept an eye on our canoe and camping gear while we prepared for our next river trip, which involved driving to the place where we intended to end up later by canoe. This was the Yukon hamlet of Carmacks, at the confluence of the Teslin and the Stewart Rivers. There we parked the car and took the Greyhound bus back to

Johnson's Crossing, where we had stashed the canoe. The following day, Irma and I embarked on our 15-day adventure down the Teslin, the headwaters of the Yukon River, which drains much of Alaska and Yukon. The Teslin's ancient aboriginal name is Hootalinqua, which has a nice cadence to it, evocative of water and waves.

Although the river's current is placid and steady over the approximately 400 kilometres of our planned route, we were warned about the Roaring Bull Rapids halfway down. Their menacing roar could be heard from afar and worried us enough to pull in to shore well ahead of the rapids for a look through binoculars. The white-crested standing waves looked awesome against a vertical wall of rock. To our immense relief, the heavily laden canoe danced through without trouble and glided out in the smooth waters beyond.

For most of the journey, we were bedeviled by rain and strong winds. And when the weather seemed to improve, the sky stayed grey and dark for days due to smoke from distant forest fires. Mosquitoes and no-see-ums spoiled many an evening, and we saw next to nothing in the way of wildlife. In contrast to my previous Yukon visit, when the population cycle of snowshoe hares had been at its peak, we saw no rabbits at all, and as a consequence, no avian raptors either. Goshawks and great-horned owls, which had been common during my earlier explorations, seemed completely absent or very scarce. So much for my boasts and high expectations about boreal wildlife populations.

For our next canoe trip we stayed in Alberta and chose the Peace River, largely on the advice of Edo Nyland, a fellow Dutch immigrant who had become the superintendent of the huge Whitecourt Forest. An experienced canoeist himself, he had discouraged us from floating the Athabasca River, which was dangerous and dirty on account of driftwood, eroding mud banks, and wandering channels.

The Peace River did much to restore my belief in the enjoyment of canoe travel on Canada's northern rivers. Our starting point was the bridge of the Alaska Highway over the Peace River, some 650 kilometres northwest of Edmonton and 25 kilometres south of the town of Fort St. John. We parked the car on the downstream side of the bridge and carried the canoe and camping gear to the river bank below the bridge, hiding them in the bushes. Climbing back up to the car, we drove to the terminus of our planned trip, which was the Dunvegan River bridge, about 200 river kilometres downstream. Across from the bridge was a roadside campground, one of many that were in those happy days built and maintained by the Alberta government as a free service to its outdoor-loving citizens. There was nobody around. So we left a note on the windshield of the parked car to the effect that we were out on a canoe trip and would be back later. We then waited by the highway for the Greyhound bus back to Fort St. John. Late in the afternoon, we were let off at the Alaska Highway bridge, the starting point of our trip. To our relief, the hidden canoe and camping gear had not been disturbed, by people nor bears.

With the sun at our backs, we drifted down the most beautiful river valley we had ever seen. To the left, south-facing slopes, several hundred metres in height, were golden with dry grasses, brightly lit on this warm August afternoon. On our right, the slopes were darkly wooded. On both sides, the deep blue river was rimmed with sandy beaches. Before long, we spotted a black bear, the first of about a dozen seen during our six-day trip. We found some of them by scanning the open hills through binoculars. One bear swam across the river right in front of us. Others ambled along the shore. A mother with three small cubs provided a few comical moments when they clambered up the steep bank.

One evening, when we were looking for a good spot to land, we had just passed a bear walking on the same side of the river. By nightfall, as is my habit, I covered the food box with a tarp and placed it well away from the tent. Checking for fresh tracks in the morning, we were pleased to see that the bear had given our tent and the box a wide berth.

Earlier that night, or in the small hours of the morning, we had not heard the shouts of a man and a young woman, who drifted by in their aluminum skiff with a defective outboard motor. With only one short paddle, the man had trouble keeping his craft in the current, and later that day we found them stuck on a midstream sandbar. We helped to get them afloat and from then on we drifted down side by side. Around midday, a silver aircraft began circling overhead. Apparently, the couple had been reported missing. The amphibious airplane touched down on the river and pulled up to a point where we joined the crew of two RCMP officers.

When Irma and I were ready to leave and resume our journey, the owner of the boat handed us a micky, a partly full plastic bottle of whiskey. Later we learned that having open liquor in a boat was illegal in Alberta. Obviously, the man had wanted to get rid of the evidence. To us it became an unexpected stimulant in an interesting day.

Continuing our peaceful float, we passed the bottle back and forth on our paddles, the first whiskey we had ever tasted. The alcohol added to our euphoric reaction when we spotted five wolf pups gamboling on the shore. Landing at once on the opposite bank, we planned to stay a few days for observation. But the weather had become excessively warm and there was no shade on our beach. After two days of watching we ended up with just a brief view of one adult wolf in addition to the pups. Once, during early evening, when we had crossed the river in the hope of getting a close-up view of the pups, we were startled by the growls of an approaching animal that turned out to be a huge black bear. Shouting to alert him to our presence, we pushed off again and returned to our blistering hot campsite.

Early the second morning, just after we had finished our usual breakfast of oatmeal and tea, we were surprised to hear an approaching motorboat, an aluminium skiff. The craft landed just upstream from our campsite. Two young men got out, rifles strung over their shoulders. They had seen our tent from a hill on the valley rim and wondered what we were doing. "You guys looking for gold?" Their demeanor was far from friendly, and we were relieved to see them leave soon again. They could have been poachers.

Well before noon, we packed up and resumed our trip. By the time we reached the big bridge at Dunvegan, the heat wave appeared to be ending. Ominous clouds were building, and thunder was rumbling overhead. There was, again, no one at the campground, and the car was untouched. Driving away, we were glad to have gotten off the river just in time, because the thunderstorm developed into a very heavy downpour.

While the memories of the Peace River trip remained vivid for many years, we were shocked to learn that Dunvegan was slated as the future site for a gigantic hydroelectric dam, the third on the upper Peace. Scheduled for construction in the 2020s, the dam would hold back a very large reservoir and was bound to drown out all of the beautiful shores we had so much enjoyed.

In August of 1965, Irma and I canoed down a section of Alberta's Peace River. This beautiful valley might be flooded in the near future by a planned powerdam.

On the way to Jasper's Snake Indian Valley I often made a shortcut by crossing a section of the Athabasca River that stayed unfrozen most winters.   Photo Brian Genereux

CHAPTER 4
Backcountry Camping

Our first winter in Edmonton turned out to be exceptionally cold. By December the temperature had already dropped to minus 30 degrees Celsius and snow had accumulated to more than knee-deep. Reporting on the cold snap, the Edmonton Journal featured an interview with a government biologist, who had talked with a trapper. Wild animals were having a very difficult time too, he said. "They are not moving at all, just digging a deep hole in the snow and staying put." The biologist then added a statement that he may have come to regret: "Anyone facing a wolf pack this winter is taking his life in his hands."

Wolves a threat to people? When I called the Alberta Fish & Wildlife Division and asked for the quoted biologist by name, he was kind enough to come to the phone. His informant was a provincial trapper, he said. The man had actually climbed a tree to save himself from a pack of wolves that were following him on the trap line. "Didn't he have a gun?" I asked. "Just a twenty-two," the biologist said, and he added: "Who are you with?"

I told him that I was a new immigrant from Holland and very keen to see wolves in the wild. What was the closest place to Edmonton where I could go and look for tracks? He mentioned the Bigoray Creek valley, west of Edmonton. "Why don't you contact a fellow countryman of yours, a great big Dutchman, who is the superintendent of the Whitecourt Forest. His name is Edo Nyland. He recently reported wolf sign in his neck of the woods."

Looking at the provincial road map, I found that the Bigoray Creek was bridged by a side road to a hamlet called Cynthia. The turn-off from the Yellowhead Highway was about 120 kilometres west of the city, not too far for a day trip. After the temperature had moderated, I went there in a hopeful mood and drove down the snow-covered road to Cynthia for about twenty kilometres, looking for wolf sign on the shoulder and in the ditch. If I were to find tracks, I intended to park the car and follow them. Walking in deep snow might take a lot of energy. But I had purchased a set of snowshoes, the time-tested kind made with rawhide webbing stretched across a wooden frame. They should make the way back easy, and following my own trail I could not get lost in the woods.

That first visit, I was elated to come across the fresh tracks of two wolves. In subsequent years I tracked packs of up to eight members in those extensive woods and muskegs. The wolves saved energy by moving in single file and stepping into each other's footprints. They liked to travel along the higher ridges, where mature spruces sheltered the ground and kept the snow to a minimum. But when the wolves started to pursue prey, I usually lost them all too soon and had to backtrack for another look, particularly when they had passed under and through bushes with leaps of five or six metres. I never came across a fresh kill. Deer that had been chased got away. A moose that was roused from its day bed had simply outlasted its pursuers, and a small herd of elk seemed to have stood off the confrontation by keeping their vulnerable back sides against a dense thicket of spruces, as indicated by broken branches.

In addition to the wolf trails, I sometimes followed the characteristic pads of lynxes, which were quite common that winter. Spoor of their bigger cousin, the cougar, was rare. Of special interest were the tracks of fisher, a mid-sized member of the weasel family that adapts its gait and track pattern to the depth and firmness of the snow.

One day, in the absence of wolf tracks, and instead of striking out at random through deep snow, I walked the packed trail of a local trapper, who owned a snowmobile, a very recent invention at that time. Although I feared coming across a trapped animal, I was morbidly curious about the business. At one site I found the skinned carcass of a lynx. The trap had been reactivated and the bait consisted of a skinned beaver that was placed at the base of a huge spruce tree. To further sadden and depress me, I found a dead rough-legged hawk in the bushes, its legs broken. This open-country raptor had evidently been hungry enough to go for something to eat in a tight spot under the tree, probably alerted by the comings and goings of magpies. Later, someone who was familiar with the business of fur trappers said that so-called accidental by-catch like hawks and owls is all too common. The unintended victims are called 'trash' and no records are kept or made public. Alberta trapping regulations specify that sets need to be checked daily, but the professionals as well as weekend hobbyists generally ignore the regulations and check their traps once a week or so, weather permitting. Shocking details are known from the sub-arctic, where traps are placed on slight knolls in the flat tundra landscape that are kept free of snow by the action of wind. These baits or poison sets are intended for arctic foxes, but they also attract scavenging eagles, gyrfalcons, or snowy owls.

The suggestion by the provincial wolf biologist to contact Edo Nyland proved very productive. When I phoned him, he was quick to invite Irma and me to come over for the weekend and stay at the huge chalet-type house he had built himself in the forested outskirts of the town of Whitecourt. He was indeed a big man with a generous attitude and very knowledgeable about local vegetation and wildlife. Later that winter, he and a colleague were planning to make a snowmobile trip in the McLeod forest, and instead of taking two skidoos, he could let us have one machine to go where we wanted.

The late March day turned out to be clear and warming up in the afternoon. After we got the tricky snowmobile to start, Irma and I proceeded up the solidly frozen McLeod River, frequently stopping to investigate tracks. We found the fresh footprints of two wolves and the remains of three deer. How these fragile herbivores had died was impossible to say. They could have been killed by wolves, or they might have succumbed to starvation due to the deep snow. Attracted by the carrion, there were several eagles soaring over the valley hills, goldens as well as white-headed bald eagles. At the end of the day, we were pleased to return the snowmobiles to the starting point at the appointed time. Long after we got back home, the sound of those extremely noisy machines reverberated in our ears. Edo and his colleague had actually seen a wolf that day, fleeing from them on the river bank just after they had left us.

On a subsequent visit to Whitecourt, Edo gave us a key to the Oldman cabin, deep in the backcountry forest. Upon our arrival, we found that the hut was set well back from the road, and that it had not been used for a very long time. I ended up digging a long trench of nearly one meter deep to the door. The sturdy log cabin was empty of any furniture; no table, no chairs, no bedsteads. But there was a barrel stove, which proved to be very much needed, for that night the outside temperature dropped to minus 30 Celsius. The trip was a worthwhile experience, though, and to my great relief the Beetle started fine in the colder-than-cold morning.

As to wolf sign, we were happy to find fresh tracks of a pack of seven on a forestry cut line. Following them in the deep snow we didn't get far, but at one point we heard barking and howling in the distance. A week or so later, when we told Edo about our find, he said that a local trapper had just reported the capture of seven wolves in the Oldman forest. How, I wondered, could the trapper have captured the entire pack? Much later I learned about their methods. On all access trails through the bushes, they surround a bait site with hidden foothold traps or steel snares. If one of the wolf family is caught, the others may circle about until they too, inevitably, are caught. Another routine wolf-killing method that may result in the capture of entire packs is by poisoning the bait or by scattering poison pellets.

Having been confronted with so much depressing reality about the way trappers operated in Alberta's forests, I stopped going there altogether, disgusted by what I had learned. From now on, Irma and I abandoned the provincial foothills and moved on to the national parks, where trapping and hunting were prohibited. Even there, we were in for more shocking details about the way wolf control was handled in adjacent mountain valleys.

My routine inquiries about the occurrence of wolves in Jasper Park were unsuccessful until a park employee remembered that the Willow Creek warden had recently filed a positive report. His name was Norman Woody. I mailed a letter to him at the park's head office in Jasper town, and wrote that we were interested in wolves and would like to visit him on the weekend of July 24-25, 1965. As it turned out, the message did reach him, and we were told that the warden would be at his backcountry cabin on that date. His wife and young children were with him, for their school holidays had just begun.

To reach the starting point of our hike to Willow Creek, we drove to Rock Lake, about 70 kilometres northwest of the Yellowhead town of Hinton. A few kilometres past the provincial campsite at that big, pristine lake, we left the car at the locked gate of the ancient aboriginal trail that skirts the front ranges of the Rocky Mountains and continues north all the way to Grande Prairie. A little way past the gate, the horse trail to Willow Creek forks off from the main trail and turns south into Jasper National Park. The distance to the warden station would be about 12 kilometres. Part way down the trail, we were confronted with Rock Creek, a fast, ice-cold stream about 50 meters wide that we needed to ford. For tenderfoots like us, the natural choice was to keep our Kodiak boots on. On the opposite shore was a wide gravel bar, where we sat down on a driftwood log to make a fire for brewing a cup of tea, toast a sandwich, and dry our footwear.

Presently, we were startled to see a black bear openly approaching us, directly in line with the drifting smoke of our fire. Jumping to our feet, we shouted and waved our arms. To our relief, the bear halted and turned around, but he did not retreat very far and sneaked about just inside the trees. Worried by the fearless behaviour of this "wilderness' bear, we doused the fire and put our boots back on to continue our hike. Double-checking the map, we wondered why the red line representing the trail indicated a sharp turn to the left and ascended to the valley rim, whereas I knew that the Willow Creek warden station was situated in the valley bottom. Clearly, the map could not be relied upon.

Uncertain, we bushwhacked through the trees and to our relief soon came upon a well-worn horse trail. The next little puzzle arose when we were stopped by Willow Creek, a much smaller stream than Rock Creek. Although it was no wider than a couple of steps, it was quite deep, and we decided to take our boots off to keep them dry. Proceeding a little farther down the trail, we ended up having to take our boots off two more times. On the way back, we realized that we could have walked around the first meander and forded the creek just once.

After passing through a wide belt of mature spruces, we were delighted when the valley opened up into a mosaic of montane meadows with, here and there, a copse of aspen trees or spruces. The gently flowing creek was lined with low willow bushes and dwarf birch. Without further problems, we arrived at the warden station and found the family at home. Norman Woody took all the time in the world to sit down with us and talk about wolves. Last winter, when he snowshoed in from Rock Lake, he told us, he had seen nine wolves on the ice. Next day, back at his log cabin, he had received a radio call from a local trapper who had been hired by the Alberta government to conduct wolf control in the region. Seven of the nine wolves had taken his poison bait and were now dead. Fortunately, Norm also had better news. In late March of this year, he had seen two wolves in his yard. One was a large, black male, much bigger than his grey companion. Throughout the summer, on calm nights, he had often heard wolves howling west of his place.

When we told Norman about the black bear that had approached us at the Rock Creek crossing, he had an explanation. It probably was a translocated animal from the Athabasca Valley. Individual bears that had lost their fear of people and habitually raided camp sites in the main valley or near the town site were captured and trucked to Rock Lake. Other problem bears were netted and slung under a helicopter to be transported and released farther away into the backcountry. Unfortunately, these spoiled 'wilderness' bears could then show up as unwelcome visitors at the tents of long-distance hikers.

We set up our pup tent near Willow Creek, just outside the warden's yard. Next day we made an exploratory hike down the horse trail west of the station. Checking muddy spots along the route, we were delighted to find the paw signatures of wolves at several locations.

Over the next 15 years, I made many repeat visits to that same trail and eventually became quite successful at observing wolves and their pups at a local den site. However, what I really wanted was to learn how the wolves hunted, and how elk and deer managed to cope with their predators. That kind of interactive observation proved to be practically impossible in this predominantly wooded environment. In discussing my objectives with Edo Nyland, he suggested that the mountains farther north would be much better for long-distance viewing because there were extensive open subalpine slopes devoid of trees. The place to go would be Eagles Nest Pass, some twenty kilometers west of Rock Lake, and to get there we just had to follow the Indian Trail.

In the meantime, on the way back from our first trip into Willow Creek, we met Archie, the Alberta forest ranger who lived at Rock Lake. He knew about the seven wolves that had been poisoned on the lake the previous winter, and he had much more bad news to tell. The same trapper had set baits at Eagles Nest Pass, but the deep snow of this past winter had prevented him from checking the results until early May. He had been shocked by what he eventually found. "Seventeen dead wolves! We didn't know we had that many." In addition, there were numerous other casualties: grizzly bears, wolverines, lynxes, coyotes, eagles, and several smaller carnivores and scavengers.

When I mentioned to Archie that I would very much like to see the open mountain slopes of the Willmore Wilderness, he offered to drive me to Eagles Nest Pass. "Saves you a long walk," he said. "I go there every once in a while to check out things." His generous offer was postponed until August of 1967. By that time, Irma was seven months pregnant, but her doctor had assured us that she was healthy and fit for travel, including hiking. On the appointed day, Archie probably drove as fast as usual, bouncing over the uneven surfaces, and when I peevishly told him to please slow down a bit because Irma was pregnant, it did not seem to make much difference. A few kilometres past the gate of the Indian Trail, we descended to the Wildhay River, a clear stream of some 100 metres wide. The shoreline was quite flat, and Archie hardly slowed down, gunning the engine over the rocky bottom, until we heard a sharp bang and the truck came to a full stop in the middle of the stream. "Oh-oh," he said. "Probably the fan belt again." He was proven right. Fortunately, the station was within reach of his mobile radio. Less than half an hour later, the assistant ranger arrived in his 4x4 truck and attached a tow line to Archie's stuck vehicle. In less than twenty minutes they had installed a new fan belt and we went on our way again. I am always impressed by the efficiency of professionals in coping with emergencies and solving mechanical problems. Thanks to Archie and his assistant, Irma and I could make the most of this welcome opportunity to see new country. Passing by a pleasant succession of woody hills and grassy openings, we splashed through several small side streams until the Wildhay River valley widened, and we arrived at a fork in the trail. The branch to the left was the horse trail to Eagles Nest Pass.

At three sides the alpine slopes were open and miles wide. I could just imagine hearing a pack of wolves howling far away and, after scanning the mountainsides through binoculars, watching them without fear of causing undue disturbance. When I expressed my hopeful excitement to Archie, he chuckled indulgently and wished us a good time. He would be back in three days to pick us up again.

Excited to be here, Irma and I found a level spot to erect our tent, unconcerned that we were blocking a game trail. After dragging a log to sit on by the fire, we had a pot boiling in no time and enjoyed a relaxed lunch, while feasting our eyes on the mountain scenery around us. Not far away was an open meadow with Columbian ground squirrels, a rodent that can be locally common at this elevation and constitutes ideal prey for golden eagles.

Scanning the skies, it did not take long before I picked up a soaring eagle, which reminded me of another reason why I had been so keen to visit this place. A classic book on the golden eagle published in 1955 by Seton Gordon, a Scottish expert, mentioned that the only locality where this normally territorial eagle was reported to nest in a colony was in the Rocky Mountains of western Alberta. The name of the site was Eagles Nest Pass. Gordon had obtained that information from Professor William Rowan, the dean of biology with the University of Alberta. In turn, the professor's knowledge was based on hearsay from First Nations hunters, who had seen the nests. Unfortunately, when Rowan set out to investigate the rumor, he had been forced to turn back before reaching his goal because the trail to the pass was blocked by deep snow.

When Irma and I walked the short distance to the summit of the pass and looked up at the imposing wall of rock on the south side, we could see two very large piles of branches on the cliff, which we assumed were the nests of eagles. On one of the nests, we spotted a pair of adult goldens and an almost fully grown youngster. A well-known fact of eagle biology is that the territorial occupants of traditional sites each year add sticks to some nests until they may become two or more metres high. Eagles also tend to construct more than one nest and use them alternately, which probably was the explanation for the local rumour of a nesting colony at this imposing cliff site.

During our stay the weather was calm and clear, with afternoon temperatures climbing above 25 degrees Celsius, but the nights dropped to below freezing. We spent our days walking the horse trails and looking for tracks. Wolves had passed by in both directions, and here and there we found the footprints of grizzly bears. As to animal sightings, we spotted a band of bighorn sheep high on a ridge, two mule deer, and one large bull moose. Each evening, a moose cow stood looking at us from the opposite side of the valley. We did not realize that all she wanted was to follow the game trail that we had inadvertently blocked with the tent. On the last night, she gathered her courage and her approaching footfall had us paralyzed with fear. One of her hooves touched a guy line of the tent with the twang of a plucked guitar. Taking a quick look outside, I just caught a glimpse of her hairy rump going down the creek bank, leaving us much relieved to know that our visitor had been a moose instead of a grizzly. In the morning, when we packed up the tent, we saw that one of my creek-fording shoes had been gnawed by a mouse, which explained a nighttime noise that had been startlingly loud in the stillness of the night.

Archie did not show on the date when he had promised to collect us. Waiting in vain for another day, we decided to hike out the next morning. Irma's sister and friends would no doubt be very worried and report us missing. From the start, they had been doubtful about the wisdom of our plan to go camping in the backcountry.

It did not take us long to dismantle the tent and leave all camping equipment in a neat pile by the edge of the trail. With the sleeping bags strapped to my pack and carrying some food for lunch, we began the long walk back to Rock Lake. The weather was great, and the trail was mostly downhill, so that we ended up enjoying the day and the scenery. The ranger was quite surprised, even embarrassed, to see us again. He had thought that we would be okay out there, since the weather had been fine. Besides, he had been duty-bound to remain on station alert because of the high forest fire hazard during the heat wave.

In subsequent years I made other trips to Eagles Nest Pass in the company of Peter DeMulder. By that time, I had obtained permission to overnight in the local forestry cabins. Since the distance involved was well over ten kilometres and the trail rather smooth, I raised the idea of using bikes. As I had no bicycle myself, Peter loaned me an older one belonging to his daughters, and with the packs secured on the carrier, we greatly enjoyed the ride. Especially the way back, which was easy and mostly descending, enabling us to stay ahead of the mosquitoes and horseflies. To my knowledge, we may have been the first-ever mountain bikers, well before this hobby became as popular as it is today.

In the alpine country, we stashed the bikes and made day trips to the headwaters of the Berland River. Animal sightings were quite rare. Apart from bighorn sheep on distant ridges, we spotted just one herd of elk, several mule deer, and two lynxes. We saw no wolves or bears, although their sign was ubiquitous. Tracks make for thin soup, hunters say, but to me, looking for tracks became a passion. To this day, I am unable to pass by a muddy section of trail without stopping and checking for animal tracks. Ironically, mud became the reason we abandoned plans for additional trips to Eagles Nest Pass. As the manager of a large medical laboratory, Peter had to plan his weekend nature trips well ahead, regardless of the weather forecast. During our last three-day trip to the pass, the rain started in late afternoon of the first day and never stopped. On the way back, parts of the horse trail had turned into a mire of mud and we ended up carrying our bikes or dragging them through swollen creeks to clear the clogged wheels.

Apart from the frustration of muddy trails, there was another reason why we stopped going to Eagles Nest Pass. The new slogan of the pro-development Alberta government was 'Roads to Resources.' The Indian Trail was to be opened up to surveyors and geologists prospecting for coal deposits and promising mineral riches. Their intrusive and messy activities became an eyesore. At Eagles Nest Pass, vandals painted their company names in huge letters on the cliffs. The highway from Hinton north was widened and extended to Grande Cache. A railway was added to service a new coal mine, which ended up becoming a financial burden for the provincial taxpayer after the export market for the mine's coal collapsed. Furthermore, the new road corridor to Grande Cache blocked the seasonal migrations of mountain caribou, which had been declared an endangered species in the province.

The original intention of designating Willmore Park had been to safeguard its 4,600 square kilometres of wilderness as a preserve for provincial horse outfitters and their clients. In 1994 it was reconfirmed as a provincial park, in which industrial development and motorized traffic would not be permitted. A major benefit of the Willmore is that this huge block of protected wilderness is adjacent to Jasper National Park, the jewel in the crown of Canadian National Parks.

CHAPTER 5
The Aspen-Elk-Wolves Equation

The tree line in the Canadian Rocky Mountains is roughly at 2,100 metres (7,000 feet) above sea level. At 1,386 metres the elevation of Rock Lake is well below that line, but a common tree like the poplar, which occurs in Canada from coast to coast, is already close to its vertical limit. Some deciduous trees are hardier than poplars and better able to cope with the thinning of oxygen at increasing altitudes or with other environmental limitations, such as drought, waterlogged soils, or extreme cold. All trees with leaves are eclipsed in toughness by those with needles, such as pines, spruces, and junipers. Around Rock Lake, the dark mantle of evergreens is only here and there enlivened by the lighter shade of green or the blazing yellow of poplars, either the slender aspen or the sturdier balsam poplar. In Jasper National Park, the aspen is an important food resource for a host of wild creatures that love its bark, twigs, buds, and leaves, or suck its sap.

A few kilometres west of Rock Lake, the horse trail to Jasper branches off from the Indian Trail and makes a sharp left turn across the eastern flank of Daybreak Peak. Much of the lodgepole pine forest on both sides was killed off by forest fires sixty or more years ago, and fallen trunks block the path after every storm. The steepest part of the trail crosses the gully of an unnamed rivulet that I call Fools Gold Creek because the bottom sparkles with glittering flakes of mica. On hot days, its clear water is good for a cool drink or a foot bath. A little way past the creek, the trail begins to descend and passes by a signpost marking the boundary of Jasper National Park. Near the bottom of the hill, the view opens up and allows a glimpse of the Rock Creek flats to the left. A marsh with an expanse of shimmering mud made me step off the trail to check it out for tracks, until I heard the explosive alarm barks of a coyote that stayed hidden in the brush. Was the coyote's alarm sparked by a bear? Proceeding with the greatest care, alert to every movement or sound, I discovered that the marsh was a partially dry beaver pond. Standing on the remnants of the dam, I was amazed by its great width: well over two hundred metres, the longest dam I had ever seen. The breach in the structure through which the water had flowed out could not have opened up more than a couple of years ago, for the bottom of the pond was still free of vegetation. On the muddy margin, I came across the footprints of deer, elk, wolves, and coyotes, as well as the scribbles of muskrats and some birds. There also were the very fresh pads of a black bear.

There was no proof that the former pond was still inhabited by its aquatic engineers. There were no living poplar trees around. Fallen trunks and cut-off stumps were much in evidence. Evidently, the colony had eaten itself out of house and home and had been forced to go in search of a new place at the risk of encountering their mortal enemies.

Returning to the trail, I could hear the rushing waters of Rock Creek, and the sound gradually increased to a menacing roar. Fording the braided channels of this turbulent mountain stream always presented a challenge. The bedding and shores were strewn with stones and gravel, so I lost the horse trail, but once I had entered a belt of mature spruces, I soon found the right path again and resumed my hike to Willow Creek. The space in between the two watersheds constitutes the lowest divide you may find anywhere. On the north side, the wetland rivulets seep into Rock Creek and Rock Lake. On the south side of the divide, meandering Willow Creek merges with the Snake Indian River, a major tributary of the great Athabasca that drains Jasper's main valley. All of these wilderness waters eventually discharge into the Arctic Ocean.

The Willow Creek valley is a delightful mosaic of montane meadows studded with spruce and willows. The west side of the valley includes a string of beaver ponds, like beads on a chain, but most are dry. Cut-off poplar stumps are everywhere, presenting the same desolate scene as on the Rock Creek side. Evidently the region had once been a major stronghold for beavers and a paradise for a host of creatures that benefit from the beaver's work, including ducks, muskrats, otters, mink, trout, songbirds, dragonflies, and aquatic invertebrates. All of this water-based community of species had vanished after the beavers had exhausted their food supply. On the opposite side of the valley, on higher ground, some copses of aspen had apparently survived, but too far away for secure access by beavers, leaving them open to ambush attacks from wolves or bears. On closer inspection, though, even those aspen stands proved to be in trouble. They were over-mature. Compared to other species of trees, aspen have a relatively short lifespan, not much more than fifty or sixty years.

The ground under the groves was littered with dead trunks, and there were no saplings or young trees to be seen. Why were these aspens not rejuvenating themselves by sending up suckering shoots, I wondered? Nowhere in the valley was there any evidence of normal regeneration, not around the dry beaver ponds, nor anywhere else on higher ground.

Years later, while I continued my seasonal hikes to the same valley, I began to get an inkling of what had brought about such a drastic change in the interconnected world of animals here. In late April or May, the aspen groves came into leaf, and during summer numerous shoots emerged around the trees. But by the following spring, I could not find a single one. Over the winter season, something or someone had killed or removed all of the suckers. It was then that I had a eureka moment, a novel insight into the dynamics at work here. The key to the aspen's demise was browsing by grazing animals. In addition to eating the nutritious aspen shoots, the elk, deer, and moose had munched the twigs as high as they could reach. Starving elk had even stripped bark from the boles.

Compounding the problem of overgrazing and adding to the competition among the native herbivores were the horses of local outfitters. Ever since the park's establishment, they had been permitted to winter their stock in the Snake Indian Valley. Well into spring or early summer, the meadows were grazed by thirty or more saddle and pack horses. Several were collared with cow bells that clanged with every step and could be heard from afar.

Elk in what is now Jasper National Park have a volatile population history, which swings on a pendulum from great scarcity to abundance and back again. According to the earliest European fur scouts, elk were common on the western plains during the 1700s and the early 1800s, but by the turn of that century, elk and all other ungulates, including their predators, were at a very low ebb, due to year-round hunting by native peoples and early European travellers. In 1811, David Thompson reported seeing no elk. He was a great naturalist and purportedly the first European to travel through the Athabasca Valley on his way to the Pacific coast.

Jasper National Park was established in 1907, and elk were reintroduced in 1920, with 88 animals that had been corralled in Yellowstone and shipped by rail to Alberta. Six years later, due to effective protection and the absence of predators, the park's elk had multiplied to about 1,000, and in 1940 the herds were estimated at 3,000. Already then, biologists with the Canadian

Wildlife Service were concerned that the elk were destroying forage on a large scale, with negative consequences for wintering bighorn sheep. During the 1960s, additional concern was expressed that the elk were invading the alpine summer range of mountain caribou, which were declining. To alleviate grazing pressure in the park's main valley, wardens culled the elk herds by shooting about 200 animals per year, mainly cows. This hard-nosed policy was started in 1949 and continued until 1970. In total, 2,100 elk were slaughtered, their meat given away to First Nations bands. Reduced to 2,000–2,500 in 1973, the estimate of elk in the park quite abruptly dropped to less than 1,000 in 1975. The main cause of the crash was starvation due to an extremely severe winter. By late March of that year, snow depth at Jasper town was still at a record 0.9 metres. Superimposed on the climatic crisis were two other critical factors: the overgrazed condition of the winter range and predation pressure from wolves, bears, and cougars.

Anthony Henday, the first European fur scout to reach Alberta in 1754, noted that wolves were common around bison on the plains. "I cannot say whether them or the bison are most numerous," he wrote. Other early travellers passing through what is now Jasper National Park made frequent anecdotal references to wolves. To protect their wintering horses, Hudson Bay postmasters began setting out poison baits in 1859. By the end of that century, wolves had practically disappeared from western Alberta. So had their prey. All of that changed for the better after the establishment of Jasper National Park.

In sync with the return of the elk, the park's wolves slowly reclaimed their former domain. Yet, while elk were reaching peak numbers and damaging the winter range, park wolves were shot on sight, their dens dug out and the pups destroyed. Professor Ian McTaggart-Cowan, one of Canada's earliest and greatest ecologists, had to admit that wolves would have to be kept down in order to protect the elk and other ungulates. In the 1940s, based on warden reports, Professor Cowan estimated the park's wolf population at 35 to 55. Official figures changed little during the 1960s, but the estimate doubled to 80–100 in 1984. Even that figure may have been an underestimate, because outfitters operating in boundary districts reported packs of 18–25 members in the Brazeau, Smoky, Miette, and Moosehorn watersheds.

In my Willow Creek study area, I watched a family of ten or eleven wolves at their den site. Over many years, with persistence and luck, I enjoyed detailed views of all pack members. About half of them were grey-brown, others black or silvery grey. Two were reddish brown with black legs and tail. Getting a glimpse of the season's five or six pups was always the highlight of the year.

By the end of the 1970s, while I was observing the Willow Creek pack, there were reports of denning wolves at higher elevations in the Snake Indian watershed and near the river's confluence with the Athabasca. Precise population data were unavailable but there was no doubt that the park's wolves had greatly increased. During the same time, elk estimates continued to drop. The causal connection between the two phenomena seemed self-evident. So was the discovery that there had been a spectacular improvement in aspen regeneration in the Willow Creek valley. Some of the suckering shoots survived the winter due to a marked decline in elk browsing, and here and there dense thickets of saplings had begun to grow taller than a six-foot man.

I also noted that dense willow bushes and other shrubs were springing up along the trail. All of this looked like good news. The valley was recovering from the calamity that began with an overpopulation of elk and its negative impact on the intertwined lives of a range of animals that depended on the aspen. After the elk population declined, beavers rebuilt some of the ponds. Eventually, ducks, muskrats and trout returned. Songbirds and bears took advantage of the berry bushes that were no longer destroyed by hungry elk. The interconnected dynamics of aspen, elk, and wolves became the subject of my 1985 research paper in the Alberta Naturalist and a chapter in my book 'Wild Hunters' published during the same year.

Another interesting story having to do with aspen and elk came from Yellowstone National Park. About 8,500 square kilometres in size, Yellowstone is smaller than Jasper's 11,000 square kilometres, but its elk population was ten times greater. As reported by long-term researcher Dr. Charles Kay, hungry herds of elk were shearing aspen stands by browsing the branches as high as an elk could reach and by devouring their sprouting shoots. The hope was that the damage would ease after the reintroduction of wolves. In 1995, after a decade of controversy and heated discussions, fifteen wolves, captured in western Alberta, were released into the Lamar Valley and allowed to work their magic in restoring the natural balance between grass and meat in Yellowstone.

With permission from Alberta's Fish and Wildlife Division, American crack biologists, flying helicopters, were successful in dropping nets on fifteen wolves in the provincial foothills not far from Jasper's east boundary. Based on my experience in Jasper, I predicted (1) that the wolves would cull Yellowstone's elk herd; (2) that aspen and willows would get a chance to rejuvenate; (3) that habitat and food resources would be enriched for beavers, fish, birds, and bears, and (4) that Yellowstone would become a great place for future observation of wild wolves because of the wide open habitat in the Lamar Valley. All of these predictions have since come true and today are popular knowledge.

In 2005, I was contacted by two forestry professors from Oregon. They had read my paper in the *Alberta Naturalist* and wanted detailed information about Willow Creek and how to get there. They intended to repeat my project. Upon arrival, they analyzed the age of the aspen trees by counting growth rings of the trunks and compared these timelines with the dates I had given them for the collapse of the local elk population and the big return of the wolves. Some time later, I was approached by a Canadian scientist who also wanted to test the conclusions I had reached at Willow Creek. In subsequent years, these scientists conducted similar studies in Yellowstone National Park, but to my surprise and regret, they did not credit my Jasper investigations as having been the catalyst and inspiration for their ecological discoveries. Yellowstone's wolves have become famous as the keystone predators of the world's first national park, where runaway elk numbers had been destroying the park's aspen, with serious secondary impacts on a range of other wildlife. The wolves' role in the interconnected food chain between plants and animals has received abundant and widespread publicity and has become known as a trophic cascade. An enthusiastic reporter even came up with the fanciful notion that wolves were changing rivers. The way to explain this is that the reduced browsing pressure from elk was expected to result in the regrowth of bushes along the river's edge and thus reduce bank erosion.

Since then, a number of biologists who were aware of my longstanding interest in wolves but did not know that I had been first to describe the aspen-elk-wolf equation in Jasper National Park, excitedly approached me with comments like this: "Have you heard that the Yellowstone wolves are playing a key role in the regeneration of the park's aspen poplars? Did you know that they are improving the habitat for a range of other wildlife?"

I recently learned of an interesting update to the Yellowstone situation. Based on continuing research by ecologists Drs. Charles Kay and Cliff White, the aspen and willows of Yellowstone's northern range have actually shown little regrowth. Although the park's elk herd has declined by some 60%, there was another player in the equation, namely a growing population of 5,000 bison, which was keeping parts of the northern winter range heavily overgrazed and locally bald.

The explanation of why the aspen-versus-elk dynamic played such a dominant role in Yellowstone and Willow Creek is that poplars are relatively scarce in this high elevation ecosystem. Aspen groves in particular are limited to pockets of suitable habitat. It explains why elk herbivory at Willow Creek is so severe, much more so than away from the park's montane. For instance, east of Jasper Park, at lower elevations in the Edson or Whitecourt forests, poplar stands are in no way vulnerable to elk because there are just too many poplars and too few elk there. The only herbivore that periodically can have a locally devastating impact on the regeneration of poplars and willows in Canada's boreal forest is the snowshoe hare, particularly during years when its numbers reach a cyclic peak.

On the way to the Devona flats, I often walked along the north shore of Jasper Lake. The imposing mountain front is the DeSmet Range.   Photo Brian Genereux

Thirty years ago, the slope below the Devona lookout hill was open. Today, the grass is studded with spruce seedlings.

Crossing frozen Jasper Lake was always risky, with or without snow shoes..

Long-time companion Mister Intrepid by the winter tent.

Prior to the 1970s, wintering herds of browsing elk prevented the aspen groves in the Willow Creek valley from rejuvenating. After the big return of wolves, elk declined and aspen recovered. The meadow in the foreground was kept free of bushes and trees by the horses of the Willow Creek park warden.

A traditional rendezvous-site of the local wolf pack.

CHAPTER 6
How Grey is the Gray Wolf?

In the standard textbook of Canadian mammals, written by Ottawa zoologist A.W.F. Banfield, the common species name of *Canis lupus* was just wolf, while the American name has always been gray wolf. Unfortunately, the American label, including its spelling, has now also been adopted in Canada. Which is a pity, because this colour-based name is clearly a misnomer.

Half a century ago, provincial biologist Dewey Soper described five different subspecies of wolves for Alberta, while Banfield recognized 17 for Canada. The number of subspecies inhabiting all of North America, based on physical characteristics and geographic range, ran to several dozen. More recently, however, by scientific consensus, the continental total has been drastically whittled down to only three or four subspecies. These include the gray wolf, the white arctic wolf, the red wolf of the American southeast, and perhaps the Mexican wolf.

The present range of the gray wolf extends right across the continent, from Montana to Minnesota and from Alaska to Labrador. But there is a marked difference between east and west. With very rare exceptions, all eastern wolves are tan-grey, resembling the coyote. By contrast, the pelage colour of western gray wolves shows extreme individual variation. For instance, in two 1950s wolf control campaigns by government agents in Alberta and British Columbia, in which a total of nearly one thousand wolves were poisoned, the respective percentages of black were 31% and 33%. The proportion of blacks in Alaska is in the same order of magnitude.

Apparently, black wolves were not uncommon in Mississippi and Florida. More than half a century ago, the renowned American wolfers Stanley Young and Edward Goldman named two smallish southern subspecies *Canis niger* and *Canis niger rufus*. This indicates that the subspecific name red wolf actually is a misnomer, too.

In our Rocky Mountain National Parks, melanism has always been common. In the 1940s, 55% of 80 wolves seen by park wardens were described as black. In the summers of 1966–1985, I saw 132 wolves at their dens in Jasper's upper Snake Indian Valley, and the black percentage was 53%. In Yellowstone National Park, where wolves from western Canada were reintroduced a decade ago, the black contingent of the current population is about half.

As a volunteer wildlife watcher in Jasper National Park, I have monitored wolves and their prey species on a wintering range in the lower Athabasca Valley over 35 years. My methods were simple and required no more than patience and luck to be in the right place at the right time. Each day, around sundown and just after dawn, I spent an hour or so on a ridge overlooking the semi-open Devona flats. Over the years, as of 1998, I saw wolves on about 150 days of the 600 or so spent in the field. Quite often, the sighting involved just a single animal, at other times a pack. The size of the local wolf pack changed from year to year and varied from five to thirteen, except for 1983, when it declined to two. Mean or average pack size was 7.9 members. Seventy-four percent of all wolves seen were black. This is the highest proportion ever reported anywhere. In 1992, all 13 members of the local pack were black. And between 1992 and 1996, I failed to see a single grey wolf.

From 1999 to 2013, I recorded another 68 wolf sightings, of which 82% were black, but in 2014 and 2015 the Devona pack of respectively six and eight members was evenly split between the two colour variants. Elsewhere in Jasper, park wardens reported an all-grey pack of six. Then, in September of 2018, I was sent a video of 12 wolves, of which 11 were jet-black. This rare footage was filmed by Raoul Voshaar, the instructor of a Dutch Buitensport School, who had been on a wolf-finding trip to Alberta's Willmore Park. He and a dozen of his students were lucky enough to observe the wolves from a viewpoint overlooking Rock Lake, on the north boundary of Jasper National Park. The largest wolf in the pack was white, and the blacks included five pups of the year.

Black puppies often feature a white spot on the chest. Black adults may have white feet or a whitish face, and after one or more years, the dark pelage of nearly all blacks fades to bluish-grey, brown-grey, or silver. Some even turn white, which was closely observed in Yellowstone National Park. There, two radio-collared black wolves, transplanted from Alberta, became practically white after just two years. Extreme bleaching of black wolves has also been reported in captive situations.

While the colour of a grey wolf changes little with age, Jasper's high percentage of blacks may be indicative of a young population. The mortality rate of these park wolves is believed to be high because they are subject to trapping and hunting on the park boundaries. Inside the park, this fleetfooted predator runs afoul of vehicles and trains. Warden Wes Bradford, who kept track of such data, reports that the average yearly number of fatalities over the previous decade was around four, with a peak of ten casualties in 1996. The traffic toll of hoofed mammals as well as of wolves is expected to grow as the highway and railroad corridor that transects the park becomes even busier.

Interestingly, based on historical records, the wolves of the American frontier, prior to their final extermination earlier this century, included black animals as well as whites. In a paper published in the *Canadian Field-Naturalist*, biologists Philip Gipson and Warren Ballard reported that one-third of 59 notorious cattle-killing lobos of the Old West were white. Several of these crafty survivors became adept at avoiding traps and poison, and they were known to have reached an old age of 15 years. Apparently, having your hair turn silver or white with increasing age is a characteristic that we share with the wild ancestor of man's best friend.

A press release titled 'Black wolves have evolutionary edge over their grey cousins' hit the Canadian newspapers in February 2009. Written by Ottawa journalist Tom Spears, this article misrepresents the research findings of a group of 15 biologists and geneticists, who published a paper in the *American Journal of Science* (323:1339-1343) under the title: 'Molecular and evolutionary history of melanism in North American Gray Wolves.' The scientists linked black fur in gray wolves to a mutation that was lost to wolves in ancient times, before they split into wolves and dogs. They further speculated that the black gene was subsequently re-acquired after wolves hybridized with domestic dogs. And this was most likely to have happened, the scientists thought, some 15,000 years ago, after wolves crossed over from Asia into Alaska via the land bridge that developed between the two continents during the Pleistocene ice age.

In my opinion, the scientists exaggerated the significance of their finding by claiming that black wolves are better adapted than their grey cousins to climate change, because black fur, they said, would be an advantage for forest-dwelling predators. Black wolves would gain in camouflage if climate change leads to the northward expansion of tree cover. This argument is questionable in view of the fact that the role of climate change may be entirely different in its effect on the North American landscape. Instead of expanding the forest belt, a warmer and dryer climate may locally result in the demise of forests and create more open terrain, so that the so-called advantage of being black would be lost. At any rate, in my 60 years of experience in Jasper National Park, black wolves were at all times more visible than grey ones, even among the trees. Yukon biologist Bob Hayes, who has conducted three decades of field research of wolf predation on moose and caribou, advanced the theory that having black fur would be a camouflage advantage during the long northern night. His viewpoint makes sense if wolves were indeed to do most of their hunting after sundown, which is not a question I can answer.

Melanism in North American wolves pre-existed well before wolves crossed over from Asia into North America. Fossil evidence pointed American professor Ronald Nowak to the idea that the forebear of all wolves is the red wolf of the American Southwest. It includes a black variant that was given the scientific name of *Canis niger*. Wolf colour was examined again with a lot of data from Yellowstone and Jasper in a research paper published by Hedrick and others in the *Journal of Heredity* (2014.105:457-465). The questions they raised had to do with possible differences in mate selection and reproductive success between the two variants.

Interestingly, some years ago at a wolf meeting in Holland I met a Russian wolf biologist who said that black wolves were unknown in his country or elsewhere in Europe. Interestingly, in North America melanism is not limited to wolves. It is also common in red foxes, where it can have nothing to do with hybridisation, since foxes and dogs cannot interbreed because their chromosome numbers are different. Melanism also occurs in the grey squirrel. After this large eastern species was introduced near Vancouver, the sight of black squirrels has become routine in Stanley Park. Black fur has even been reported in the common Richardson's ground squirrel, or gopher. Colonies of blacks have been recorded near Edmonton, in the Yukon and in Jasper National Park.

Black coyotes are apparently very rare, and the only ones I ever saw, or knew about, were the product of hybridisation with a farm dog. My records date back to August 1995, when I was walking the open pasture lands along the west shore of Beaverhills Lake. To my great surprise, I came across six coyote pups of the year, all jet black. To me, they just looked like miniature wolves.

During subsequent visits, I glimpsed one of the adults; a white-and-black border collie! In 1996, in the same general area, I saw several lone black coyotes, and three together in 1997. One of these was all black, the second dark grey, and the third featured white on the chest and tail.

So what is so important about black fur in wolves? For me as an observer, the fact that the Jasper wolves come in two very different colours has added greatly to the joys of watching them. In a pack dominated by blacks, it was the exceptional grey wolf who became special, and vice versa. The proportion of black versus grey and the individual variations between them have been important clues in recognizing individual wolves and telling one pack from the other. Seeing a wolf that I have seen before gives me a feeling of meeting an old friend.

The majority of wolves in western Canada are black. Yet, their official species name is grey wolf.
Photo Brian Genereux

Wolves often feed on road kill. This big grey was photographed along a highway near Jasper. Note its swollen belly,
Photo Keith Lengle

CHAPTER 7
Mule Deer versus White-tailed Deer

Scientists have described the perennial contest between prey and predator as an arms race, in which the prey continually improves its defences while the predator strives to overcome those defences. Another often-made point is that the slender legs of the deer have been sculpted by the wolf. Each of the seven species of hoofed mammals native to Jasper National Park has its own method of coping with predation. For a deer, it's a question of running for 'dear' life.

There are two kinds of deer in Jasper: the native mule deer and a fairly recent invader from eastern Canada, the white-tailed deer. While the former has declined, the latter has greatly increased. Can the difference be explained in relation to their respective vulnerability to their predators? Is the white-tail perhaps better able than the mule deer to cope with the danger posed by wolves?

During 35 consecutive winters of watching wildlife at Devona in the lower main valley of Jasper National Park, I have counted all deer seen and compared the frequency of mule deer sightings per day to white-tail sightings. My tally of all deer came to over 400. And each year I have been lucky enough to see the local wolf pack, which has averaged ten members. But direct observations of wolf and deer interactions have been uncommon.

One March afternoon, while walking along a game trail on an open ridge above the Snake Indian River, I spotted a female white-tailed deer bounding along toward me. I stopped and she halted two metres away, her mouth agape, tongue protruding. Her eyes seemed glazed over with fatigue and fear. After a moment of hesitation, she darted by at arm's length to resume her headlong flight. Suspecting that she was being chased, I moved aside a few steps behind a spruce tree. Seconds later, a grey wolf, red tongue lolling, came loping down the trail. Just a few metres away, he suddenly spun around and dashed back the way he had come. As much as I dislike interfering in the lives of wild animals, I had involuntarily saved the life of this defenceless deer.

Over much of North America, deer are the optimum prey species for wolves. Compared to moose or elk, deer seem easy to kill, even for a single wolf, but catching one is another matter. From the air, David Mech, the famous American wolf researcher, once followed an exceptionally long hunt by a radio-collared wolf, which, with two companions, began to chase a white-tailed deer. Two hours later, the plane had to return to base for refuelling. In the meantime, the collared wolf had lost his companions but he was still hot on the trail of the deer, and by that time he had already covered a distance of just over 20 kilometres through the snowy forests of Minnesota. David Mech never learned the outcome of that long chase.

In Jasper National Park, over 50-plus years, I have seen several wolves in hot pursuit of deer, but the final act was always hidden from my view. Once, when I came across the remains of a freshly killed deer and back-tracked the wolf, I discovered that the chase had actually been very short. The successful wolf had stormed down a steep slope and intercepted its prey in deep snow at the base of the hillside.

Zoologist Valerius Geist points out that mule deer, in hilly habitat, may be less vulnerable to pursuing predators than white-tails. Fleeing in their characteristic high bounding gait with all fours off the ground, which is called stotting, mule deer can clear hurdles in rough terrain and quickly ascend steep slopes where predators lag behind. Fleeing over open ground, though, might be risky. Bigger and heavier than the white-tail, a mule deer buck can put up a good defence as long as his vulnerable back side is protected. His forked rack has a greater span than the antlers of a white-tailed buck and can be turned into a lethal weapon.

On a very cold November morning in 2010, a companion and I were looking at the partly wooded mountainside west of Jasper Lake. Scanning the slopes through binoculars, we discovered three wolves—two blacks and a grey—hanging around by a dense clump of young evergreens. Their hesitant behaviour seemed puzzling. Another black wolf was lying asleep higher up on the crest of the slope, as if he or she was recovering from a long chase. After some 20 minutes, the three wolves joined the single wolf and all four disappeared over the wooded ridge, where snow lay deep. Elated to have seen the local wolf pack, we kept scanning the slopes, and presently, to our surprise, a big-antlered mule deer buck stepped forth out of the evergreen bush by which the three wolves had been loitering. The way I interpret this happenstance observation is that the dapper buck had managed to save his life by pressing his rump against the protective screen of spruce branches and presenting the pointed daggers of his huge rack to keep the wolves at bay.

The following week, in the same general area, sharp-eyed Wes Bradford, a retired Jasper park warden who was guiding a nature film crew, spotted two black wolves sleeping on frozen Jasper Lake near a downed mule deer buck, which appeared to have sustained a bloody wound in his rump. Later that day, the same observers saw a large grey wolf approach at a trot. The buck quickly got to his feet and unhesitatingly gored the charging wolf, which yelped in pain and limped off. Next morning, there were four wolves asleep on the ice and the deer had been consumed. Later that winter, on two memorable occasions, I saw the pack of four again, travelling down the Snake Indian River Valley; the three blacks in the lead, the big grey following at some distance. Every now and then the blacks waited for their limping companion to catch up.

The native ungulate fauna of North America includes the white-tailed deer and the black-tailed deer. The white-tail is originally an eastern and southern species that was at a very low ebb in the 17th century, due to unlimited hunting, but the species has since greatly increased and expanded its range. The white-tail is now the most common ungulate in North America. Valerius Geist attributes the white-tail's success to its resistance to parasites and diseases that limit its potential competitors in the northern climate. No doubt, timely legal protection and sound management have been of essential importance, too.

The black-tailed deer is a western species of the family and its largest subspecies is the mule deer, which ranges from California to Arizona and north to Yukon. Mule deer and white-tails can interbreed and produce hybrids, which may or may not be fertile. The two species eat the same foods, and on sympatric range there is no inherent conflict between them. In the long run, though, the white-tail appears to dominate. For instance, in southern Manitoba prior to European settlement, the original deer population was composed almost solely of mule deer; the present situation is reversed, with a preponderance of white-tails.

In Alberta, white-tailed deer were only rarely seen in the southwest of the province during the 1950s, until they gradually spread northward. White-tails began to appear in the Rocky Mountains of west-central Alberta in the 1940s, and the earliest record for Jasper National Park is 1943. The population increased during the 1950s and 1960s, particularly in semi-open habitats of the lower Athabasca valley. At Willow Creek, where I began a 20-year mammal survey in 1965, I recorded the first white-tailed deer in 1980.

Mule deer were scarce in Jasper until the park's establishment in 1907. Protected from hunting, they became common in the valleys and seasonally at higher elevations. Professor Cowan reported the densest concentration of mule deer at Devona in the lower Athabasca Valley, where I began a yearly census of large mammals in 1981. Over 35 winters, between October and March from 1981 to 2016, I spent 718 observation days in that district, frequently accompanied by (the late) Peter DeMulder or Brian Genereux. Getting there on foot, we arrived in the afternoon of the first day and left again in the afternoon of the last day. A three-day trip involved two overnightings and was counted as two complete days in the field, because it included two mornings and two evenings of observation time. From a hillside lookout, we scanned the semi-open montane meadows and the river flats at the base of the hill through binoculars or a telescope.

Of the 425 deer spotted, 270 (64%) were white-tails and 155 (36%) mulies. Sightings of white-tails increased significantly from 0.08 per day in 1981–1985 to 1.08 per day in 2010–2016. In contrast, over this same time span, mulies declined from 0.40 sightings per day to 0.06 per day. When added together, all deer, either mulies or white-tails, increased from 0.48 per day in the first five years to 1.13 per day in the last five years. Total sightings of deer more than doubled over time, indicating that the decline in mule deer was offset by an increase in white-tails.

These results clearly show that white-tailed deer have increased over the past 35 years and that mule deer have declined. However, the primary cause of these opposing trends in abundance is not clear. One possible factor is predation, but, as mentioned, whether mule deer are more at risk than the white-tail is unknown. The main predators of deer are wolves and coyotes, and wolves are known to kill coyotes. Between 1981 and 2016, while wolves were common at Devona, my coyote sightings declined from 0.2 per day in 1981–2001 to 0.03 in 2001–2006. In 2007–2016, the sighting rate dropped to a mere 0.02 per day.

Cougars also prey on deer. I have seen six of these big cats at Devona, and their tracks in snow could be found each winter. In a published study from southern British Columbia, cougar predation was found to have a disproportionate effect on mule deer compared to white-tails, but the impact of cougars on deer in Jasper is not exactly known.

The opposing population trend of the two deer species recorded at Devona can be compared to a list of 191 deer killed on roads and highways, and picked up by Jasper park staff. Although these casualty figures may be somewhat compromised by the likelihood that mammalian scavengers, such as bears and wolves, tend to drag carrion into cover, thus reducing the chance that it is found by park wardens, the road kill data roughly parallel my results. The traffic toll of white-tailed deer rose from zero in 1980–1984 to 17 in 2010–2014. However, these figures are no true reflection of deer population trends in the park's traffic corridor, for they are affected by the increasing traffic on the roads that transect Jasper. Vehicle counts on the Yellowhead Highway in the lower Athabasca Valley have more than doubled from 0.8 million per annum in 1980 to 1.7 million in 2014. No doubt further increases have occurred since then.

Deer inhabit semi-open terrain and tend to avoid closed forests. Tree clearing along an oil pipeline corridor in the Devona district may well have played a role in attracting deer, and the white-tail is believed to be better able than mule deer to take advantage of man-made openings in wooded terrain. Forest maturation and plant succession have been progressing naturally in Jasper ever since the park's establishment in 1907. Repeat photographs taken from my observation hill show that formerly open meadows and slopes are increasingly invaded by spruce seedlings, while mature spruces growing on the flats have restricted the view from the lookout hill. Notwithstanding the above, over 35 years, my deer sightings have more than doubled from 0.48 per day to 1.13.

The influx of white-tailed deer has not only coincided with a decline of mule deer but also led to an increase in the total deer population at Devona. Based on statistical analysis, the difference in population trends of the two deer species is highly significant, but whether the one species is more vulnerable to their predators than the other remains unclear. The amazing fact is that the white-tail has managed to expand its range continent-wide and that it is now thriving in the western mountains despite the presence of wolves and cougars.

As mentioned earlier in this chapter, Valerius Geist has suggested that the white-tail seems less susceptible to disease than other ungulates. The most serious long-term threat to deer populations, including elk and moose, is spongiform encephalopathy, or chronic wasting disease (CWD). First recognized in 1967 in Colorado, the cause is a prion or bacterium in the central nervous system, and the symptoms are progressive weight loss with fatal results. The disease has since spread across the United States into Canada. Fortunately, the disease is not considered transmittable to humans. So, eating deer meat is okay for hunters.

From captive herds in a Saskatchewan game farm, CWD has spread into wild deer populations in that province. In attempts to stop the infection at the border, the Alberta Fish & Wildlife Department began a campaign of pre-emptive herd reduction and disease control in eastern regions of the province. Starting in 2005, deer numbers were culled by shooting from helicopters and vehicles. Hunters cooperated by turning in the heads of harvested deer for analysis. At the program's termination in 2008, a total of 7,591 deer had been collected. Interestingly, the proportions of mule deer and white-tails were close, with 3,663 mulies and 3,928 white-tails. In this regard, and of particular relevance to the question raised earlier in this chapter, is the fact that there are no wolves in the disease control region!

The incidence of CWD in the two species proved to be different. The percentage of mule deer tested positive for CWD was 8.2% compared to 1.9% for the white-tails. The possibility that the disease might have influenced my deer count at Devona is unlikely, though. As of 2018, all dead JNP deer tested for CWD have proved to be negative, which indicates that the feared disease has not (yet) spread as far west as Alberta's Rocky Mountains.

The open bluff above Jasper Lake is called Ram Pasture. In 1969, there were 25 mature bighorns wintering on these slopes, but by 2016 the band had dwindled to two or three members.

The white-tailed deer is the only hoofed mammal that has increased in Jasper Park during the past fifty years.

Photo Mark Bradley

This coyote was observed stalking and killing a bighorn lamb. Disturbed by curious people, the coyote abandoned its fresh kill, crossed the highway and hunted down a second lamb. Coyote sightings have declined precipitously in Jasper's backcountry, while the wolf population has fluctuated.

Surrounded by ravens, a wolf is cleaning up the leftovers from a deer kill on the frozen Snake Indian River.

Photo Brian Genereux

CHAPTER 8
Wolves and Caribou

America's war on wolves started four centuries ago, soon after the arrival of English and French settlers in the 'howling wilderness' of the New World. In Alberta, the war has continued to this day for the purpose of wildlife management and to save the last of the woodland caribou.

This chapter presents a review of the heated controversy since the 1980s, when it became known that the provincial caribou population was in trouble. Purportedly, the quickest way to stop their decline was to remove *Canis lupus*, the wolf. Shooting wildlife from aircraft is illegal in this country, but Alberta's biologists obtained permission from their political masters to hunt down wolves from helicopters. When the survivors of this modern 'management tool' learned to take cover at the sound of approaching aircraft, the frustrated biologists shamelessly reverted back to the callous and indiscriminate methods of the past, including strychnine poisoning. Wanting to reduce wolf numbers by the most responsible method possible is one thing, but setting out poison baits is quite another, and it adds a scandalous dimension to the job of these professionals, who are actually aggravating the chaotic destruction of wildlife on public lands. According to available information, from 2006 onward, the number of wolves killed in the foothill forests of Alberta has surpassed 2,000. The toll of incidental victims, including carnivores and scavengers, such as foxes, lynxes, wolverines, martens, weasels, ravens, and eagles can only be guessed at. To justify their methodology, government biologists say that their only goal is to protect the dwindling caribou. Concerned conservationists immediately countered with the charge that the real enemy of the caribou is the provincial government itself, because its representatives continue to sell permits to industrial companies for the destruction of more foothill wilderness, the caribou's ancient habitat.

To add perspective to the ongoing controversy, the following includes a brief review of wolf control campaigns in Alberta, based on historical literature and scientific reports. Alberta's on-again off-again war on wolves started soon after the arrival of European immigrants, but what sealed the predator's doom was the simultaneous destruction of its prey base. By the end of the 19th century, human greed had killed off most of Alberta's wildlife that could either be eaten or traded as fur. Superimposed on the relentless hunting pressure was a series of extremely severe winters, which led to the starvation deaths of thousands of cattle in southern Alberta and practically wiped out the remnant elk and deer.

A gradual change for the better began with the enactment of game laws and the establishment of national parks. Hoofed mammals made a slow comeback, but the return of the wolf was viewed with misgiving. In the 1940s, wolves were even shot on sight in the national parks. During 1952–1960, the war on predators was stepped up a notch. The catalyst was that rabies had been identified in foxes in northern Alberta. To stop the feared disease from spreading south, the province unleashed the most intensive poisoning campaign ever, anytime, anywhere.

A more respectful era for wildlife dawned in the 1960s. Among the increasingly urban public, nature appreciation grew and embraced all of our fellow creatures, including the formerly despised and persecuted carnivores. Celebrated in magazines, books, and films, the big bad wolf of lore went through a complete metamorphosis and became as popular and beloved as Bambi. Attitudes among professional wildlife managers changed, too. Their slogan was inspired by the Beatles. Let it be. Human hunters had no reason to begrudge 'brother wolf' its prey. In a well-balanced ecosystem, large predators were said to function as agents of health, weeding out the weak and unfit among their prey species.

From 1966 onward, Alberta's wolves were allowed to stage a spontaneous recovery, and they did so with a vengeance, so to speak, because their prey base was super abundant. Breeding wolf packs repopulated the foothills and dispersed into farmlands. There, quite understandably, the Fish & Wildlife department had to draw the line, and setting poison baits became routine. Hunters, on the other hand, had little reason to complain. Due to the previous scarcity of predators, coupled with a series of mild winters, hoofed mammals were not hard to find on wilderness lands and bag limits were generous.

The armistice in the war on wolves did not last long, and the pendulum of tolerance soon swung the other way again. Wildlife communities are subject to cyclic highs and lows. In the mid-1960s, and particularly in 1973–1974, herbivores were hit hard by severe winters. Food-stressed and harassed by expanding numbers of wolves, bears, and cougars, elk and moose suffered a population collapse. Eventually, their numbers dropped to a fraction of what they had been a few years earlier.

After many detailed field studies on predation, wildlife managers changed their minds again. Too many wolves were killing too many hoofed mammals, in direct competition with human hunters and outfitters. Calls for remedial action became increasingly demanding. For instance, on December 29, 1982, the *Edmonton Journal* ran a story under the headline "Wolf population explosion raises howls for controls."

The war on wolves resumed full blast during the 1980s, beginning in Alaska. Canada's Yukon Territories and British Columbia soon followed. The objectives were upfront and straightforward: to make more venison and trophies available for human hunters. However, this time around, government biologists shied away from the use of poison. Instead, they reverted to a method considered more selective and humane: search and destroy with helicopters, inspired by the Vietnam jungle war.

The imagery of government personnel shotgunning a spooked pack of wolves from the air shocked a largely non-hunting public and sparked a tidal wave of protest in the national and international media. It led to a frenzy of demonstrations in California and tourism boycotts in Alaska. But despite an escalating chorus of protest, led by environmental crusader Paul Watson, the regional biologist in British Columbia persisted in shooting wolves. However, in the spring of 1986, he was quite suddenly reined in by his political masters. The stop order followed on the heels of a press release by Friends of the Wolf and their American affiliates, who were planning a major tourism boycott at Expo '86, to be held in Vancouver that summer.

In the spring of 1988, to calm the turmoil and open a public debate, the University of British Columbia, in partnership with government departments and private conservation groups, organized a wolf management symposium. In a terse presentation, a provincial biologist reported that he had personally shot 996 wolves from the air over two winters. Barely three years after the carnage, he considered his efforts to have been a waste of time. The wolves were back at their former strength, he claimed. The total expenditure of the campaign, in helicopter rental and manpower, was on the order of $2,500 to $3,000 per wolf. Similarly high costs were reported by the equally candid biologists from Alaska. There, support for the controversial wolf kills had come mainly from people who were concerned about the shrinking inventory of moose, a subsistence staple in that northern state. However, the Canadian focus was mainly on woodland caribou. A Yukon biologist supported a regional wolf cull and said that the economic importance of caribou, in pounds of meat, was greater than the monetary value of wolf fur sold. Another pro-control argument was voiced in B.C., where researchers claimed that local populations of woodland caribou were especially hit hard. The reason was that alpine habitats, formerly the exclusive domain of caribou, were increasingly invaded by moose, which in turn had attracted more wolves. Furthermore, they claimed that predation pressure was proportionally heavier on caribou than on moose. The only way to save the remaining caribou from extinction, the researchers warned, was to reduce the number of predators. This view soon became the mantra of government biologists in Alberta.

The fuse for the current wolf control campaign was lit more than thirty years ago, when the *Calgary Herald* of November 4, 1986, ran a news item under the headline 'Report outlines plan for major wolf kill.' It was based on a leaked and confidential government document titled 'Restoration Plan for Woodland Caribou in Alberta.' The report's author, a biologist with the Edson Fish and Wildlife Division, wrote that a herd of migratory caribou that summered in the alpine region of Jasper and Willmore Wilderness Park had dwindled from an estimated 1,700 in 1968 to less than 300 in 1986. The report outlined a number of causes for the decline, but it failed to place the population fluctuation in a historical and realistic perspective. The biologist did not explain that the high caribou numbers of 1968 were linked to the extreme wolf poisoning campaigns of the 1950s. The resulting scarcity of predators, in combination with a decade of mild winters, had led to a cyclic high in ungulate prey species—not only caribou, but also moose and elk. Furthermore, the down cycle in the 1980s was to be expected, given a series of very cold winters and the resurgence of the once-decimated wolves.

In 1986, soon after the 'Caribou Restoration Plan' had been broadcast by the media, the Honourable Don Sparrow—then Alberta's minister of Forestry, Lands & Wildlife—began receiving an avalanche of letters condemning the proposed wolf cull. On December 4, 1986, the Sierra Club of Canada organized a protest meeting at the Calgary Auditorium. The star attraction was illustrious author Farley Mowat. After his hard-hitting presentation, the supportive audience of over one thousand was shown the film *Never Cry Wolf.* The meeting received wide coverage on provincial and national television, which contributed to the government's early capitulation.

The controversy ended as abruptly as it had begun. On January 9, 1987, the minister announced that the wolf kill was not going ahead and had only been a last resort. In a newspaper interview, Sparrow expressed his personal dislike for the plan: "Shooting wolves from a helicopter is too much like fishing in a barrel."

Nevertheless, the wolf controversy did not die. In March 1988, the University of Alberta invited the courageous activist Paul Watson to speak at a public meeting in Edmonton. Formerly with Greenpeace, Watson was now captain of the *Sea Shepherd*, and his current passion was the fight for whales, dolphins, and baby seals. However, a year or two earlier, he had played a pivotal role in halting the infamous government wolf kills in British Columbia. Following Watson's address, a senior Alberta biologist who had personally poisoned wolves in the 1950s and 1960s bluntly told Paul that he was not welcome in this province. Notwithstanding, throughout the mostly hostile, two-hour question period, Captain Watson remained courteous, and his replies often earned him the applause of the public. Later that evening, at an informal get-together with local members of the Canadian Wolf Defenders, this 'environmental guerrilla,' as the press labelled him, proved to be a very gentle soul.

Behind the scenes, demands for wolf control remained strong in hunting circles. At its 1988 annual convention, the 17,000-member Alberta Fish and Game Association (AFGA) passed a resolution urging the government to cull wolves in the foothill forests, with the ultimate goal of enhancing elk populations. In response, LeRoy Fjordbotten, the new minister of Forestry, Lands and Wildlife, hinted that wolf control might be given over to private interests. A government biologist had informed the minister that the province's estimated 5,000 wolves were taking down 50,000 hoofed animals annually.

The following year, frustrated by continued government inaction on the wolf issue, AFGA came up with an idea of their own. Based on the most recent data, Alberta's total wolf population was said to be between 3,500 and 5,500, and the average yearly take by registered trappers was 500 wolves. AFGA wanted to increase that kill to 1,200. To that end, they would pay trappers a bonus of $150 per wolf. AFGA's executive director said that only a fringe element of society would oppose such a plan. As it happened, one of the first people to turn down AFGA's offer was government minister Fjordbotten himself. The scheme raised a chorus of protest among the general public and reverberated across Canada and beyond. 'Stop the Wolf Bounty' became the slogan of a new Alberta group calling itself 'Friends of the Wolf.' On February

3, 1989, they organized a protest rally and march to the Alberta Legislature, which received considerable press coverage. Members of the Canadian Wolf Defenders, as usual low-key and well informed, collected a petition with over 30,000 signatures, which they presented in person to LeRoy Fjordbotten. The minister shrugged off the wolf worries with an indulgent smile. At the time, his department had more important business at hand. Alberta was signing away the cutting rights to thousands of square miles of boreal forest to foreign-owned companies, with ominous but unmentioned implications for all of its wild denizens, including wolves. As it turned out, the AFGA bounty scheme fizzled. Due to a shortage of donations for the proposal, the bounty was reduced from $150 to $100 per wolf and the target lowered to a maximum of 50 payments.

The flames of public indignation over the never-ending wolf complaints were again fanned on January 18, 1990, when the *Edmonton Journal* ran the following headline: 'Alberta ponders killing up to 1,200 wolves to free up game for hunters.' The journalist had based his information on a leaked government document titled 'Draft Management Plan for Wolves.' The plan was intended to eliminate wolves near Grande Cache and along the boundaries of Banff and Jasper National Park, and the method used would be aerial gunning.

On February 8, 1990, to expose the long-festering issue to public scrutiny, I organized an open forum and panel discussion at the Alberta Provincial Museum. Local members of Canadian Wolf Defenders distributed posters throughout the city, and the meeting drew the largest crowd ever to gather at the museum. The 400-seat auditorium was filled to capacity. In addition, an estimated 150 people had to follow the proceedings in the museum's foyer via closed-circuit television. Many others were turned back at the door or unable to enter the parking lot.

The six panel members included two senior zoologists from the University of Alberta, the executive director of the hunting group, the deputy minister of Alberta Wildlife, and the president of the Alberta Federation of Naturalists. The moderator was Garnet Anthony, a well-known CBC radio personality and a knowledgeable conservationist.

After a brief introduction, the floor was open to the public lining up at the microphones. Their comments and questions were lively, informative, and often humorous. Ranging from computer programmers to crusty old trappers, from articulate politicians to bright-voiced schoolchildren, the audience comprised a wide spectrum of Albertans. Perhaps not surprisingly, the most passionate voice protesting government wolf kills and pleading for more protection of our wildlands came from a young member of AFGA. The meeting ended with a showing of the film *Following the Tundra Wolf*, narrated by Robert Redford.

During the winter of 2005–06, twenty years after the start of the caribou controversy, the Alberta government went into action again and allowed its staff to shoot wolves from the air in the hill country northwest of Hinton. On March 5, 2006, the *Edmonton Journal* included a feature story titled 'Alberta's War on Wolves.' The writer had interviewed half a dozen independent wildlife experts. All of them condemned the wolf cull as futile and a waste of time, money, and animal lives. Like similar campaigns in other jurisdictions, once the killing ended, the wolves were predicted to bounce back to larger numbers than before.

In contrast to 30 years ago, the general public recently has largely remained silent on the issue of killing wolves on wildlands. Why? Have they become immune to such drastic cruelty, the way we have become inured to the killing of innocent citizens on foreign soil, as long as we are told that the war is just? Propaganda experts advise that the most effective way to get public opinion onside, in politics and advertising, is to repeat a lie until it is taken for the truth. The oft-stated rationale behind the current wolf kill is that the woodland caribou is on the road to extinction unless we protect it from its arch-enemy, the wolf. Therefore, so says the Alberta government and its Fish & Wildlife department, the predators need to be controlled.

But wait a minute! The fact is that Alberta's wolves have never been completely out of control. Hunters bag them at every opportunity, and trappers "harvest" them for their pelt value. In our foothill forests, the wolf population is hit hard by secretive capture methods. A common practice is to dump the carcasses of traffic-killed deer and moose at bait stations hidden in the bush and on the boundary of our national parks. After the wolves have become habituated to a free meal at these sites, the local trapper closes off all access with steel snares. This has resulted in the capture of entire family packs, who mill about in confusion until all members choke to death. These hidden tragedies take place each winter on the boundaries of Jasper National Park, out of view of the general public, and sanctioned by government departments that help supply the carrion. Rumour has it that some trappers even had the gall to ask park staff for their road kills.

In 1980, the Alberta government wisely closed the hunting season on woodland caribou. Unfortunately, the causes of random mortality include traffic accidents, poaching, and hunter error in animal identification. But the most important peril affecting the caribou population is the fragmentation of its preferred habitat, leading to large-scale ecosystem degradation. Clear-cuts bulldozed by petroleum and forestry companies are spreading, coupled with motorized access on roads and trails pushed through formerly closed forests. In the past 40 years, commercial deforestation and destruction of our foothill and boreal forests has intensified, bringing tears to the eyes of all who love wild nature.

As to the future of Alberta's woodland caribou, there's no doubt some herds will be decimated and vanish. One of nature's basic edicts is that life is ever evolving. Animals that are unable to adapt to change will be replaced by other species. Since the last ice age, long before humans entered the equation, the southern limit of caribou range has shifted farther north, a trend that seems to be continuing.

The caribou's official designation as a species at risk forces government agencies to take measures in the hope of limiting further losses. One immediate consequence has been that aerial research has been stepped up, with most of the money ending up in the pockets of aircraft companies. In a recent newspaper interview, one of Alberta's foremost biologists candidly said: "I don't know if there is any point in spending millions of dollars trying to save a caribou herd when the chances of success are minimal."

Indeed, we must be pragmatic enough to accept the fact that some scattered herds may be on the way out. On the other hand, mountain caribou that are spending most of their year in the north end of Jasper National Park and the Willmore Wilderness seem certain to survive. The reclusive 'grey ghost of the north woods' has been around for eons, and all it needs from us is to be left alone.

In the final analysis, we must keep pressing for protection of caribou habitat. With responsible management, clear-cuts left behind in the wake of resource extraction will grow back to mixed woodland and become prime feeding grounds for deer, elk, and moose. Unfortunately, Alberta's disastrous war on wildlife will continue. Forestry companies intend to kill off all deciduous young growth of poplars, birches, and willows, so as to lessen competition with conifers. Again reminiscent of the Vietnam jungle war, aerial crews are spraying their pine and spruce plantations with massive amounts of poisonous herbicides. These forest scientists, sanctioned by government permits, are destroying the food base for a wide range of herbivores and other wildlife.

After a calf in the Devona elk herd had been radio-collared, park warden Greg Slatter checked its location on a daily basis, and I compared the signal with my visual wolf observations. The data showed that the elk fled back and forth across the Athabasca valley to avoid wolves. The herd's flight path covered four or more kilometres and included crossing a railway, a busy highway, and the open outlet of Jasper Lake.

Fresh tracks of eight or nine wolves that had crossed Jasper Lake in pursuit of the Devona elk herd.

Photo Richard Dekker

In 2018, the elk population of Jasper National Park was estimated at about 300, a major decline from more than 2,000 in 1970. The principal causes were highway and train fatalities superimposed on predation.

Photo Martijn de Jonge

If attacked by wolves, mule deer bucks have been seen to defend themselves effectively with their dagger-like antlers. Photo Mark Bradley

CHAPTER 9
Hit or Myth?

The first scientist who warned the western world that the peregrine population was being decimated by the sub-lethal effects of pesticides was a British ornithologist by the name of Derek Ratcliffe. Ironically, the reason he had undertaken his study was that England's pigeon fanciers had complained that peregrines were killing too many of their prized racing pigeons. As it turned out, it was not the pigeons that were in trouble but the falcons. Ratcliffe's report showed that the country's peregrine population was in free-fall. Despite his important and critical studies, Ratcliffe had little to say about the falcon's hunting habits.

In his 1980 handbook *The Peregrine Falcon*, he wrote that "the study of food by direct observation of peregrines in the act of killing prey is not really a practical proposition; a vast amount of time would be needed to collect a reasonable sample of observation." Bully for him, but I have clearly outdone his most pessimistic expectations. After sixty years of field observations, I have amassed about 500 sightings of prey capture. As he predicted, though, it has indeed taken me a vast amount of time, in fact more than half a lifetime.

A foremost authority on peregrine biology, Ratcliffe has done a great deal of field work, such as counting nest sites and collecting eggs, but he did not spend much time actually looking at what these superior flyers did in the air. Based on the peregrine's reputation as the fastest living animal in the world, Ratcliffe assumed that falcons pursued their prey high in the sky and struck them a violent blow from their talons that sent the victim tumbling down to the ground, either dead or mortally wounded. He even claimed that the force of the strike could be so great that the prey was decapitated.

In my experience, that conclusion is a misinterpretation of the common practice of prey-carrying peregrines to deliver just-captured prey a *coup-de-grâce*. In flight, the falcon bends its head down while briefly bringing its feet forward. With its strong bill, it then bites through the neck vertebrae of the prey. Decapitation may be postponed until the falcon has landed. If you happen to come across the freshly plucked remains of a gull or a shorebird, you generally find the head separate from the carcass.

Unfortunately, Ratcliffe's inaccurate opinions are often repeated in the popular literature on the species. His idea of the classical aerial strike may be typical for peregrines that are flown by expert falconers. Released over open fields or moorland, these birds are trained to 'wait on' high overhead while the falconer and his helpers, assisted by dogs, attempt to flush a grouse or partridge out of the vegetation. The falcon then stoops down hurriedly to overtake the fleeing bird before it drops back into cover. Raked by the falcon's claws, the wounded prey falls down.

There is, however, a big difference between the hunting habits of trained and wild peregrines. The wild ones have to create their own opportunities, and they very seldom strike their prey in flight so that it plummets to earth, dead or wounded. The reason they don't just smack the flying target is that these prey would be lost if they fell into bushes or reeds. In the vast majority of the successful hunting flights that I have seen during half a century of watching, wild falcons grabbed the prey in their feet and carried it down to a convenient plucking post.

Nevertheless, the very first serious hunt that I saw was indeed a singular aerial strike. It featured an adult female peregrine pursuing a pigeon high in the sky. After two stoops that narrowly missed the target, she scored a hit that resulted in a burst of feathers, but the pigeon flew on and took shelter in a copse of birches. On the mossy ground under the trees, I soon found the pigeon, stone dead, with a large, bloody wound in the chest. That falcon's aerial hit was probably just a clumsy attempt at seizing the prey.

My second observation of a successful hunt was very different. An adult male peregrine took off from a high perch on a power pylon, flew down low over open meadows for some distance and, point-blank, seized a wigeon sitting in the wet grass. After a struggle, the falcon began to plume the duck.

Both of these sightings took place in Holland in the 1950s. In those days, peregrine populations were in catastrophic decline in all of western Europe, due to the lethal and sub-lethal effects of DDT and other toxic chemicals used in agriculture.

My chances of observing peregrines greatly improved after I moved to Edmonton in 1959. There, too, the local breeding population was close to dying out, but numerous northern falcons still came through on their migrations to and from arctic regions.

A good place to spot them was Beaverhills Lake, in those days a fabled mecca for Alberta's birdwatchers, although, when questioned, they appeared to know little about peregrines. But a waterfowl hunter said that he had recently seen a 'duck hawk'. Flying very fast along the shore, the falcon had hit one duck after the other and just dropped them dead into the water. With a look of contempt on his face, the man added that the hawk had not even attempted to pick up its kills.

In subsequent years, I learned that plunging down with a great splash is indeed the instinctive reaction of ducks that are attacked by peregrines over water. It might then look as if they had been hit, but dropping down is just the routine way flying ducks have of evading an attack. On the other hand, flying ducks that are overtaken over land may be seized in the falcon's feet. Grappled together, predator and prey then fall to the ground.

Arctic peregrines on spring migration pass through central Alberta from mid-April to the end of May. Assuming that the early morning would be the best time to see them hunting, I used to start my shoreline walks just after sunrise. If I spotted a peregrine perched on a fence post, I sat down on a convenient field stone and kept the bird under observation in the hope that it would soon become active. But that could take most of the morning. After the sun had warmed the air temperature, the falcon would finally spread its long wings in the leisurely, almost sensual way characteristic of the species, holding them fully extended for several seconds. When it jumped off the post, the falcon dropped down to just above the grass, and with quick, sculling wingbeats climbed higher into the breeze. It then began to soar, drifting downwind and gaining altitude. Eventually, it flexed its wings at a sharp angle, resembling an arrowhead, and turned north in a long glide until it dissolved into the distance. Apparently, instead of hunting, these peregrines resumed their migration to arctic breeding grounds.

During my early morning walks, it was not unusual to come across the plucked remains of ducks lying in the grass, but there was no telling at what time of day they might have been killed. Could it have been near dawn, or perhaps the previous evening?

To find out where migrating peregrines spent the night, I kept an immature falcon under observation until well after sundown. It was perched on a fence post by the lakeshore. At dusk, it suddenly took flight, flew low over the grass and made an upward try for a pair of ducks that were heading inland, clearly visible against the cloudless evening sky. The ducks evaded the attack and the hunting falcon flew on, disappearing from sight in the deepening dusk.

On another day, also near sundown, I watched a peregrine circling high over the lakeshore until it suddenly stooped to tackle a flying duck and tumbled down to the ground. Trying to locate its kill, I involuntarily approached too closely, so that the falcon flushed and flew away. That evening I parked my station wagon on the pasture and camped for the night. At the crack of dawn, I set up the telescope and saw that the falcon was back at the kill site. Its head movements indicated that it was feeding.

The late timing of these observations explains why I so seldom had seen falcons hunt in the early morning. Apparently, most of their foraging had been done during the previous evening. These peregrines entered the night with a well-filled crop and could take life easy the following morning, prior to resuming their migration.

Up to the 1990s, the size of internationally famous Beaverhills Lake was 140 square kilometres. When you stood on the south shore looking north, water touched the horizon. By 2006, the entire lake had dried up.

Cooking Lake with the avocet islet. Marsh ragwort is the first plant to colonize the muddy shores in spring.

The greater and the lesser yellowlegs. The only other such combo of two bird species that are similar in plumage but of different proportions, are the raven and the crow. Yellowlegs are hunters in their own right, picking up aquatic insects by sight. Photo Steve Knight

With their sensitive upturned bill, avocets sweep the water and collect their food by feel. In flight, the black-and-white plumage of a flock of avocets dazzles and deters attacking falcons. Photo Dawne Colwell

CHAPTER 10
Fast but Vulnerable

The peregrine is the world's fastest living creature. People who have seen this falcon in pursuit of pigeons have estimated its speed at around one hundred kilometres per hour. In 2005, an imaginative falconer conducted a decisive flight test using sophisticated instrumentation. His name was Ken Franklin, a practiced skydiver as well as a falconer. He and his captive-raised peregrine, named Frightful, were taken up in an aircraft to an altitude of close to 5,000 metres. When they bailed out, Ken held a lure baited with meat in his outstretched gloved fist. In free-fall, the pair reached a carefully measured 389 km per hour (242 miles per hour). Air speeds of that magnitude, buffeting a living, feather-covered body, are truly mind-boggling. Just before reaching maximum velocity, the falcon tucked its shoulders even tighter into its streamlined body and assumed an asymmetrical shape, one shoulder slightly ahead of the other. During my field observations at Wabamun Lake in central Alberta, I was astonished to see wild peregrines in attacks on gulls high in the sky do the same sort of thing. They would suddenly accelerate to a blurred streak in the last split-second of their stoop.

In years past, falconry was the sport of nobility and Holland was renowned for the skill of its professional falcon trainers, who were hired by the royal courts of Europe. Growing up in Holland, my favourite birds were the hawks and falcons that represented all that was truly wild and natural in this densely populated country. Peregrines did not nest in the Lowlands, but they came down from northern breeding grounds during late summer and fall, following the flocks of migrating songbirds and waterfowl. The Dutch name for the peregrine is slechtvalk. In the old days, the word slecht meant common or numerous. That classification changed drastically after the 1940s, with the invention and application of pesticides such as DDT and other chemicals used in agriculture. Residues of the toxins built up in seed-eating birds foraging on the fields, and the chemicals accumulated to harmful levels in their avian predators. The tendency of hunting falcons to capture the slowest and least fit of their prey species now worked against them. Songbirds, gulls, and waders with the highest toxic load were the first to be caught. Furthermore, irresponsible farmers who saw their crops raided by hordes of pigeons or crows spread malathion-soaked grain to kill them. By the mid-1950s, persistent pesticide poisoning had brought the peregrine close to extinction in all of western Europe. Dreaming of a more pristine environment, I made the difficult decision to emigrate. Upon arriving in Calgary in 1959, the first thing I wanted to find out was whether peregrines were still breeding in this part of the world.

In Holland I had befriended a practicing falconer who shared my passionate interest in birds of prey. He and his associates were routinely the most knowledgeable people for information about peregrines. In July of 1959, wishing to contact an Alberta falconer, I placed a personal advertisement in the *Calgary Herald*, which in those pre-computer days was the standard avenue for that sort of inquiries.

The ad produced two replies. The first call was from a hunter who did not like falconers at all. According to him, falconers could capture as many partridges as they wanted because there was no bag limit and no closed season for them. When I told him that I was a new immigrant and just wanted to see wild falcons, he was kind enough to invite me for a birdwatching tour west of the city. According to him, the Calgary region was not the right habitat for peregrines, but he was going to take me to a place where there were prairie falcons.

Finding the nesting sites of falcons in wild country is easy. Their natural choice is rocky cliffs, visible from miles away. It explains why peregrines have been so vulnerable in the past to people who wanted to shoot them or collect their eggs and young.

Along a narrow, semi-open coulee north of Cochrane, an hour's drive west of Calgary, we passed several prominent stony outcrops, and as a sure sign of occupancy some were streaked with 'white-wash.' At three locations, one or more prairie falcons were flying around or perched on the rocks. The sight of these handsome falcons did not seem to please my guide very much, though. By way of explanation, he said that peregrines were migratory and left the province by late summer, whereas prairie falcons stayed around all year and their common winter prey were partridges (or huns, as he called them). He casually added a remark that was to haunt me the following year. One of his hunting buddies was a hawk hater, he said, and if that guy were to be told of the many falcons in this coulee, he might want to do something about it.

In 1960, the Cochrane coulee became one of my birding hotspots, and all three cliffs were again occupied by prairie falcons. From the valley floor it was possible to see that there were chicks in the nesting cavities. But later that summer I came in for a shock. Except one, all of the adults had been shot. So too were four newly fledged young, and at two sites the carcasses of juvenile falcons were lying on the nest ledge, either shot or starved to death. The hillside below the cliffs was littered with spent shotgun shells.

I wrote a protest letter to the Calgary Herald, describing the carnage. There was no comment from anyone, except from the second person who had responded to the newspaper message I had placed the previous year.

His given name was Bill. Not a practicing falconer himself, he knew of two local people who had obtained juvenile peregrines from nests along the Red Deer River, some 150 km north of Calgary. Bill had personally been involved in taking nestlings from that river to be sent by air express to falconers in the USA.

In the fall of 1959, Bill introduced me to two Americans who had come to western Canada with six captive falcons that were supposed to be flown at grouse or partridges. Surprisingly, they admitted that none of their falcons was actually fit enough to be entered at game. The only birds their peregrines had ever captured were pigeons released below the flying falcons. As to a request from these guys for more peregrines from Alberta, Bill said to me in confidence that it would be like offering the proverbial pearls to the swine. To properly train a falcon is a demanding project, an every-day commitment. The majority of modern-day falconers lack the time and skill to do their captives justice. They are in fact little more than glorified pet-keepers. But for the best of falcon aficionados, their hobby becomes a way of life.

In the spring and summer of 1960, I spent a lot of my weekends along the Red Deer River scouting for nesting peregrines. Approaching the scenic valley from the county roads, I parked the car and hiked long stretches of riverbank to locate cliffs and rocky outcrops. At three locations, I discovered a pair of adult peregrines. At two other sites there were prairie falcons. At all three peregrine cliffs the nest ledge was in good view from across the river, which was little more than a hundred metres wide. On the opposite shore, in the partial shade of some trees or bushes, I sat down to observe the birds through binoculars. The big question was whether these beautiful falcons were still breeding successfully and producing young. In addition, I wanted to see how they hunted and what kind of prey they were bringing in to feed the nestlings.

The first question could eventually be answered in the affirmative. All three pairs fledged healthy chicks. But my hope of seeing the adults hunt and catch prey ended in disappointment. It turned out that these falcons rarely if ever attacked birds flying over the river. While the female stayed on the nest, the adult male was usually perched on the cliff or a treetop. When he finally flew out over the partly wooded valley, I kept him in the binoculars for as long as possible. On clear days, he began to soar over the valley rim and sailed out over the agricultural plains beyond. But despite countless days of watching, I never saw more of his hunting habits than a distant dot stooping down and disappearing from view.

After an hour or so, calling excitedly, the male returned to the cliff. The female rose at once from the nest to meet him in the air and to take a small prey from his feet. From my low point of observation, most items could not be identified, except the odd red-winged blackbird, robin, killdeer, or tern.

When I reported my discoveries to Bill, he wanted to come along to see the nest sites himself and band the young falcons. On the appointed day, I was happy and proud to show him my precious discoveries. While I anchored the rope, Bill worked his way down to the nest ledge and succeeded in putting numbered leg bands on eleven chicks.

The following year, again hiking the banks of the Red Deer River, I was pleased to see that the peregrines had returned to their former nest sites. But that summer I did not have the opportunity to check on the production of young, because I left in May on an extended holiday to the Yukon. Exploring the Canadian wilderness was a dream come true for me. The adventure ended abruptly in September with a serious canoe accident on a remote stretch of the Big Salmon River. Having lost all my backcountry gear, I was grateful to get out of there with my life. Later that month I flew back to Holland.

Three years later, upon returning to Alberta, I took up contact again with Bill and learned that he had obtained a new job as manager of the Alberta Game Farm near Edmonton. When I reached him on the phone, he at once recognized my voice and we very quickly got down to the subject of peregrines. He then said, in his own words, that he had to admit to a dastardly thing. As part of his job, he had returned to the Red Deer River and robbed the nests I had shown him in 1960. The juvenile falcons were sold to falconers. For the same purpose, and at the direction of the game farm's owner, Bill said that he and his helpers had flown or boated down other rivers in northern Canada. (Both Bill and the owner of the Alberta Game Farm have passed away.)

By the end of the 1960s, the peregrine had disappeared as a breeding bird from central Alberta. Fortunately, northern populations survived. And exactly thirty years after I had seen the last nesting falcons along the Red Deer River, there was again an adult pair on the very same cliff as before. This happy event was the crowning success of an imaginative initiative by falconers who had used their special knowledge and hands-on expertise to take peregrines from the wild and breed them in captivity with the ultimate objective of releasing their progeny into the wild. Due to their dedicated efforts, coupled with a reduction in the use of toxic chemicals such as DDT, three or four pairs of peregrines returned to their traditional breeding territories along the Red Deer River, despite serious nest site competition from prairie falcons.

Alberta falconers also played a positive role in starting a breeding population of peregrines at Wabamun Lake, some seventy kilometres west of Edmonton. There, nest boxes were installed on the smokestacks of three powerplants around the lake. From 1998 onwards, I spent many spring and summer days to watch a banded and captive-bred pair of falcons at the former Wabamun plant until it was dismantled in 2004. Each year the pair successfully fledged three or four healthy juveniles, which provided me with a unique opportunity to observe the cooperative foraging habits of parent peregrines and their brood.

At the time, scientific opinion was divided on the question of whether parent peregrines actively taught their fledglings how to hunt, or conversely, whether the juveniles needed such instruction. The latter point was convincingly settled after numerous peregrines had been let go from breeding facilities. As long as these youngsters were supplied with plenty of food for a period of several weeks after release, they proved quite capable of making it on their own. Nevertheless, my observations at Wabamun showed that parent falcons indeed played a very big role, not only by providing their fledglings with adequate food, but also by showing them how to capture it themselves.

The Wabamun pair hunted prey of two size classes, varying from ring-billed gulls to cedar waxwings. If the adults were accompanied by one or more of their fledged young, both parents demonstrated that they were aware of the different needs of the two genders. Roughly a third bigger than their male siblings, female falcons can tackle larger prey than males. To assist a female fledgling in catching a Franklin's gull, the adults would set the target up by making a close pass at the gull, sometimes striking it in the air or holding fast for a moment and letting go again. If the juvenile fumbled the catch, the adult might provide the youngster with another chance.

Male juveniles were coached in a similar way during cooperative hunts aimed at small passerines and shorebirds, although the parents' help did not always turn out as intended. One day, when two just-fledged males were chasing an erratic snipe, their father, soaring high above, interfered with a vertical stoop, hitting the snipe a solid blow. The youngsters dived after the falling bird but were unable to secure it before it fell into reedy vegetation, lost to all.

The adult pair also cooperated with each other. Setting out as a team, the male accompanied his mate, but he stayed at a much higher altitude than his partner. If she began to chase a gull, the male came down in a terrific stoop to hit or grab the prey, which he surrendered at once to the approaching female.

Capable of extreme speed and agility, adult male peregrines are not above lowly kills that one would not expect of these superior flyers. For instance, one day the Wabamun male came down from his high perch on a smokestack to attack a family of buffleheads swimming in a settling pond on the plant site. Hovering low over them for a second or two, the falcon's aim was not the mother duck, but one of the tiny ducklings, which he lifted from the water's surface and carried back to the power plant.

At a cliff breeding site on the Red Deer River I saw several times that the adult male scooped up young cliff swallows on their first feeble flight out of the clay nest cups attached lower down to the rock wall. The peregrine collected these morsels with casual ease and sometimes he did not even pluck them, but deposited the tiny carcass on the nest ledge. Storing excess food or leftovers is routine for nesting falcons.

Another surprising discovery about the foraging habits of breeding peregrines dates back to 1994, when the late Wayne Nelson—a passionate Alberta falconer and peregrine researcher—invited me for a two-week stay on Langara Island, the extreme northern outlier of the Haida Gwaii archipelago on the Pacific coast of British Columbia.

Wayne had monitored the Langara peregrine population for many years, although the search for nest sites and banding the young had left him with little time to actually watch the falcons on the hunt. Ranging far and wide over the ocean, the main prey of these maritime peregrines were small alcids, such as auklets and murrelets, which were intercepted when these sea divers flew to and from island nesting colonies. The falcons were believed to strike them a mortal blow in flight so that their prey fell down into the sea. Wayne had often watched peregrines retrieve dead or wounded alcids from the water. But his assumption that they had been hit in flight proved to be wrong.

In August of 1995, I returned to Langara accompanied by Ludo Bogaert, a birdwatcher friend from way back and a fellow immigrant from Holland. Our specific mission was to look at the hunting methods of these coastal falcons. Our observation point was a 30-metre-high cliff by the Langara lighthouse.

The peregrines that we saw in pursuit of flying auklets or murrelets just grabbed them in the air and carried them back to land. Much more often, though, the falcon's tactic was quite different and aimed at swimming sea birds. Launching a surprise attack from a high coastal spruce, the falcon would descend to very low over the water and sail the final fifty or so metres with wings set, skimming the waves. If the targeted bird became aware of the danger in the nick of time, it could save its life by submerging in a flash, but if it failed to do so, the falcon struck the swimming bird a glancing blow from its talons. Rising steeply with spread wings to brake its speed, the falcon then turned around and tried to grab the crippled alcid from the surface. This was a tricky manoeuvre, especially in a heavy ocean swell. Most of the time, the falcon had to try again and again before it succeeded in making contact with the thrashing diver.

The details of our unique observations were subsequently published in the *Journal of Raptor Research* (1997; 31:381-383). My paper elicited an appreciative response from Dr. Tom Cade, the dean of American falconers, who had played a key role in initiating the captive breeding programs that have led to the return of this once endangered species. Tom had studied falcons in Alaska and sent me a personal email to say that my observations explained what he had seen wild peregrines do in the Aleutian Islands of that northern state.

A second interesting discovery at Langara was that the peregrines were relentlessly parasitized by bald eagles, which were locally ubiquitous. If a falcon needed to make more than two or three attempts to lift the wounded prey from the waves, a hurriedly approaching eagle would seize the struggling auklet or murrelet in a flash.

Alcids weigh a little less than a pigeon, and the Langara peregrines, which are among the largest subspecies in the world, had no trouble carrying their prey away from pursuing eagles as long as the falcon had a timely start and gained some altitude.

Although my paper was cited in a comprehensive handbook published in 2013, (*Peregrine Falcons of the World*), its authors ignored our discovery and stuck to the inaccurate assumption that the Langara falcons were hitting their prey in flight so that they fell into the water, dead or wounded. The failure of the book's authors to acknowledge our contrary findings was a disappointment to me, and again proves that David Suzuki was right when he wrote in one of his newspaper columns about the myth that scientists are always objective and open to new ideas.

Peregrines that are using nest boxes placed on Alberta's power plants have been very successful in raising three or four young each year.   Photo Gordon Court

The major prey of a pair breeding near Wabamun Lake are Franklin's gulls.

Photo Don Delaney

CHAPTER 11
Peregrines Caught in the Act

In spring and fall, at any moment of the day, migrating peregrine falcons, soaring among the clouds, may come down like a bolt from the blue to attack ducks or other prey. But after years of scanning the clouds over Beaverhills Lake I had learned that the surest strategy for seeing a falcon hunt high in the sky required patience as well as luck. It was a question of watching falcons that were perched on a field stone or fence post around the lake, and of waiting until that bird took flight of its own accord. To avoid disturbing it, I had to keep my distance.

One of the most impressive high-altitude duck hunts that I ever saw occurred on April 23, 1972, during a memorable walk around the lake's north shore accompanied by the late Loran Goulden, a novice birdwatcher from Nova Scotia who later became a prominent member of the Edmonton Bird Club. Loran had been keen to join the group's traditional excursions to the south shore of Beaverhills Lake, and like most club members, he did all of his birding from a vehicle. But one spring day, he accompanied me on a long hike around the rather remote north end of the lake.

The timing was great. After a long, cold winter, some county roads were blocked by meltwater, forcing us to park the car well short of the lake. We began our walk in midmorning and did not get back until sundown. For me, it was a routine field day, but for Loran it became a new experience. He later recalled it as the best day he ever spent at the lake. A big, heavy-set man, not used to walking much, he did not complain because I often halted to scan the country ahead through binoculars to search for peregrines. My relaxed pace allowed Loran plenty of time for a rest and a snack. His lunch included a huge bag of kubasa sausages and a fistful of liquorice swizzles.

Our day was filled with birds. The sky above was alive with sandhill cranes and geese. Ducks of half a dozen species massed on flooded fields, and we spotted the first migratory waders such as yellowlegs and Hudsonian godwits. Passerines called everywhere, including blackbirds, larks, buntings, and longspurs. Rough-legged hawks and bald eagles seemed common, and one dark brown eagle turned out to be a rare golden eagle. Harriers and short-eared owls were performing their acrobatic courtship flights over the fields, and on the still frozen lake, six snowy owls were waiting for nightfall.

What made my day extra special was finding a peregrine perched on a fence post some three hundred metres ahead. We did not approach any closer but did not have to wait very long for action. The falcon took flight soon and began to soar, circling high into the lightly overcast sky. Suddenly, he folded his wings, keeled over and fell perpendicularly, his aim at a pintail drake flying lower over the lakeshore and on his way inland. The drake narrowly evaded the stoop by an abrupt change of direction, veering upwards. He then descended at great speed, while the falcon tried to overtake him. The pursuit covered hundreds of metres of open pasture land until both birds dropped low over the ground and became lost to our view. A day later, roughly on the spot where the chase had ended, I found the plucked remains and wind-blown feathers of a pintail drake.

Another opportunity to see a high-altitude duck hunt—but not to its conclusion—took place in the same general area on an April day when flocks of migrating pintails were passing over. High above them, a soaring peregrine was a tiny speck in the binoculars. Sitting in the grass, leaning against my pack sack, I had to turn around and bend over backwards to keep the falcon in focus while he circled overhead. I ended up lying flat on my back. Each time the falcon launched an attack, the ducks side-slipped his stoop with a quick upward manoeuvre. They then descended like a meteor. Pintails and other ducks can drop almost as fast as a falcon can stoop. Out-flown, or half-hearted in his approach, the falcon aborted every attack, but I expected him to capture a duck at any time. Unfortunately, I had become conscious of not being alone. Supine on the ground, I was surrounded by curious cattle. Their stomping and snorting kept coming closer until I thought it wise to end my predicament and jump to my feet. The herd of cows and heifers stampeded off, but when I scanned the skies, I was unable to relocate the falcon.

The first time I actually witnessed the final capture of what I thought was a duck occurred much later. One spring day, after scanning the lakeshore through binoculars and a telescope from the northwest corner of the county roads, I spotted an adult male peregrine sitting on a fence post. The distance was too great to see him with the unaided eye (my sight is not that sharp). When another birder stopped by and asked what I was looking at, I suggested that we cooperate and walk closer to the peregrine. While one of us kept him in the binoculars, the other walked a hundred steps farther and halted again. Alternating in this cautious way, we managed to cut the distance in half, while the falcon had stayed on his post. Suddenly, he took off in hurried flight, his aim a duck flying from the lakeshore to an inland slough. Just before the duck could reach the safety of water, it was overtaken and seized. Clutching his prey, the falcon dropped down into the grassy vegetation on the edge of the slough. I felt like shouting for joy. I had seen my first successful duck hunt! Or so I thought.

Oddly, after a little while, instead of beginning to pluck his catch, the peregrine flew away. Walking up to investigate, I found that his prey wasn't a duck but a coot. Why the falcon had not eaten the coot remains an open question. Perhaps he was not hungry enough? The coot had been an easy catch. And peregrines are always quick to take advantage of the straight and unbending flight of waterbirds such as coots and rails. Apparently, he had not been able to refuse such an easy target. But perhaps he just did not feel like eating coot?

How keen peregrines actually are on a meal of duck became clear one day when I saw an adult male rob an immature male of a just-caught robin. The adult peregrine carried his ill-gotten booty to the flat top of a wooden power pole and sat on it for several minutes, just looking around. As it turned out, he was waiting for a better meal. Leaning forward with fluttering wings, he presently took off and ascended rapidly to meet a high flock of ducks approaching over the skyline, some two kilometres away. Turning back down in hot pursuit of a teal, he seized it low over the ground. After a few minutes of looking around for possible pirates, he began to plume his catch.

Next morning, the dead robin was still lying on the pole until a gust of wind brought it down, giving me a chance to examine the carcass, which was untouched. This incident took place one winter day on Vancouver Island, but the same duck-hunting strategy is commonly used by migrant peregrines around Beaverhills Lake.

To see a peregrine increase the tempo of his wing beats to meet a flight of faraway ducks is a riveting sight. Swooping upward at his prey, the falcon prevents it from using evasive tactics and seizes the duck from below. He then brings the prey to the ground, but whether he gets to feed on his catch depends very much on what happens next. Anywhere in open country, the sky has eyes, the envious eyes of other raptors and scavengers. I once watched an immature male peregrine catch two teal in ten minutes. He lost the first teal to a bullying red-tailed hawk, and the second one to a Swainson's hawk. The falcon then sat on a fence post until sundown before resuming activity again. Evening hunting may be a tactic to avoid piracy by buteo hawks.

Male peregrines are about one-third smaller than females, and a pintail drake is a rather heavy prey for any peregrine. One spring day, when an adult male had just seized a drake in flight, he was robbed by a pair of red-tailed hawks. The peregrine retreated to a fence post some distance away. After the red-tails had eaten their fill, the remains of the pintail were taken over by three harriers. But here the peregrine drew the line. One vigorous swoop was enough to drive the scavengers away. Bigger and more powerful than their mate, female peregrines can handle thievish harriers as well as buteos, but they, in turn, are at the mercy of larger pirates such as gyrfalcons and eagles. On the west coast of Canada, near Vancouver, where I have studied the hunting habits of wintering peregrines over twenty years, falcons of both genders have stopped hunting ducks and now capture only small sandpipers such as dunlin that can be carried away at the approach of the increasingly numerous bald eagles.

To maximize my chances of seeing peregrines hunt shorebirds I have spent a lot of time around wetlands, especially during the migration seasons when northern sandpipers can drop by on their way to or from arctic breeding grounds. Not wanting to disturb them, I stay well away from the waterline and find a convenient spot to sit down. As I got older, I acquired the habit of carrying a low footstool. Sitting down and looking all around, with or without binoculars, I enjoy the ambiance of water and sky, while I depend on the birds to warn me if a falcon is sighted. With many eyes sharper than mine, the sandpipers are quick to take evasive action when danger threatens. Suddenly flushing all at once, they draw together into a dense flock, careening back and forth. It takes luck to spot the attacker, a streak upon the sky. One swoop and he's away again. The action may be over in a split second, and what actually happens can be difficult to see in detail. If the falcon missed his target, you should keep him in the glasses for as long as possible, for he may launch another attack in good view. Even if it's more than a kilometre away, distant observations add to your understanding of a falcon's hunting methods.

Soaring in the blue, in slow circles, it may not look like the falcon is on the lookout for prey. But it may suddenly flex its wings and descend in a parabolic dive, levelling out low over the ground or water. Its common tactic is to take its prey by surprise. Suddenly aware of their peril, panicked sandpipers flush in the nick of time. Birds that are directly in line with the attack instantly plunge back down, with the falcon hissing by overhead. It might then look as if these birds were struck by the falcon's claws, which may indeed be the case, but in my observations, more often than not, these sandpipers got up again in an instant and escaped in the opposite direction.

The surest way to accurately interpret these split-second attacks is to watch the hunting sequence from start to finish. It's important to keep your binoculars still, and the best angle to see what actually happens is to have the falcon travel directly away from you so that you are in a straight line of sight of any shorebirds that flush just ahead of the falcon. Some prey may be seized the moment they spread their wings. Others drop back onto the ground to get up and away again in the next instant, while the falcon overshoots the mark. What follows varies from one event to the next. The peregrine may give up at once and continue its low hunt or put on the brakes with an abrupt somersault to reverse direction and pursue the fleeing birds. More rarely, I have seen falcons slow down to the speed of a harrier and quarter the ground, head turned down, searching for sandpipers that refused to flush and instead crouched down in the grass. Exploding upward in the nick of time, some of these fear-frozen peep could still make a narrow escape. Such evasive tactics are typical of the least sandpiper and the pectoral, which rely on their cryptic dorsal colouration to hide and escape detection. Both of these species have streaked back feathers for camouflage, and they like to forage on drier ground than other species of shorebirds, such as the semipalmated and stilt sandpipers, which habitually forage in the shallows.

During half a century of watching, my deliberate method of observing the interaction of peregrines and shorebirds has been to sit down well away from the lakeshore on a high point overlooking miles of ploughland and open pastures containing two or more meltwater pools and sloughs. These inland water bodies attract the first yellowlegs and sandpipers of the season, well before the main lake is ice-free. The most wary sentinels among the gathered shorebirds are the killdeer and the marbled godwit. Both have a piercing alarm call, and the long neck of the godwit allows it to see over the grass. For me, the key to the arrival of bird-hunting falcons—peregrines or merlins—is when a pond or slough suddenly explodes with flushing shorebirds and gulls, rising all at once and flocking together defensively. If the uproar was caused by a peregrine, and if the attack failed, the falcon probably flew away at once again. Searching the sky above, you might find it soaring on spread wings, gradually reaching a great altitude. As it dwindles to a minuscule silhouette, continue to keep it in focus. It might come closer again and launch its next attack over the same pond or another slough within good view.

After 15 consecutive years of monitoring the migrations of shorebirds and peregrines at Beaverhills Lake, from mid-April to the end of May, 1965–1980, I published my observations in *Canadian Field-Naturalist*. The data include the fall season. In total, I recorded 958 hunting sequences aimed at waterbirds, of which the majority were sandpipers. The outcome of 30 percent of these hunts remained unknown, but in 674 attacks I could see whether or not the attack had been successful—that is, from the falcon's point of view—or whether the prey had made a narrow escape. Only 52 birds were captured, representing a kill rate of 7.7 %. This means that of every ten birds attacked, nine managed to escape.

My sample of data on peregrine hunting success from the Pacific coast near Vancouver is even larger. Between 1994 and 2015, I saw 1,369 peregrine attacks on wintering dunlins, a circumpolar sandpiper weighing about 70 grams. The number of captured dunlins was 205, which represents a success rate of 14.9%, almost double the figure recorded at Beaverhills Lake. The data were published in the *Journal of Raptor Research*. The reason these coastal peregrines were so much more successful that their kind at Beaverhills Lake may have to do with the fact that the coastal falcons were winter residents and quite familiar with the locality. Set in their habits, they knew how and where to get what they needed, whereas the migratory falcons seen around Beaverhills Lake were passing through. If hungry, they might go for a quick bite to eat, or move on, hunting along the way.

By comparison, the success rate of a breeding pair of peregrines nesting on a power plant at Alberta's Wabamun Lake was even higher, around 22%. During periods when the pair cooperated in their foraging, the rate rose to 39%, which is the highest rate I have recorded anywhere. The explanation for this is that these territorial falcons spent most of their day perched on the smokestacks of the power plant and pre-selected their prey among the many birds flying by their high vantage point. In good weather, the pair frequently went soaring together, two or more kilometres high, biding their time and waiting for the optimal moment for a cooperative attack on passing gulls.

Over the years, the total number of prey I have seen captured in Alberta and British Columbia was around 450. Over half were shorebirds, most of them sandpipers. A new and unique opportunity of watching the interaction of peregrines and peeps played out in the Bay of Fundy, where I was sent with a travel grant from Simon Fraser University. Fundy is famous because its twice-daily tides are the highest in the world, and in late summer the wide tidal flats are crowded with tens of thousands of migrants, mainly semipalmated sandpipers. Weighing about 30 grams, this species is one of the tiniest members of this amazing tribe of global travellers that make twice yearly flights between the Canadian arctic and tropical beaches in the southern hemisphere. Arriving at Fundy in August, the semipalms stay for two or three weeks to fatten up on the locally abundant mud shrimps, before resuming their non-stop over-ocean migration to South America. By the time they are ready for the long flight, they have doubled their weight with a layer of fat, which does not make them more agile in flight. On the contrary.

In August, young peregrines that have fledged from nest sites around Fundy are having the time of their life harassing sandpipers. Selecting one bird for persistent pursuit, teams of two or more falcons swoop alternately until the exhausted prey gives up and falls down on the mud or splashes into the shallows. The youngsters then try to pick it up, making pass after pass, but they seldom succeed before an adult falcon arrives, perhaps one of their own parents. This seemed an unusual situation to me. Each day at low tide, I noted a large female falcon quietly perched on a stone or driftwood log well offshore. Apparently, she was waiting for the youngsters to do the hunting for her and drive one of the sandpipers down. She then made a direct approach, stuck out one of her claws while remaining airborne, and carried the prize away. The young falcons did not seem to be much taken aback and departed at once, ready for other adventures.

As part of my peregrine studies, I collected separate data for adults and immatures. As expected, falcons of two or more years of age, identifiable by their blue-grey back and white chest, proved to be more successful than the brownish first-year birds. But the difference wasn't great. During spring, the capture rate of migrating adult peregrines observed at Beaverhills Lake turned out to be about nine percent, whereas the rate of immatures was seven percent. Apparently, after a winter of hunting on their own, first-year peregrines had gained enough experience and were now almost as good as their elders. The difference between adult and young falcons was much more pronounced during fall. In August and September, the success rate of juvenile peregrines was no more than two or three percent.

In the field, I also noted a major difference in the tactics used by the two age groups. As mentioned above, the primary hunting strategy of adult falcons was to take shorebirds by surprise. By comparison, first-year juveniles all too often failed in their initial approach. Instead, they ended up tail-chasing fleeing sandpipers over long distances—which did not seem a problem at all, though. Juvenile peregrines clearly enjoy the chase. After all, securing their food in one quick pass in the studied style of an adult would be no fun at all for a vigorous youngster.

If you watch an immature peregrine in an all-out attempt at overtaking a fleeing sandpiper, climbing higher and higher into the sky, you will be awed by their stamina and dexterity. Instead of a quick hit or miss, these two unequal contestants—a tiny sandpiper and a much larger, long-winged falcon—may spend ten or more minutes in a race of Olympic intensity. An erratic shift in the sandpiper's flight path might throw the pursuer off-course, widening the space between them. Many chases that I have seen covered so much distance that I lost sight of the sandpiper. But do not lower your binoculars too soon. The direction of the chase can suddenly change and both birds may come back into view. If stressed to the limit, the sandpiper will turn downwind and eventually plunge headlong to earth to find safety in bushes or reeds. Boosted by gravity, the falcon follows the prey down with closed wings, trying to intercept it before it reaches the protective cover of dense vegetation. Sometimes, though, it is the falcon that gives up, relaxing its frantic wingbeats and gliding away out of sight.

The most spectacular hunting flights occur when roosting and foraging shorebirds are super numerous. As the adage says, there is safety in numbers. With sharp-eyed sentinels everywhere, sandpipers flush early, frustrating the peregrine's typical attack strategy of taking the prey by surprise. Drawing together in dense globular flocks, the sandpipers careen and turn, alternately flashing their white undersides and dark backs, which may serve to confuse the attacker. Such evasive tactics might also function as a long-distance semaphore to warn other shorebirds. High over the ballooning flocks, the peregrine waits on and manoeuvres until it finds the best angle for a vertical stoop. Pulling in its long wings, the falcon tilts over and drops like a stone. To the human observer, with or without binoculars, it may seem as if the falcon stoops right through the flock, but that is very seldom the case. Its usual target is a bird on the outside or bottom end of the flock. Narrowly evading the strike, some sandpipers splash down into the water to get up at once again. A bird that stays down may have been hit by the falcon's claws, resulting in a broken wing or other injuries.

Adult peregrines have little or no trouble picking up a dead or crippled sandpiper from the water, but immature falcons frequently fail. Trying again and again, they are often joined by one or more competing conspecifics. At Beaverhills Lake and on the Pacific coast of British Columbia, I have seen four or five falcons alternately swooping at the same downed or fleeing sandpiper. The game is soon over with the arrival of an adult falcon, who quickly secures the prize or robs a young falcon that just got lucky. There is no honour among the so-called 'noble' falcons. They live by a time-tested motto that might is right.

CHAPTER 12
The Peregrine's Paradox

Ever since the heyday of falconry, going back hundreds if not thousands of years, the peregrine and other members of the falcon tribe have been celebrated as the 'noble' long-wings who tend to approach their prey openly, high in the sky. By comparison, short-winged forest raptors, such as the Cooper's hawk and the goshawk, do their hunting under the cover of trees and catch their prey by stealth close to the ground. The peregrine's noble predicate also has to do with the quick way it dispatches captured birds. With its strong bill, which features a special notch or tooth, the falcon twists the prey's neck vertebrae apart and delivers a *coup de grace*, resulting in instant death. The accipiters, buteos, and harriers lack such a killing tooth and instead dispatch their catch by kneading it with their talons. They may start eating their prey while it is still alive.

In the previous chapters we have seen how the peregrine's hunting success stacks up. Based on direct observation in the field, the capture rate data I found may seem surprisingly low for a falcon that has become famous for being the fastest animal in the world. A critical question that I have often been asked is this: How did you know whether these peregrines were actually seriously hunting? Maybe they were just playing or fooling around?

For any predator, especially the young, it's a thin line that separates play from work. The state of a falcon's appetite is 'up in the air,' so to speak, but the seriousness of its intent can be deducted from its behaviour. On the breeding grounds, adult peregrines adhere to a primitive imperative of bringing food home for their nest-bound partner and young. Intolerant of competitors, territorial pairs have been known to kill conspecifics. Away from the nests, though, falcons are birds of leisure. One good meal a day is all they need. And, being rather lazy, they steal from each other or take what comes easiest, by hook or by crook. Adults of both sexes are quick to rob the little merlin or harass a hard-working harrier carrying a vole to its nest in the marsh. Paradoxically, the noble peregrine is not above feeding on carrion. At Beaverhills Lake, I have seen them scavenge on the washed-up carcasses of ducks that had died of botulism. Others picked up lake flies from the shoreline. In captivity, as long as they are given enough to eat and drink, falconry birds spend most of the day sitting on a perch and looking around, letting the world go by. But wait until you see a wild falcon in action, high in the sky!

Peregrines are creatures of habit. Migrant females that pass over central Alberta in early spring may hang around for a week or so. If you watch them over several days, you get to know at what time they are in the mood for some serious duck hunting. By mid-afternoon, I find them perched on the posts of certain strategic fence lines with a wide view of lakeshore and inland fields. The tedium of waiting for action can be agonizing when the April wind is cold. The strain builds after an hour or more of peering through binoculars or telescope. Resting my weary eyes for a spell may cost me the one moment that counts, when she finally spreads her wings. Searching high and low, left and right, I curse my lapse of attention. Minutes later, she may be back on her post. Perhaps she just dropped down into the grass to pick up a worm or insect? With renewed hope, I wait until the tension is finally relieved and she takes off. Following the falcon in the glasses, her outline dwindles over the wooded horizon. But wait! She is turning back downwind and climbing.

My most treasured memories are of seeing a falcon come from afar and pass by with deceptively shallow wing beats, which tells me she is holding back but ready for instant acceleration if prey is spotted far ahead. The final stage of the attack may carry the bird out of view, two or three kilometres away. With luck, I may get a glimpse of the target. If the duck reaches the lake in time, I might see a metre-high spout of water. Lucky duck! Although she missed the target, there was no doubt about this falcon's intentions.

Individual peregrines differ in hunting style. An experienced falcon may let common prey species go if they evade a casual pass. Easy come, easy go. In contrast, young falcons may be more persistent and tackle waterbirds hiding in reedy marshes where they would have been safe from adult falcons.

For instance, on a cold and windy May afternoon, I was standing in the lee of some willow bushes near the lake, hoping to see a peregrine flying by. As I scanned the shore through binoculars, she was given away by a distant flicker of long wings. She turned out to be an immature female. At her approach, a number of ducks flushed from a wet pasture, and the falcon suddenly dropped out of view between the sedges. Presently, alerted by the raucous calls of crows, I suspected that a kill had been made. Wearing rubber boots, I waded into the flooded meadow, and after a long search the falcon flushed in good view. On the spot where she rose out of the vegetation, I located the partially plucked carcass of a gadwall duck, almost totally submerged.

Adult peregrines may do surprising things, too. One early May afternoon I was sitting on a field stone watching a flock of dowitchers foraging in a pool of snowmelt when they suddenly panicked and took off. One of them plunged back into the water to dodge a high-speed attack by an adult male peregrine. Instead of rising at once again and making its escape into the opposite direction, the dowitcher had dived and stayed under water, out of sight. Hovering over the spot for three of four seconds, the peregrine could probably see the submerged wader holding on to the bottom vegetation. Diving down feet first, like an osprey, he dropped chest-deep into the pool and emerged with the dowitcher in his claws. Observed at close range, this was one of my rarest observations of peregrines hunting shorebirds.

How to explain this very unusual event? His successful capture leaves no doubt as to this falcon's seriousness. Was he starved after a long migration flight? Or just exceptionally clever?

Casual interactions with potential prey are easily misinterpreted. A playful pass at a Canada goose or snow goose, which reacts by dropping down into the water or grass, should not be seen as a serious attempt at capturing that goose. Some observers might claim, though, that they saw the falcon 'knock the goose down.' Observations of peregrines making half-hearted swoops at crows, large gulls, or buteo hawks are not included in my records. But then, a falcon's mood is hard to fathom and some of my interpretations may have been wrong, too.

Sixty years ago, people who disturbed falcons at their nest site were quite safe from attack. Peregrines had learned the range of a shotgun. The survivors might vent their rage on innocent passersby, though. The late Edgar Jones, a local bird photographer, told me that he once saw an excited and angry peregrine, disturbed at the nest, score a direct hit on a passing red-tailed hawk, which dropped down out of the sky. Reports from Alaska tell of defensive peregrines hitting and downing snowy owls. Dogs are terrified of peregrines that stoop to turn the mammal away from the nesting cliff.

Falcons that have been raised in captivity and are habituated to the comings and goings of harmless people can become dangerous. One day, when the supervisor of the Alberta falcon breeding program accompanied his helmeted biologist to check on a pair of city peregrines, he ended up with a long bloody scratch on his bald skull. The peregrine is not alone in his fury in the defence of nestlings. In wilderness settings, goshawks can cause nasty problems for anyone approaching the nest tree. Interestingly, in Holland, where birds of prey are now fully protected after centuries of persecution, even buzzards have reverted to their inherent spunk. In some popular parks, hiking and biking trails had to be closed to protect unwary visitors from aggressive hawks that attacked intruders from behind. Sixty years ago, Dutch buzzards were so shy that one visit to the nest could result in their abandonment.

The question of how serious peregrines are when attacking prey came up again during my peregrine observations in Holland in 2008–2010. Some northern falcons wintering on the coast of the Wadden Sea are much larger than most Canadian peregrines, except the Peale's falcons of the northwest Pacific coast and Alaska, which are the biggest peregrine subspecies in the world. Female weights of these North American falcons are between 1,200 and 1,400 grams. During my field studies in Holland I saw very large falcons tackle prey as heavy as shelduck and black brant. Even bigger waterbirds have been recorded killed, including cormorants.

During a period of cold, overcast, or foggy weather by the Dutch Wadden Sea I kept a sedentary adult female under observation in the hope of seeing her hunt. When I found her on one of her usual coastal lookout points, I stayed in the parked car to get away from the wind, while she sat low on the ground. As seen from behind, her tapered profile looked as big as a great blue heron. When she finally went into action, my heart skipped a beat. Following her in the glasses, I saw her steadily climb toward a distant black dot that turned out to be a crow approaching high over the sea. It looked like a sure thing. But the crow changed course and managed to reach the coast. Pursued over an inland pasture, the crow evaded four or five stoops until the falcon gave up and left him alone. On subsequent days I saw two similar hunts aimed at distant crows approaching high over the sea. One escaped into the protection of a large tree, and the other one dropped into a tangle of tall weeds. The falcon viciously swooped at the spot, time and again, but she was unable to flush the crow into the open. She then retired to a fence post. Perhaps she was waiting for the crow to reappear, but he did not, and after some time the falcon flew away.

When I described these crow hunts to one of Holland's most experienced falconers, he said that the falcon I had seen could not have been serious. "Otherwise, she would have grabbed that crow when it dropped down into the weeds." Although I disagreed with him, I began to understand his viewpoint when he invited me to accompany him on one of his exploits in the same general area.

The favourite targets for his adult female falcon were grey partridges, which had become very scarce in the agricultural polders of Holland. But carrion crows were common. On the appointed day, we followed a narrow track through coastal grassland. Steering with one hand, he carried the loosely hooded falcon on his gloved left, and the side window was open. Upon spotting two crows some distance ahead, he slowed down and used his teeth to remove the falcon's hood. Incredible as it seemed to me, the next instant the falcon shot out of the open window and raced away, directly aiming for the crows. Both of them flushed and one of them narrowly dodged the sudden assault, as well as several additional passes. In defence, the crow's mate swooped at the falcon, which instantly switched targets. Trying to find cover under a barbed wire fence, the harassed crow eventually sought refuge by the base of the last post where the fence ended against a wall of shoreline reeds. Without a moment's hesitation, the falcon slammed right down on the same spot, disappearing from view between the vegetation. The violence had taken mere seconds. In the meantime, the falconer had jumped out of the car, a knife in his hand, and ran as fast as he could to the last fence post. Bending down to his knees, he stabbed the crow to death and lured the agitated falcon onto his gloved fist with a piece of meat.

To explain his interference in the drama, he said: "Crows can put up an effective defence with their bill and their feet. Besides, other crows might come in to help. And I want the action to be over as quickly as possible, before a buzzard or goshawk arrives to fight and rob the falcon of its prey."

To me, neither the spectacle nor the method of killing could have been classed as 'noble.' Clearly, wild peregrines behave quite differently than falconry birds. If their intended prey manages to escape into protective cover, I am sure a wild falcon would have let it go, in what I would consider to be fair play.

CHAPTER 13
Falcons Great and Small

On my first Christmas day spent in Canada, sixty years ago, I received an unexpected and most memorable present: the observation of a gyrfalcon, the only one of that northern species reported that year during the continent-wide Christmas bird counts. As a new immigrant with nothing better to do, I had gone for an afternoon drive on the bleak county roads east of Calgary. The temperature was well below freezing, and the view on the snow-covered fields on either side was utterly devoid of any life, until I suddenly came across a spectacular scene, a large hawk in hot pursuit of a running jackrabbit. Each time the hawk swooped, the big white hare jumped up vertically, several metres high, to meet its attacker in mid-air, sending the powder snow flying. Harassing the fleeing hare, the hawk repeated its vicious swoop half a dozen times until the chase ended abruptly when the hare took shelter under the strands of a barbed wire fence. Its attacker landed on a wooden post a little distance away. After I had stopped and aimed the 10x50 Zeiss binoculars, I slowly came to the gladdening realization that this raptor was a large falcon, a gyrfalcon. Presently it fluttered down to the base of the post and retrieved a food item, which turned out to be the frozen leftovers of a grey partridge, probably one of the falcon's earlier meals.

My second gyrfalcon sighting was equally unexpected and enchanting. On a clear and windy February afternoon of that same first winter in Calgary, while exploring the lower valley of the Bow River, I casually noted a distant white bird soaring over the steep, sixty-metre-high bank. Assuming it to be a gull—which would have been a very rare winter sighting indeed at this location—I resumed my walk. Presently, half a dozen magpies flushed from some carrion on the shore, and a large falcon swooped down in futile pursuit. Soaring back up on the brisk westerly wind, the white falcon sailed high over the riverbank, resplendent in the blue winter sky. For size comparison, it was joined by a prairie falcon, pestering its much bigger cousin in a playful manner.

In subsequent years, I learned that winter sightings of gyrfalcons were not uncommon in central Alberta. Their usual prey were partridges, but near open water they were attracted by the ducks that managed to survive the sub-arctic cold on stretches of river that remained unfrozen downstream from the city due to sewage effluents.

Another surprising discovery was that gyrfalcons were winter visitors on the Pacific coast. Between 1980 and 1994, I spent three weeks or so each winter on the Martindale flats of Vancouver Island. My main focus was a territorial female peregrine. One day, when she wasn't perched on her usual lookout tree, a lone sycamore, I went for a walk along a wood lot bordering on ploughed land. Briefly halting by a reedy ditch, I had raised the binoculars to scan the fields when I was alerted by the click of claws on wood. Looking up, I discovered a large raptor that had evidently just alighted on a bare maple branch overhead. The bird fearlessly returned my stare and remained on its perch. Its whitish chest and belly were boldly marked with heart-shaped dots. Thinking *peregrine*, I focussed the glasses on its head and noted the absence of a black cap or a prominent malar bar. Instead, there was only a narrow moustache stripe accentuating the dark eyes. Impressed by the bird's large size, it suddenly dawned on me that this was a gyrfalcon. Stepping back for a better view of its profile, I inadvertently flushed a cock pheasant that thundered up and away out of the reeds, and the falcon went after it in long-winged pursuit. Just before it was overtaken, the pheasant reached the opposite side of the field and dashed into the safety of woods.

In ensuing days, visiting the same area, I again spotted the gyrfalcon perched on a prominent tree, and hoping to see more action, I deliberately flushed ducks from the ditch and an irrigation pond. As expected, the falcon immediately took off in pursuit, although without much success, for the ducks managed to splash down into another body of water before being overtaken. At our next meeting, the falcon seemed to anticipate his opportunity, and to get a head start on fleeing prey, he flew some distance toward me when I entered the field. Alighting on a strategic tree, he waited for me to flush the ducks. However, the mallards, buffleheads, pintails, and teal refused to rise. Apparently, they too had become wise to the risk. As soon as the ducks saw me approach the pond, they rushed to the farthest shore and stayed put.

The above encounters illustrate the natural tendency of hunting falcons to team up with humans. Once they overcome their fear of people, birds of prey readily become partners in the ancient practice of falconry. Since the middle ages, long before the invention of the shotgun, hawks and falcons were trained to capture food for the table or for sport. The noble gyrfalcon was the favourite of kings and emperors, who financed expeditions to Iceland to collect young birds from cliff nests. Other falcons were caught in nets or baited traps during their southward migration.

Having read some of the classic literature on the subject, and after befriending an experienced falconer in Holland, I toyed with the idea of becoming one myself, but decided against it. Keeping a bird of prey and doing it justice is an extremely demanding task that often ends in disappointment if the precious captive escapes or succumbs to disease or accident. Far easier and more rewarding, in my view, was the study of wild birds. To learn how a falcon catches its wary prey is just as fascinating as the question of how prey species manage to cope with the fastest creature on earth streaking down like a bolt from the blue.

In America, the gyrfalcon's breeding range is restricted to Alaska and Canada, with the closest known nest sites roughly a thousand kilometres north of the international boundary. A portion of the population, including immatures as well as some adults, start wandering southward by early September. They may show up anywhere, but it stands to reason that migrant falcons, in their search for productive hunting grounds, should not have to go farther south than necessary to wait out the winter months. The remarkable but perhaps not really surprising fact is that Canadian gyrfalcon sightings are concentrated near centres of human population. Of course, the obvious correlation is that birdwatchers are more numerous around cities than in rural environs. Another reason is that cities abound in falcon prey.

My fervent wish to learn more about the hunting tactics of the gyrfalcon was realized after I had settled in Edmonton, which straddles the North Saskatchewan River. At this high latitude, most of the river is frozen solid all winter, except a section of ten of more kilometres just downstream from the city. Several hundred hardy mallards manage to survive here, but to find something to eat they have to venture out over the frozen stubble fields. If the snow deepens, they become dependent on area farms where beef cattle are fed with silage or grain. Favourite sites are visited daily and may attract the attention of their predators.

As soon as a gyrfalcon sighting has been reported on the Edmonton birding hot line, interested residents and visitors alike zero in on the chance to add this sought-after species to their life list. During the winters of 1999–2002, four or five different gyrs were frequently seen at a cattle feed yard on the city's eastern outskirts. Most of these falcons looked quite large and were assumed to be females. In those years I was periodically bothered by sciatic back pains that severely limited my ability to walk. So, I was quite content to sit in the car within view of the farm and wait for falcon action. As an independent wildlife watcher, I took advantage of the opportunity and watched every day unless it was extremely cold or snowing. On weekends, I met up with local raptor expert Gordon Court and wildlife photographer Gerald Romanchuk.

In 2003, with Gordon as co-author, I published a paper in the *Journal of Raptor Research* (37:161-163), detailing 70 gyrfalcon attacks on ducks, of which 16 were successful. Just over half of these hunts were the result of surprise attacks on feeding ducks. Approaching low in the cover of bushes or buildings, the falcons tried to seize the prey just after the panicked ducks flushed, or even before they had a chance to get off the ground. Too heavy to be carried away, the duck was plumed and eaten where it fell. The feeding falcon often ended up surrounded by curious cows or steers. If the cattle approached too closely, the falcon left. She might come back later to finish her meal or to capture another duck.

In the meantime, the panicked flock had flown back to the river. At the cattle feedlot, the farmer had shot several of the raiding ducks, which proved to be very skinny and close to starvation. Compelled by hunger, the flock would eventually return to their manure-covered feeding ground despite the risk of falcon attacks. However, if they were harassed too often, the ducks delayed their foraging flight and did not leave the safety of the river until sundown. If there were no ducks at the feedlot, I waited for their arrival, and like me, some gyrs seemed to have the same idea, quietly watching from a distant fence post.

The low stealth tactics of foraging gyrfalcons are well described and emphasized in the professional literature. However, I found no reference to a much more spectacular hunting method which involved the pursuit of ducks high in the sky. I got to watch many such flights after keeping my telescope focussed on distant falcons. Well before I saw any ducks flying in from the river and still miles away, the falcon locked them in her superior sights. As soon as she spread her wings and took off, I put the telescope aside and focussed the binoculars. Gradually accelerating, she began a long climb. My heart skipped a beat when I spotted a straggling line of ducks, tiny specks vibrating against the winter sky. Aware of the approaching danger, the flock broke up and veered out of the way, while the falcon singled out a target. Closely pursued, the duck descended to find cover on the ground. Some were intercepted and seized in the air. Others managed to plunge into bushes, in a weedy roadside ditch, or on the grassy median of a four-lane highway.

The gyr's success and determination in securing downed ducks varied. Some falcons tackled the prey without hesitation; others swooped several times in a futile attempt to flush it out of hiding. One falcon walked over the crusted snow of a roadside ditch, apparently searching for a duck that had taken cover under bushes. In another incident, a mallard drake that had landed on the shoulder of a highway put up an effective defense, lunging with gaping bill each time the falcon made a pass at him.

As a side show, it was fascinating to learn that the gyrfalcons were shadowed by bald eagles that spent the winter along the same open stretch of river. One or two adult eagles could often be seen perched on trees within view of the cattle feedlot where the ducks were known to gather. Soon after a falcon began plucking her kill, an eagle would commandeer the carcass. If a falcon failed to catch a duck and flew away to hunt elsewhere, the eagle followed at a distance.

Prey theft by eagles was also commonplace in the Fraser River delta near Vancouver. There, from October to March, bald eagles were seldom out of sight. The result was that hunting falcons, peregrines as well as gyrs, hardly ever got much of a chance to consume their own catch, and a duck was too heavy to be carried out of the reach of pirates.

Miechel Tabak, a Vancouver birdwatching friend and a skilled photographer, has seen more than a dozen instances in which gyrfalcons were robbed of just-caught ducks. In our experience, gyrfalcons had become very sneaky, and to hide from eagle eyes, they hunted low over the fields and along the weedy growth of irrigation ditches. Similarly pressured by eagles, coastal peregrines had stopped hunting ducks over the tidal flats. They now exclusively capture lightweight prey, such as sandpipers. Even then, they run the risk of losing them to pursuing bullies.

In much of its nearly worldwide range, the peregrine's commonest prey are pigeons and doves. How does the gyrfalcon do with these speedy flyers? Arthur Cleveland Bent's classic treatise *Life Histories of North American Birds of Prey* contains a telling anecdote from 1910. During an expedition to the Canadian arctic, the crew of a sailing vessel reported that their messenger pigeons were violently pursued by one or several gyrfalcons, although they never succeeded in capturing any. The conclusion was that pigeons were more than a match for the gyr. Bent's informants added that expedition members had shot 40 falcons and seen five times that many during their autumn journey.

Some years ago, the Edmonton birding hotline reported that a gyrfalcon and a prairie falcon had been seen hunting rock doves (feral pigeons) in an industrial area of town. Generally speaking, the business centre of a city is not a mecca for birdwatchers, but I decided to take a look anyway because my back had not yet healed, forcing me to forego my usual country walks. After driving downtown, I sat for hours in the car on a snow-covered parking lot between the train tracks and a busy highway, often while the engine was kept running because of the extreme cold. On many a morning, the overnight temperature had plunged to minus -30 C. But my ordeal resulted in a unprecedented series of observations, including the discovery that gyrfalcons have a novel way of catching doves not described before in the literature and quite different from the methods used by prairie falcons.

Straddling the railway was a grain-loading silo, where spilled grain had attracted some 500 feral rock doves. Their nervousness and frequent flushing proved that they had seen the enemy. As soon as the panicked flock burst up from the ground or from the building, I craned my neck in hopes of spotting a falcon before its hunt was over. During a period of 44 observation days, I tallied 141 attacks by gyrs and 104 by prairie falcons. Respectively, they captured fifteen and twenty-seven doves. This means that the prairie, an adult female, was about twice as successful as her big cousin.

A primary objective of both species was to take the doves by surprise. Approaching at speed and rounding the corner of the building, or racing low over the railway, the gyrfalcons managed to grab six doves immediately after they flushed. The prairie succeeded in eight surprise hunts. But an interesting difference in style showed up in aerial attacks on flying flocks that had spotted the falcon in time and were careening back and forth in alarm.

Soaring and sailing high above the flocking pigeons, the prairie took her time to select a specific target on the outside edge of the dense formations. Keeling over with furled wings, she stooped like a falling stone and seized her target at once, to carry it down to the snow-covered ground. In contrast, the gyrfalcons initiated their attacks with a fast, winging descent. Then, using their momentum, they swooped steeply upward into the middle of the dense flock and tried to grab a dove at random. If the strategy failed, the gyr could repeat the tactic several times, rising and falling like a pendulum.

During my observations, the granary doves were hunted by at least four different gyrs. All appeared to be females. One was a very large and nearly white adult, two were light grey adults, and others were dark grey-streaked immatures. Unlike the two grey females, the white gyr never used the pendulum method, but persisted in pursuing small flocks and single pigeons, in which she proved quite unsuccessful. Over two days, including a total of five hours of observation, she made 32 attacks and succeeded only once.

By contrast, the immature falcons took it easy. Searching the lower roofs of the granary complex, they picked up dead doves, which might have died after hitting the air circulation fans. Others could have been struck and wounded by falcon attacks. Carrion feeding is a common trait of gyrfalcons, a practical adaptation to lean times in their harsh northern environment. However, it comes at the risk of eating poison baits. In the Canadian north, gyrfalcons are known to die on traps set for arctic foxes. In Russia, gyrs become entangled in snares set for ptarmigan.

In February of 2011, the university of Boise, Idaho, hosted an international conference titled "Gyrfalcons and Ptarmigan in a Changing World." Its focus was on the ecology of these iconic birds in relation to climate change. In view of the predictions for continued warming of the arctic tundra, it will be interesting to see whether we can expect a change in the number of gyrs migrating south in winter. In my opinion, there is little reason to worry about the future of the gyrfalcon. This hardy and versatile hunter has been around far longer than the human race, and over the eons, gyrs have been able to adapt to all major environmental upheavals, from one ice age or warming cycle to the next.

The merlin is often seen as a small version of the peregrine, but in taxonomic terms, such as relative length of its toes, the merlin is not akin to the peregrines of the world, but closer to the desert falcons, which include the circumpolar gyr, the American prairie falcon, the African lanner, and the east European saker. The last three are medium-sized species that inhabit semi-open habitats. In body length—bill to tail tip—the merlin measures roughly half of the gyr's size, but the gyr is ten times heavier. The weight of the smallest male merlin is about 170 grams, while female gyrs may tip the scales at 1,700 grams. Having watched the dapper merlin in action over ocean shores, prairies, and city streets, I see this tiny tyke as a gyrfalcon in miniature, and in dash and dexterity I tend to rate *Falco columbarius* as superior to all of its bigger cousins.

Having watched merlins at every opportunity, my notes contain numerous hunting flights aimed at sandpipers and small songbirds, but the only research paper I ever wrote about the merlin is based on my first 22 years in the field. The data were published in the 1988 *Journal of Zoology* (66:925-028), in which I compared the merlin's records with a set of hunts by peregrines observed over the same time span. The merlin data include 354 hunts with 44 kills, representing a hunting success rate of 12.4%. The peregrine's comparative score is 647 hunts with 53 kills, for a success rate of 8.2%. One way to account for the difference in the two values is that the peregrine records were collected during migration times, whereas many of the merlin observations occurred during summer, when adult males do most of the foraging for their breeding mate or nestlings. Adult male falcons of any species can be expected to be better hunters than immature falcons during their first year on the wing.

In their open habitat, merlins are quite approachable, and all it takes to see them in action is to be patient. Unlike peregrines, they seldom dawdle on a fence post for hours and hours. Merlins are active birds, and after a brief rest, they are off again, just to another lookout spot or to launch an attack. Typically, they race low over the ground to flush a sparrow from the grass and grab it the moment it rises. Using the same stealth tactics, merlins prey on sandpipers. On days when gale force winds are blowing, they hunt upwind and very low over the mud flats. Facing into the strong wind, foraging shorebirds are vulnerable to surprise attacks from behind and slow to react. Taking advantage of an opportunity to hide its approach, one merlin aimed for a sandpiper sitting among a dozen ducks. The ducks were not alarmed by the little raptor that seized the sandpiper point-blank.

Walking the pastures at Beaverhills Lake during a wet summer when the grass had grown tall, I was shadowed by a merlin that launched attacks on sparrows I inadvertently flushed out of the rank vegetation. In the past, despite their small size, merlins were used in falconry. The literature on the species mentions that the Russian Empress Katherina had dozens of wild merlins captured and trained each fall by her retinue of professional falconers. The merlins were flown at skylarks that took the chase high into the sky. In those days, small songbirds were considered food for the gods. At the start of winter, after the falconry season ended, the empress ordered all of her merlins set free again.

Both at Beaverhills Lake and on the Pacific coast I have greatly enjoyed watching merlins and peregrines in long flights after sandpipers. Peregrines are overpowered and tend to overshoot the erratic twists and turns of small prey, but merlins follow-chase the dodging target with better precision. Rising hundreds of metres into the sky, the chase may cover long distances, until the prey is captured or gives up and suddenly plunges straight down to earth to find protection in a dense tangle of reeds or bushes.

A common problem of merlin life that I hate to witness is to see the little guy robbed of its hard-won prize by a greedy peregrine. Nowadays, though, the most common freeloader on the west coast is the bald eagle. I remember watching one prey-carrying merlin pursued over the ocean by three bald eagles. Refusing to give up its prey and evading every pass by the gigantic bullies, the merlin carried its just-caught dunlin to the Boundary Bay dike, hopped over it at top speed and disappeared from sight between the bushes of a farmyard. I felt like clapping my hands in applause.

Feral pigeons that collect around city granaries may attract birds of prey. In Edmonton, gyrfalcons compete with prairie falcons. Their respective hunting success rates were 16% and 26%. Also their hunting methods were different.   Photo Don Delaney

A rare shot of the two species of falcon together.   Photo Don Delaney

The merlin is the smallest of the falcon tribe, but its hunting style is as dashing as the peregrine's.
Photo Gordon Court

If an immature goshawk seizes a flying duck over a pond or ditch, the hawk might fall back into the water with its prey. This one landed on the ice.
Photo Miechel Tabak

CHAPTER 14
Bald Eagle Lore

Half a century ago, when Irma and I settled in Edmonton, pesticide poisoning of raptors was a worldwide concern. The American bald eagle had already become scarce over its continental breeding range. A few years earlier, while living in Calgary, I had seen many eagles -- golden as well as bald -- migrating along the Rocky Mountain foothills, and wintering bald eagles were still common along open stretches of the Bow River east of the city. But how the species was doing in Canada's vast boreal hinterland was not exactly known. A topical question raised by the scientific community was whether these eagles were still fledging young, or whether their progeny had been compromised by the toxic residues of chemicals used in agriculture and other industries.

The move to central Alberta opened up a new opportunity for bald eagle watching. From 1964 onward and continuing for the next 20 years, I kept notes of all eagles sighted in the lake-studded parklands east of the city. Fall migration began in the second week of September and lasted until the end of December. Return flights took place from mid March to mid May. Most of my observations were made around Beaverhills Lake. But during late fall and early winter, I spent many days at Cooking and Hastings Lakes. Their water level was about two or more metres higher than today, and some county roads gave open access onto the shore. Sitting in the parked car, I scanned the partly frozen lake through binoculars or a telescope in the hope of observing eagle interaction with the last of the ducks.

The following information is gleaned from my 1984 paper in Blue Jay (42:199-205) published by the Saskatchewan Natural History Society. During the fall migration period, I spent a total of 463 days afield, compared to 435 days in spring. The respective numbers of eagles sighted were 626 and 187, which amounts to 1.35 sightings per day in fall and 0.43 per day in spring.

The fact that I saw a lot more eagles on their way south than coming back in spring needs an explanation. Part of the reason might be that the migrants were subject to a high mortality rate on their wintering grounds. But the main reason is that the fall movement is quite leisurely, with the eagles stopping off on Alberta's prairie lakes to hunt waterfowl. By contrast, in spring, the adults hurry to reach their northern breeding grounds in competition with other pairs.

The good news coming out of my twenty-year project was that the south-bound flights included a remarkably high percentage of immature eagles. The fall data were as follows: 231 immatures, 215 adults, and 180 unclassified birds. The percentage of immatures was even higher during the return migration: 116 immatures, 47 adults, and 24 unclassified bald eagles.

Bald eagles spend most of their day in idleness, just sitting on a tree for hours on end or soaring in the blue. Their lifestyle is geared toward energy conservation. With a staple diet of fish, their winter menu includes any kind of carrion, and where bald eagles are attracted to concentrations of waterfowl, they are known to pick off ducks and geese crippled by hunters. Apart from robbing gulls and parasitizing peregrines, they aggressively compete with each other and fight over the smallest bits of food. Yet, once they shake off their lethargy, bald eagles are very capable hunters of waterfowl.

If approached directly, ducks and geese take to the air, but when the lakes begin to freeze up, and the remaining waterfowl are concentrated in patches of open water, they seem reluctant to flush. Some or most of these laggards might be sick or crippled. I have seen flightless ducks leave waterholes on their own, walking or sliding along the ice on their way to the shore. A few managed to reach and hide in the reeds, others were intercepted by eagles. One was killed by a coyote..

By mid November there might be more than a dozen migrating eagles resting on the ice of Cooking Lake. My highest day count was November 11, 1977, when there were 15 eagles on Cooking, 7 on Hastings, and 5 on Beaverhills. From time to time, one of them flew toward swimming ducks. Whether or not these flights represented a serious attempt at capture was not always clear. If the eagle passed over massed ducks at a height of one metre or less, I counted that as a hunt. Of 118 such flights, 60 involved swoops at diving or splashing targets, 9 included a brief hover, and 3 resulted in a short pursuit of fleeing birds. Fourteen of these attacks ended in a catch, representing a success rate of 12 per cent. On 15 additional occasions I saw eagles carrying or eating ducks which might have just been caught. Prey theft and aerial chases were common. Most food items 'changed hands' repeatedly. If a prey-carrying eagle was forced to drop its duck, the item was often retrieved by another eagle in the air before it hit the ground. Intraspecific piracy and commensal feeding were also routine at Boundary Bay on the Pacific coast near Vancouver, where wintering bald eagles have become super abundant.

During November 1976, the waterholes in Cooking and Hastings Lakes were about 300-400 metres distant from my point of observation and remained open later than in other years, which created exceptional opportunities for detailed observation. Following are some examples of successful hunts showing a variety of methods.

October 3, 1965. 09:00. Beaverhills Lake. An immature eagle flying at a height of about 10 metres, flushing numerous waterfowl, suddenly swooped at a swimming coot, which dived and kicked up a splash. The eagle described a tight circle and swooped again when the coot surfaced. At the sixth swoop, the eagle seized the coot and carried it to the muddy shore. Prior to this hunt, the same eagle had made two similar but unsuccessful series of swoops at other birds, possibly also coots.

November 6, 1976. 11:00. Hastings Lake. Flying at a height of about 10 metres against a strong wind, an adult eagle approached an open waterhole in which some 100 ducks, mostly lesser scaup, were massed together and splashing about. A lone female mallard flushed well ahead of the eagle and dropped back into the water just after the eagle had passed by. In a very swift manoeuvre the eagle doubled back and seized the mallard.

November 6, 1976. 12:30. Beaverhills Lake. An adult bald eagle sitting on the ice, flew up and approached a waterhole with some 60 mallards. All of them left except one. The eagle grabbed the lone duck and took it away.

November 14, 1976. 12:30. Cooking Lake. An adult bald eagle that had been standing on the ice for some time, flew at a height of 2-3 metres to a waterhole. About 80 ducks, mostly scaup, standing on the edge of the ice hurriedly entered the water. The last bird, a drake scaup, was seized by the eagle in one foot.

November 15, 1976. 12:00. Hastings Lake. An unidentified duck left a water hole and flew low over the frozen lake for about 0.8 km before descending onto the ice. Immediately, two immature eagles that had standing some distance away, flew toward the duck, which was grabbed by the first eagle. At the approach of the second one, the captor flew away carrying the prey, but dropped it into the ice. Both eagles turned back, fighting over the duck, and were joined by a third eagle.

November 19, 1976. 14:00. Hastings Lake. In about one hour, an adult eagle made 12 low passes over a waterhole with some 200 ducks, each time returning to the ice and resting for 3-10 minutes. During six over-flights the eagle either briefly hovered over the massing ducks or swooped at one of the ducks which dived. On one occasion, the eagle plunged feet first into the water, sinking up to its belly, but rising without prey. After a few minutes rest on the edge of the hole, the eagle walked into the water until breast-deep and returned dragging a duck along with one foot.

November 20, 1976. 13:00. Cooking Lake. Two immature bald eagles hovered against a strong wind 2-3 metres over a waterhole. They were approached by an adult eagle that landed on the ice nearby. The immatures each swooped several times at the same duck, probably a female mallard, which dived each time. After a brief rest on the ice, the two immatures resumed the attack until one of them plunged into the water and lay on the surface, wings extended. After half a minute, it rose, holding a duck in its feet. Landing on the ice, it was rushed by the adult eagle. The duck was released and escaped into the water. Presently, the two immatures again hovered over the waterhole, swooping alternatively until one of them plunged down. Rising with apparent difficulty and swooped at by the other immature, it dropped the duck. After a rest, the two eagles resumed hovering with the same result as before. One of them plunged into the water to lie on the surface for half a minute. When it rose, holding the duck, the eagle had trouble getting out of the water and twice fell back. On the ice, the wing-flapping duck was surrendered to the adult, which killed and consumed it, flanked by the two immatures. A third immature cleaned up the leftovers.

November 21, 1976. 12:30. Cooking Lake. One adult and three immature eagles were standing on the ice near a small waterhole in which 15 ducks, mostly mallards and scaup, were milling about. One immature flew low over the hole, while the ducks kicked up water and dived. After some ten minutes the same eagle again hovered briefly over the hole and plunged in, submerging up to its neck. Coming back up, it lay on the surface for a few moments, then 'rowed' to the edge of the ice about six metres away. With apparent difficulty, the eagle climbed out of the water, holding the duck in one foot and pulling it up further with its bill. The eagle fed on its prey, while the others stood around to snatch a severed wing or a leg, and clean up the remains after the captor flew to shoreline trees.

In several interactions, bald eagles attempted to overtake ducks that flushed at close range, pursuing them until the target abruptly changed course.

On November 13, 1978, an immature eagle flushed a flock of ducks from a waterhole of Hastings Lake. All ducks returned to the water except one that flew out over the frozen lake, climbing at first, then dropping low over the ice, to be chased by an immature and an adult eagle. In a close pursuit of some 800 metres, the adult and the immature alternately seized the duck, holding on for a minute. When the other eagle swooped at the one holding the prey. the duck was released and flew on. It eventually reached the cover of shore vegetation.

Apart from their focus on waterbirds, the bald eagles opportunistically added small mammals to their diet. On April 10, 1966, I watched four immatures standing on the ice of Beaverhills Lake, facing a muskrat. Over some 20 minutes, the rat defensively dodged five or six pounces until the eagles gave up the siege. On April 8, 1972, there were four immatures, plus one adult bald and one golden eagle, picking up meadow voles that had been flooded out of their burrows by snow melt. Numerous gulls, crows, and harriers were taking part in the feast. In Jasper Park, I once saw an adult bald eagle feeding on a rabbit, still in its white winter fur, which must have been an eye-catching target on a snow-free slope.

In the intervening years, the return of the bald eagle to its former breeding range across the continent ranks as one of the greatest conservation stories of our time.

Adult bald eagles have a varied menu but spend most of their day at rest.   Photo Miechel Tabak

Immature bald eagles are not as skilled as adults at catching waterbirds and fight over every scrap of food.
Note the falling prey item released by one harassed eagle, while another eagle turns to catch it in mid air.

Photo Miechel Tabak

CHAPTER 15
Saga of the Riverside Eagles

Soaring in the blue, its white head blinking in the sun, there is no more majestic sight in the avian theatre than the American bald eagle. A century ago, this heraldic symbol of freedom had become scarce. Shot up and poisoned from Alaska to Florida, it was on the point of vanishing altogether from its formerly continent-wide range. The bald eagle's relatively recent recovery, together with the return of the peregrine, is one of the greatest wildlife stories of our time.

Year-round, the eagle is seldom far from water, and the only reason a few of them overwinter in frigid Alberta, where lakes and rivers are locked in ice for six months of the year, is because a section of the river downstream from the big cities stays open due to their sewage outflow.

Over many winters, I have enjoyed walking the banks of the North Saskatchewan River on Edmonton's eastern boundary, overlooking the magnificent valley. The view hasn't changed much in 300 years, since the time when the first European explorers ascended this wilderness highway. The river valley is just as beautiful and pristine today, although much of the land higher up on either side of the river has been cultivated for agriculture or mined for gravel.

Sometime after the turn of the last century, at least one adult eagle hung around all year. It was one of the shyest eagles I have ever known, no doubt having become wary of people with rifles who occasionally frequented the same river bank. When she saw me coming from afar, she left her treetop overlooking the stretch of open water where some four or five hundred mallards spent the winter. Going by her large size, I assumed that she was a female, that she was on territory, and that this same eagle stayed around from year to year.

Since the late 1990s, I had kept an eye on a huge stick nest in a mature poplar. One day, I saw an eagle in the trees nearby and hoped that the nest would be used, but when I checked later that spring, it was occupied by a pair of red-tailed hawks. The following year, I discovered another nest just downstream from the open water of the sewer outflow. An eagle was perched nearby. To avoid possible disturbance, I stayed away until April of 2004, when I saw a second eagle, a slightly smaller one, an adult male. Upon spotting me, he chittered in protest. Several days later, looking through binoculars, I could see the white head of an adult sitting low on the nest. Retreating at once, I was sure I had found the first occupied nest of a pair of bald eagles in greater Edmonton.

I did not visit the area again until May 25. Approaching from behind a belt of trees, I took care to stay out of sight until I could see the nest, screened by tree branches. The binoculars revealed that there was indeed a bird on it, sitting low in a brooding attitude. But the thrill of discovery quickly changed into disappointment when the occupant turned out to be a Canada goose. Apparently, the eagles had abandoned the nest.

In subsequent years, there always was one adult eagle on location, but I saw no evidence of a mated pair until March 2009. The nest was in a difficult spot for observation and I did not want to get too close. But in June, watching through the telescope from across the river, I glimpsed two downy eaglets. Unfortunately, on July 18, 2009, the area was hit by a near-tornado. Two days later, when I checked the nest site, the local devastation was shocking to see. Many poplars had been uprooted or broken, including the nest tree. On the ground below, a great packet of branches lay buried under broken trunks and debris. The parent eagles were still in the area, but there was no sign of the young. Some distance downwind, I found a secondary wing feather, its broken shaft still in the blood-gorged growing stage. I feared the worst.

As of July 26, at least one of the two eaglets had evidently survived the storm. Flying on and off, its wings looked undamaged. But where was its sibling? On August 9, there was still only one youngster around, and I had given up all hope of ever finding out what had happened to the other one. Then, on August 16 and again on August 30, there were two immature eagles in the air. And I noted that one of them, when it soared overhead, was missing a wing feather.

In September and October, the young were absent while the adult eagles stayed around. I was wondering whether they would build a new nest. And yes, already by the end of November there was a nest under construction in a mature poplar tree, close to the broken stump.

During the previous summer, Strathcona County had built a new hiking trail on the riverbank. It was posted and fenced to keep out motorcycles and snowmobiles, which had earlier done much damage to the terrain. But instead of following a route along the outside of a shoreline belt of old-growth trees, the contractors cut a path right through them, exposing the nest tree to full view from the trail.

On April 3, my first visit of 2010, it was apparent that the nest had been greatly enlarged. I could just make out the white bonnet of a brooding adult, and on June 6, the fluffy heads of two chicks protruded above the nest rim, while the female eagle was perched on a branch above. Presently, her mate arrived with a fair-sized silvery fish. Later that month, when the river crested and ran brown with silt and debris, I wondered how the eagles managed to catch any fish at all. Interestingly, I twice saw them bring in a small prey item that appeared to be a ground squirrel. By this time, the chicks could feed themselves and took turns eating. They were generally well behaved and docile, gazing about sleepily, quite different from other young birds of prey, such as peregrines, which never seem to keep their heads still.

Watching the nest from a safe distance, many days went by without any activity. For instance, on July 10, I sat there for five hours and saw no food deliveries at all. By the middle of the month, the youngsters were jumping up and down, exercising their great wings and climbing into the branches above the nest. On July 31, both of them had fledged.

During the summer of 2010, very few hikers were using the new trail and most of them showed only a passing interest in the big nest, high in a poplar tree. Meanwhile, the eagles seemed to have become less alarmed by the occasional passerby. But all this changed the following summer. The pair of eagles was back at the same site, and there were three eaglets standing on the nest rim in good view. The news spread quickly via a photo website on the internet. On July 30, I met five different camera-toting birdwatchers, and all of them walked right up to the nest tree. Despite the increased attention, the young fledged successfully. However, what this kind of human disturbance was going to do next spring, when the eagles would be in the early stages of nesting, remained to be seen.

Another negative aspect of the new trail was that it attracted more and more dog walkers. One day I met two parties of women who had eight dogs between them, including three rottweilers with an aggressive attitude. Complaining to the county office about them, I was told that the trail was going to be posted as dogs-on-leash-only. While the number of visitors increased, the signs were vandalized, and the trail became a free-for-all. Interestingly, the eagles stayed in the same vulnerable spot and became ever more tolerant of people. Some photographers walked right up to nest and the brooding bird would not flush.

By way of comparison, it is interesting to note how other countries have dealt with the recent return of their sea eagles. In Denmark, after a century of absence, the white-tailed sea eagle began recolonizing some regions in the late 1990s, and by 2010 the recovery had surged to 37 breeding pairs. To protect occupied nest sites, all human activity was prohibited within a radius of 300–500 metres, but viewing platforms were set up at a safe distance. In Holland, which can now boast of fifteen occupied eagle nests, public access is even more restricted, the same as in Scotland after sea eagles had been reintroduced.

The newly rebuilt nest on the North Saskatchewan River fledged two young in 2010 and three in 2011. Sadly, in the spring of 2012, the sewage treatment plant contracted a pest control company to poison the ground squirrels on its property. There were just too may holes in the ground and people driving the yard had complained. The area was treated with chlorophacinone, an anti-coagulant blood poison that renders the entire carcass of expired ground squirrels toxic.

By July 5, I noted that something had happened to the two half-grown eaglets. In response, the Alberta Fish & Wildlife Department sent someone to check out the nest and climb the tree. He collected some remains of the eaglets but the exact cause of death remained unknown.

It so happened that the Edmonton Wildlife Rehabilitation Society had just received a young orphaned bald eagle—a fully feathered female from northern Alberta. Manager Holly Duvall agreed to have the eaglet placed into the empty nest. It turned out to be a good decision. Big mama eagle adopted the new kid, a day or so after it had been sitting in the nest forlornly gazing up at the sky. On August 2, during a violent rainstorm, the eaglet spread its huge wings into the wind and lifted off on her maiden flight. She stayed out of sight until August 16, when she and an adult were seen perched in the nest tree together. The story of the orphan had become an unqualified success.

The following summer, there were again two chicks on the nest. They attracted the attention of many photographers, some of whom were callous enough to stand for hours on the riverbank directly below the nest, waiting for adult eagles to bring food to their young.

In 2013, I observed the nest from a shady vantage point on seven days in July and six in August, each time for about four hours. My goal was to see what kind of food the parents were bringing in and to record the fledging date of the young. Their maiden flight might have taken place one or two days earlier, but by July 26 both youngsters had left the nest. In ensuing days, I saw them perched in a tree or soaring over the opposite riverbank. However, they often returned home. On August 1, both were lying down on the nest as if they had never spread a wing. On August 10, there was one eaglet on the nest, while its sibling was perched in the wood behind my observation post. Every few seconds, it whistled a plaintive call, urging its parents to bring food. At 3 p.m., just as I was ready to leave after three hours of watching and seeing no action at all, I happened to glimpse an adult coming in from behind the trees. He touched down on the rim of the nest and was gone again before I could focus the binoculars.

While the sleeping youngster rose to its feet, its sibling that had been calling from the woods rushed up at once and pounced on whatever was brought. However, he took his time before starting to eat, reinforcing my impression that the eaglets were never ravenously hungry. Nor did I ever see them fight over food. Most food items that I saw brought to the nest appeared to be small, hard to identify in the big feet of the eagle. A few items looked like the remains of a partly eaten fish. But on July 23, the female parent delivered a bird, probably a duck. Curiously, the young eagles, which were sitting on a branch just above the nest, did not display any obvious interest. After a few minutes, the adult female carried her prey back to a tree perch. I could now clearly see that it indeed was a duck, obviously still alive, for it was vigorously flapping one wing. Presently, the eagle took her prey to a more convenient plucking spot. When she returned to the nest rim, she dropped the partly eaten duck and left at once. Again I was impressed by the lack of eagerness on the part of the youngsters. It took a while before they began nuzzling the food brought.

To actually see the eagles hunt and catch prey was rare. After many days of watching, I could count my successful observations on the fingers of one hand. Several times, a low-flying eagle picked up a small item from the water and flew out of sight. Only once I was lucky enough to see the male eagle fly down over the river, lower his feet in a fluid, classical move and swipe a fair-sized fish. He carried it to a tree limb and spent the next 25 minutes eating the entire thing, leaving nothing to take to his obviously well-provided-for chicks. Some deliveries to the nest were photographed by other observers and turned out to be sticks or lumps of mud and vegetation.

In each of the following three breeding seasons, 2014 to 2016, the eagle pair fledged three youngsters, an exceptional record for the species anywhere. In the meantime, they must have kept on adding building material, because in the spring of 2017, I was struck by the enormous size of the nest. In 2017 the pair produced two young, and on June 6 the provincial Fish & Wildlife Division added two other young eagles of about the same age. These two had been collected in another part of the province after their nest tree broke during a wind storm. All four eaglets, now nearly fully-grown, added their combined weight of several kilos each to the massive bulk of the nest. On June 26, the river valley was hit by a gusty storm and the entire top-heavy structure ended up on the ground. When it was discovered and reported by a dog walker, three of the young eagles were found to have been crushed. The one surviving youngster was removed by government staff and added to another eagle nest in the province.

The parent eagles stayed around for some time, but they soon abandoned the area. Concerned personnel of the county, who had become fond of their eagles, got together with some prominent birdwatchers for advice. The group decided to construct an artificial nest platform, ignoring my unsolicited opinion to the effect that the eagles would build a new nest themselves if they felt like it, and that it would be interesting to see what they would do. The group hired a contractor, who secured a door-sized platform on top of a telephone pole erected between the shoreline trees. After several years, no eagles seem to have shown any interest in the contraption. The interesting saga of the riverside pair had come to an end, at least for now.

In 2013, a pair of bald eagles nesting near Edmonton produced two or three young per year until their top-heavy nest blew down in a summer storm.   Don Delaney

Wintering bald eagles are numerous along the Pacific coast near Vancouver. They often parasitize peregrines, which have stopped hunting ducks and now concentrate on light prey such as dunlins that can be carried away at the approach of eagles.   Photo Miechel Tabak

CHAPTER 16
Shorebird Seasons

As the preceding chapters have made clear, falcons are my favourite animals, but if you were to ask me what kind of birds I actually like best, my answer might be surprising. Shorebirds. And in particular the little sandpipers. By way of explanation, I hurry to add that the main reason has to do with their open habitat, the ambience of the ever-changing vista of water and sky. Secondly, I enjoy watching these trusty dwarves because they allow intimate and close observation, very much unlike other little birds, such as the warblers that flit in and out of view in the foliage of trees or stay hidden between the reeds. Added to the suspense of waiting for a falcon to come down like a bolt from the blue is the realization that these tiny bundles of feathers are the champions of long-distance travel on the planet. Another wonder is their physiological diversity, in body size, the length of their legs, or the shape of their bills, a diversity that brings to mind the famous finches of Charles Darwin.

Departing from England in 1831 on a voyage around the world, the good ship Beagle anchored in the Galapagos archipelago, giving Darwin, as the onboard naturalist, the chance of his life to explore a range of pristine islands. Each one was home to a different kind of small passerine, for a total of 15 species. Their bills showed a gradation from thick and stubby to thin and sharply pointed. Darwin posited that all of them had developed from the same ancestor, a nondescript brown finch. The diversity of beak shape and function was proof of a process he called evolution through natural selection. Over the millions of years of isolation, the beak of each type of finch had been modified by the kinds of foods the birds commonly fed upon.

What I am thinking of here is that a similar process of evolution must have been at work in the shorebirds. All of the varied species frequent the same habitat, the relatively narrow strip where water and land meet, called the littoral zone. In an ecological sense, this biotope is very rich, with a super abundance of organic nutrients released by decaying plants and algae. The water is turbid and alive with swarms of bacteria and tiny crustaceans, including water fleas and shrimps, as well as aquatic insects and the larvae of midges and mosquitoes. They are the reason shorebirds frequent the littoral life zone. It is a meeting place for thirty-six kinds of shorebirds that congregate in the shallows to take advantage of a seasonal feast.

Since all are dependent upon the same food base, how do these different species of shorebirds avoid competition with each other? By dividing the seating at the table, so to speak. To lessen strife, the various kinds stick to their own specific niche. Birds with short legs stay close to the land, those with longer legs can wade out farther from shore. Additionally, each has its own unique set of utensils. Plovers have short, straight bills, sturdy enough to root out bugs between the pebbles. The avocet, with its thin, up-turned bill, scythes the water by feel. Dowitchers probe the bottom with a long beak that features a neat little hinge at the tip, like a pair of pliers that opens and closes to grab worms deep in the mud.

Easy to find in season and because of their open habitat, if approached with some caution, most shorebirds stay down long enough for a birder to aim a high-powered telescope or a camera with stabilizer optics for brilliant detail. Carrying just binoculars, you may be tempted to approach for a closer view. Most likely, the birds will react by flying off and landing farther away. A more productive tactic is to sit quietly by the shore on a stone or a little stool, and let the birds come to you. Sandpipers that breed in the arctic and pass through Alberta during spring and fall migrations show little or no fear of humans as long as you sit still. Feeding on the go and following the shore, the birds gradually come nearer until they are at your feet, close enough to admire the fine detail of their plumage, and to share in the high-intensity life of these delightful creatures.

Shorebirds appear to have the amazing ability to focus on the ground at the tip of their beak, searching for minuscule food items, and simultaneously, with high acuity, keep an eye on the sky. Some researchers have suggested that their eyes may have separate functions, one for close-up scrutiny, while the other eye remains on alert for distant threats. Be that as it may, for them and all other wild creatures, survival depends on staying alert and concentrating on the twin necessities of eating and avoiding being eaten.

Coming and going with the seasons, all of our shorebirds are long-distance migrants, but at least ten species are known to nest in Alberta. First to arrive is the dapper killdeer. The odd one may turn up by mid-March, when ponds and lakes are still frozen. Killdeers nest on open ground, often away from water. They do not make any attempt at nest building, but lay their four spotted eggs in a slight depression, decorated with a few pebbles or twigs. At the sight of humans, the brooding bird leaves quietly and sneaks off for a short distance until it flies up and bursts out in vehement protest.

If you are too close to its treasure, the killdeer attempts to lure you away by so-called distraction display. Dragging itself along the ground as if crippled, the bird screams pitifully. Potential egg robbers such as crows and weasels may be turned aside by such behaviour, but no amount of scolding or wing-fluttering would help if the nest was approached by a steer or a cow. In a frantic attempt to halt the innocent bovine, killdeer will literally 'fly into the face of danger.'

Like killdeer, the American avocet nests on bare ground, and the breeding bird slips away from the eggs well before the approach of people. It then joins other members of the breeding colony in a collective protest. By contrast, territorial shorebirds such as the marbled godwit and the willet, which hide their nest in the grass, stay put and leave its defence to a partner who flies out to meet the intruder in a highly agitated protest. Willets swoop aggressively over a person's head in a loud rush of wings. However, the brooding bird will flush only if you, unwittingly, almost step on the nest. Some godwits or willets sit so tightly that they can be touched or allow themselves to be picked up by people for a brief look at the eggs.

Colour is very important in bird identification, but the problem with shorebirds is that the most colourful species, such as the red knot and the red phalarope, moult back into the plainest grey well before the end of summer. They are then difficult to recognize. Another example is the black-bellied plover, well-named because of its bold plumage during the breeding season, but by autumn, it turns into the dullest looking bird on the wintering grounds. The British name of grey plover for this same species may actually be more appropriate.

Leg colour, in addition to other plumage details, can be the key to distinguishing some sandpipers that look very much alike in size and shape. Most have black legs, but the least sandpiper and the pectoral have yellow legs. Bright yellow legs are a year-round diagnostic feature for two of the most recognizable shorebirds, the greater and the lesser yellowlegs. The difference in size is substantial, but size can be difficult to judge in the field unless you see these two together.

The eggs of shorebirds are relatively large and perfectly peryform, or pear-shaped. Four of them, the usual number in a clutch, fit together like wedges in a pie, taking up the smallest possible space under the brooding bird. Unlike ducks, both members of paired shorebirds share incubation duties. The eggs hatch in 17 to 24 days, and the chicks are precocious. Within hours of birth they are quick on their feet and capable of catching insects. As soon as they can fly, they are fit to travel, and with or without their parents as guides, they start the long migration southward.

To speed up the breeding cycle and to share parental duties even more fairly, the Wilson's phalarope has reversed the gender roles in the care of eggs and young. Unlike most other birds, the male phalarope is the drab-coloured partner, while the female is the one with the fancy plumage. The male does all of the brooding while the female spends her time loafing about and fattening up to recover from the energy loss associated with producing her large eggs. She soon loses all interest in family business and departs early for distant winter quarters. By the end of June, most local shorebirds have fallen silent. Some already leave on migration in July; a few stragglers stay around into September. First to arrive and last to go, the odd killdeer may hang on until freeze-up.

Bird migrations in North America take place along three major flyways: the Pacific, the central, and the eastern flyway, which partly converge over central Alberta. Travelling mainly at night, shorebirds follow a timetable that is as predictable as the seasons, but their route may depend on the weather. With thousands of miles to go, the flocks depart on a tail wind. Northbound migrants take advantage of the strong counter-clockwise southerlies that precede cells of low atmospheric pressure, moving on the jet stream from west to east. Little or no bird migration takes place when the province lies under a large dome of high pressure and the air is practically stagnant. In some years, dependent upon weather patterns, the mass of shorebirds may bypass Alberta and instead choose a route over the neighbouring province of Saskatchewan.

Spotting the first shorebirds of the season, after six months of winter, is always a thrill. Invariably, killdeer and yellowlegs are in the vanguard. A few individuals of other species may be ahead of their kind and show up in April, but the first big wave of sandpipers does not arrive before the second week of May. With a staggered timetable for various species, the spring passage of shorebirds is hurried and may be over before the end of that month, unless the travellers hit on a stopover spot where food is super abundant.

The shallow wetlands of Alberta play a functional role in recycling decaying organic matter. A keystone species in this process of nutrient renewal is the chironomid midge. In flight, it resembles a mosquito, but it does not sting or suck blood, although midge larvae are called bloodworms. They are red in colour and 2–5 cm long. Their density in the muck at the bottom of the shallows can be astonishing, about 65,000 per cubic metre. Long-billed shorebirds such as the dowitcher can extract the worms from the mud. Avocets and sandpipers go for the pupae that rise to the surface and emerge as midges, locally called lake flies. On warm days, huge mating swarms of lake flies hang like a smokescreen over the shore. If the arrival of arctic-bound sandpipers coincides with a big hatch of flies, the birds tend to stay long enough to fatten up before resuming travel. Such conditions can provide spectacular opportunities for shorebird watchers.

On their return migration through central Alberta, some sandpipers are already back by mid-June, when the last of the spring migrants may still be hanging around. Ornithologists used to think that these early-returning peep were non-nesters, but that assumption proved to be wrong. They are the adults of nesting pairs. Odd as it may seem, the females of several species depart their arctic breeding grounds as soon as the eggs have hatched. The chicks are then guarded by the adult male or left to fend for themselves. The reason for the early departure of the female has to do with the timing of her annual moult. She begins the long flight south under full sail and completes moulting her wing feathers after arrival on the wintering grounds. In other shorebird species, it is the male that takes early leave.

The southward migration in Alberta can be quite drawn-out and may include sightings of some Pacific shorebirds that are way out of their normal range. Such unusual records include western sandpiper, wandering tattler, surfbird, ruff, and little stint. Whether these stray visitors were just blown off-course by strong westerly winds or got their navigation system mixed up is hard to say. The riddle of migration—how migrating birds find their way—has been a matter of scientific debate for ages, and today's consensus is that the migrants are guided by the earth's magnetic field as well as the stars.

A western vagrant that has become almost a regular in Alberta is the dunlin. A few are reported every spring and fall. This medium-sized sandpiper, weighing about 70 grams, travels the ocean shores of the world. It is practically the only sandpiper that spends the winter months along the Pacific coast of Canada. A very good place to see them is the delta of the Fraser River, near Vancouver.

Estimated at around 40,000 birds, these flocks have been monitored for many years by the Canadian Wildlife Service and Simon Fraser University. To collect data on the dunlins, many hundreds, if not thousands, have been netted, banded, and released again. Biologists involved in this kind of detailed studies might have seen some predation events, but no one has had the time for a serious look at peregrine attacks on dunlin flocks. This is where I came in.

After an initial exploratory stop-off at Boundary Bay on the way back from Vancouver Island, I spent my first days there in January of 1994 and made many subsequent visits over the next 25 years. I did so on my own initiative and dime, until the publication of my findings led to some grant money for travel and motel expenses. The drive from Edmonton to the coast in my aging Volvo could be quite a challenge, especially in winters when January temperatures dropped to 30 degrees below zero. Arrival at Boundary Bay was especially bitter when the coastal plains were also snow-covered. But the maritime climate and the richness of its bird life made me, as a born and bred lowlander, feel at home at once.

At high tide, when the mud flats are flooded, wintering dunlins mass together on the waterline. To lessen the danger of surprise attacks by peregrines and merlins, the flocks fly out over the ocean and stay airborne well off-shore until ebb time.   Photo Brian Genereux

Some 50,000 dunlins, migrants from northern breeding grounds, spend the winter in the Fraser Delta near Vancouver   Photo Brian Genereux

Striving to seek safety from raptor attacks, wintering dunlins form dense flight formations over the ocean. Peregrines that stoop at the birds from an overhead position tend to take their prey from the outside or the bottom end of the gyrating flock. Dunlins in the centre of the flock are safest..　　　　Photo Miechel Tabak

Based on 1,369 peregrine hunts observed over 15 winters , I have recorded the capture of 205 dunlins. This adult male was banded as a nestling on the Channel Islands. Fearful of being robbed by larger raptors, he is consuming a just captured dunlin on a power pole, so that he has a height advantage if he needs to take off at the approach of a female falcon or an eagle. For the same security reason, immature peregrines often carry their prey high into the sky and start plucking it while soaring high above the land or ocean.

Photo Miechel Tabak

CHAPTER 17
Aerial Contests

B etween forested headlands, Boundary Bay is 16 kilometres across and, at the lowest tides, 4–5 kilometres wide. Inland fields are protected from ocean tsunamis by a gravelled dike a few metres high that makes for an excellent viewing platform. Walking that road on my very first day, flanked by a restless sea under overcast skies, I felt a sense of space I hadn't experienced for a very long time. Gulls galore and dunlins in their thousands. Frequently taking to the air and landing again, the flocks seemed restless. Later, I understood why. The tide was rising. As I sat down on the edge of the dike, hoping for action, the dunlins approached ever closer. Earlier that afternoon, I had seen two peregrines, but their attention had been focussed on each other, an adult female chasing an adult male.

As the flood crested and reached the dike, the dunlins were massing at its base, jostling for dominance on the last strips of dry ground. The outside birds were standing up to their bellies in water. Suddenly, with a roar of wings, the flock flushed and flew away over the ocean. What had happened? Had I missed a falcon, coming in from behind me, low and fast? Scanning the shore, I picked up a sharp-shinned hawk flitting over the pebbles. Focusing on the dunlins again, I saw that they had drawn together into a dense flock, careening back and forth over the water. They stayed far out over the ocean, while I kept watching from the dike. After another hour or so, I left the way I had come, wanting to get back to the motel before dark.

Realizing the critical importance to sandpipers of a wide open habitat, which allows them to see an approaching raptor from afar, I understood the significance of these dunlins abandoning the shoreline after their ebb time foraging flats had become inundated by the rising tide. If the flock had settled down close to the dike, the birds would have been a magnet for any passing falcon. On later visits, I often saw peregrines take advantage of such ambush situations. The success rate of surprise hunts on the high-tide line proved to be significantly greater than attacks over the wide open flats and the ocean. The aerial manoeuvres of the dunlin flocks that stayed in the air and far out over the water were a strategy designed to lessen the risk of surprise attacks. I termed that strategy Over-Ocean-Flocking (OOF).

Over 25 winters, I have spent a lot of time watching OOF. To see thousands of dunlins cruising over the ocean at high tide in ever-changing formations is fascinating. Depending on wind speed, they drift in a loose cloud or coalesce into a dense, undulating stream, low over the waves. The flocks frequently split up and separate or merge with other flocks. Timing the high-tide OOF flights, I found that their duration depended on the height of the tide and the extent to which the intertidal zone had been inundated. High-tide flights could last as long as four and a half hours. Later in the season, when ocean tides were less high and did not submerge all of the intertidal, the dunlins did not engage in OOF. Then, the flocks roosted on the mudflats, a safe distance away from the vegetated shore.

Other factors that had a bearing on the length of time the dunlins spent in flight over the ocean were temperature and wind. During periods of frost or continued heavy rain, the flocks did not fly very long or not at all. Instead, they sat out the tide on the edge of the salt marsh or on driftwood logs. After a few days of sub-zero temperatures, when the tide flats became ice-covered, the dunlins did not have the energy for long flights. A few dozen of them might stay and roost on the ice or on the foreshore, too tired to fly, taking their chances with attacks by falcons. Their choice was a trade-off between safety and energy cost. Most dunlins might actually leave the bay and fly farther south to escape from the cold, or to sit out the frost period on steeper beaches south of the international boundary, where the shoreline was kept free of ice by the wave action of the surf.

Instead of engaging in OOF, some dunlins headed inland, especially during periods of heavy rain. Waiting for ebb time, they roosted side by side, packed closely together on a field. Inland moves could also provide new foraging opportunities on waterlogged grassland, when worms were forced to rise to the surface. Sooner or later, though, these flocks might attract the attention of a peregrine, which caused widespread panic. Most of the dunlins would then return to the ocean and join their kind in OOF.

Several years ago, I gave a PowerPoint presentation about peregrines at an international gathering of shorebird biologists. My data included a very large sample of observations of falcon attacks on dunlins at Boundary Bay. Perhaps I should not have been surprised by the critical reaction. Negative comments came mainly from people who had no personal field experience with peregrines at all, although they might have had much to say about predation as a possible factor in the decline of migrating shorebirds. One vocal biologist from the Atlantic seaboard questioned my large sample of kills. "We have plenty of peregrines on the coast these days, but all I see them do is chasing back and forth, scaring the hell out of the shorebirds. They never seem to catch anything."

Another biologist doubted that Over-Ocean-Flocking was an anti-predator strategy. "The eyesight of peregrines is supposed to be eight times better than ours,' he argued. "So how could OOF be an anti-predator strategy, when I can clearly see those dunlin flocks myself, flying openly over the water?"

This was actually a very good question. Unfortunately, during the hectic and hurried proceedings of the conference, I never had a chance to formulate my reply. The answer is to be found in the difference between individual vulnerability of dunlins that are taking part in large flying flocks, as compared to those roosting and tightly packed together on the ground. Dunlins that spend the high-tide intermezzo in a communal roost below and close to the dike or in the saltmarsh are prone to surprise attacks by falcons that grab the first bird they bump into. I have seen such captures made in a split second. Before the dunlins rose in alarm, the falcon had already turned around and carried its prey away.

By contrast, attacks on dunlin flocks in OOF formation over the ocean are subject to a selective process. Approaching high and openly, the falcon is spotted from afar and early enough to allow the dunlins time to prepare their defence. Drawing together, they form globular flocks that gyrate back and forth, alternately flashing dark and light. High above them, the falcon takes its time to decide on the best angle for a vertical attack. Although it may then look as if he stoops right through the flock, that is not the case. His aim is on the outside and bottom end of the flock. Consequently, dunlins in the centre of the flock are practically safe from attack. The question here is, which birds are in the centre of the flock? My guess is that these are the dominant and fittest members. By contrast, the hangers-on, the weaker and less fit dunlins, are on the outside of the group and thus the most vulnerable. Isn't that exactly how all predation is supposed to work, in accordance with Darwin's principle of the survival of the fittest?

In land-locked Alberta, the closest thing to an ocean view can be enjoyed at Beaverhills Lake, at least during years of high water. Sixty years or more ago, Beaverhills Lake was a well-known hotspot for migrating shorebirds, and the one species for which the lake became particularly and internationally famous was the buff-breasted sandpiper. In season, on their way from South America to their northern breeding range, these long-distance migrants were believed to stop off on two places in between, the Texas Gulf Coast and Beaverhills Lake. A notable characteristic of buffies, which made them exceptionally sought after, was that the males interrupted their rest stops with courtship behaviour, during which they flapped their open wings while facing the females.

During my early experience at the lake, buffies predictably arrived in mid- to late-May. I remember a day when the pastures on the north end of the lake, near the old windmill, thronged with them. In the company of pectoral and Baird's sandpipers, they feasted on lake flies that had dropped down into the short grass to evade the brisk wind. When the flocks flushed in alarm, I looked for and found a peregrine. Climbing high in pursuit of the buffies, it managed to catch one in a spectacular stoop. Lowering the binoculars, I saw two people approaching on the old stone house trail who turned out to be prominent members of the Edmonton bird club. Yes, they had seen the buffies, but not the peregrine. I was glad they had not arrived a few minutes earlier, which might have disturbed the aerial show I had just witnessed.

As mentioned earlier in these pages, my specific method of watching raptor attacks on shorebirds is to sit down well away from the waterline. However, the chance of seeing a peregrine in action is low if there are people walking along the shore. Nevertheless, on one memorable occasion, the arrival of another birder led to a unique observation. That evening I was standing by my parked car at the northwest corner of the lake, enjoying a wide-open view of the north and west shores. Through the glasses, I picked up a distant falcon. As it came closer, it turned out to be an immature male peregrine. When a flock of about 30 buffies flushed from a ploughed field, he made a shallow pass at them but flew on. Two or three kilometres farther, the falcon landed on a fence post. While I kept the glasses focussed, a fellow birdwatcher, whom I knew quite well, stopped by and asked what I was looking at. "A peregrine," I said, without taking my eyes off the distant speck. Getting out of his car, he set up his telescope, and I suggested that we should keep an eye on the bird, for it might start hunting again soon. It took much longer than I thought, and I relieved the strain by glancing around, scanning the lakeshore. Fortunately, my co-observer kept his scope glued on the target. "Tell me when he flies," I asked.

The evening was drawing to a close, and, at last, the falcon took off. Moving his scope, the other guy immediately lost sight of the peregrine, but when I aimed the glasses, I was lucky enough to find him, a flickering dot approaching low over the darkening fields and gradually rising above the skyline. Directly in line with his flight path, a flock of buffies flushed and drew together defensively into a dense global sphere. The falcon slammed into the compact ball of birds just at the moment when the flock had risen high enough to catch the rays of the sun, which had already set below the horizon. At the moment of impact, the flock burst apart as if it had been hit by an exploding shell. Having seized its prey point-blank, the falcon planed down to the ground, landing near a barbed-wire fence. To mark the exact spot, I counted the number of fence posts, and the following morning I found the plucked remains of a buffy, the victim of one of the most spectacular peregrine hunts I have ever seen.

In recent years, global declines of shorebirds have sparked increased attention from the scientific community. In 1992, I was approached by Richard Lanctot, an American ornithology student who had embarked on a PhD. study of the buff-breasted sandpiper. Aware of its regular occurrence at Beaverhills Lake, he paid me a visit at home to talk about my records over the years. Currently, Richard is the shorebird coordinator with Alaska's Department of Fish & Game. One of his papers is titled: 'Light-level geolocation reveals migration patterns of the Buff-breasted Sandpiper. (Lanctot, et al. 2016. Wader Study 123:29-43).

In 2012 and 2013, Richard and his associates had captured 62 buffies on their wintering grounds in Argentina and Brazil. These birds had been fitted with tiny microchips and marked with coloured flags on one of their legs. The following winter, three of these flagged birds were recaptured (shot). Their geolocator data, transferred to the computer screen, revealed how far these buffies had flown. The distances matched or outdid what had become known of other migrant shorebirds, including golden plover, red knot, and white-rumped sandpipers. Two of the buffies, both females, had logged over 30,000 km, and the male 41,000 km. Travel time between departure from the pampas and arrival on the arctic coast of Alaska was 1.5 months. Their southbound return took 2.5 months. Although these data were limited to three individuals, the path they took across the American continent, passing over central Alberta, was recently confirmed when the researchers began using GPS satellite tags. Along the way, these fragile but incredibly capable world travellers have to cope with the perils of various climatic conditions, in addition to engaging in aerial contests with 'the bolt from the blue.

CHAPTER 18
Wetland Fluctuations

S ooner or later, as an immigrant in the second-largest country in the world, and coming from the most densely populated country in Europe, I had to go through a mostly unconscious process of putting down roots. To feel good about the world, I needed to get over the loss of home place and develop a new sense of belonging. After my 1959 arrival in Calgary, it took some time before I could feel fully comfortable in the spectacular landscapes that were so very different from the misty lowlands of Holland. As related in an earlier chapter, after two years in Canada, my dream of finding the perfect wolf wilderness ended in a serious canoe mishap that could have easily cost me my life. To reorient myself and write about my adventures, I went back home.

Wanting to start over, but not alone, it took three years before I met Irma, my cheerful life's companion, who was willing to return to Alberta with me. For family reasons, though, I had to bypass Calgary and relocate to Edmonton, 300 km farther north in the province. No more spectacular foothills and shining mountains on the horizon there. All around the city, the landscape was flat or gently rolling, but woodlots, creek ravines, and the magnificent North Saskatchewan River offered visual relief and an intriguing new challenge for a naturalist. Edmonton's elevation is about 650 metres (2,200 feet) above sea level. Twenty-five kilometres east of the city, the land rises a further hundred metres or so to the Beaver Hills, also called the Cooking Lake Highlands or the Cooking Lake Moraine. As hills go, the Beaver Hills do not amount to much. Covered with woods today, their original base consists of ridges of gravel and stones left behind some ten thousand years ago, when the mile-high Pleistocene glaciers halted their southward momentum and began to melt. Piles of debris that were buried by ice later became water-filled depressions. The typical Beaver Hills landscape of wooded hills and shallow lakes is called knob-and-kettle topography.

Cooking Lake is the first in the chain of lakes that drains the highlands. In 1980, its surface was measured at 36 square kilometres, its irregular shoreline at

72 km, and its depth at a maximum of four metres. During periods of high water, the lake was connected to a series of other water bodies that are, unfortunately, no longer deep enough for sticklebacks or minnows to survive winter.

The Beaver Hills were named for the aquatic rodent that became the gold standard for European fur companies, who arrived in western Canada during the seventeenth century. They paid Indigenous and Metis trappers to take their beaver pelts to Fort Edmonton and to supply the traders with bison meat. In those early days, everybody lived high on the hog, killing bison by the hundreds until the late 1800s, when the once-massive herds dwindled. Furbearers, too, including beavers, were exterminated. This, in short, is the sad history of the region's wildlife.

Even more radical and far-reaching were the changes brought by the next wave of Europeans, who were enticed to come by Canada's generous offer of free land. Their major tool for clearing the bush was fire. Year after year, the Beaver Hills were burned. Finally, in the twentieth century the conservation idea took a tentative hold, and today the region has again much to offer in the way of natural riches.

The collection basin for the Cooking Lake watershed is Beaverhills Lake, which is about 60 km east of Edmonton. From the nearest county road south of the lake, the view is magnificent, or at least it used to be magnificent from the mid-1960s to the 1980s, when its water level was still quite high. Surrounded by agricultural lands stretching as far as the eye could see, the vast sheet of shallows was about 10 km wide and 18 km long, with a surface area of 140 square km. Walking the open south shore and looking north across the lake's longest axis, there was one point on the horizon where water met sky, which to me seemed the closest thing to an ocean view in land-locked Alberta. The view reminded me of the Zuiderzee, and I soon felt quite at home there.

Sixty years ago, while living in Calgary, I had already heard about Beaverhills Lake as a popular destination for Edmonton's birdwatchers. One summer's day in 1959, my brother Marius, who at the time was living in Edmonton, was kind enough to drive me to the lake. But approaching from the east and walking to the marshy shore across a pasture littered with manure, I was not impressed.

In 1964, having moved to Edmonton myself, Irma and I joined the local bird club. During the migration seasons, the group made field trips to the lake. Traditionally, they drove the south shore down from Francis Point. In those days there were no fences to impede progress to the southeast bay, where the group socialized and enjoyed their lunch. On that first meeting, we were introduced to several of the club's founding members, including the club's patriarch, Bob Lister. In reply to my inquiry about peregrine falcons, his brief comment was: "We see them in May, stooping at those masses of waders." *Waders* is the English term for what North Americans call shorebirds.

In the early 1920s, Bob was hired as the field assistant by Professor William Rowan, head of the University of Alberta's new biology department. During the migration seasons, they made collecting trips to Beaverhills Lake. Their carefully prepared shorebird skins were shipped to museums in England and North America. Rowan added to the lake's growing fame among ornithologists. In popular publications, he called it a 'birder's paradise.'

In Rowan's time, the lake was brimming with water, fed by snowmelt and rain from its huge watershed. His favourite study area was a strip of sandy shore on the south side, which was named Francis Point after the local farmer. The point ran west to east, just south of the main lake, and merged with the inlet bay of Amisk Creek. That shallow bay is now known as Lister Lake. The country road from Francis Point to Lister Lake is called Rowan's Route. The formerly open Francis Point has fallen dry and is now overgrown with poplar woods.

One afternoon in August of 1964, a few days after our arrival in Edmonton, Irma and I paid our first ever visit to the lake. Randomly picking a spot closest to the city, we parked the car at the corner of a gravelled county road and an unpaved road allowance. The lake was just visible a kilometre or two farther east, set in a vast agricultural plain. Walking the rutted trail, we were approached by a farmer who had been working his land some distance away. After uncoupling his cultivator, he drove to us in his tractor. "What you guys looking for?" His dust-caked face showed that he had never heard of a phenomenon called birdwatcher, but after a brief chat, he let us continue on our way.

Crossing the last fence, we entered the lakeside pasture and walked along the shore, keeping our distance from a herd of cattle. Finding a pair of suitably sized boulders to sit on, we enjoyed the view of the huge expanse of water. Bird-wise, it was an interesting season, with migrating sandpipers gathering in the shallows. Scanning the shore, I was hoping to see distant flocks climb high into the sky the way they do if attacked by a peregrine. When some birds rose in panic mode, I was thrilled to spot a fast-flying raptor. Following the lakeshore, it approached closely, but instead of a peregrine, it proved to be a parasitic jaeger, an arctic migrant seldom reported here.

At our return to the parked car, we were shocked to find that two of the tires were flat. After installing our only spare, we limped to the nearest farmhouse. The man who answered the door turned out to be the same guy who had approached us earlier. His son admitted that he was the one who had let the air out of our tires. We were lucky, he added, for he had wanted to push our car into the ditch, but the tractor was out. After they had helped us pump up the flat, the farmer was kind enough to tell us that we could park our Volvo on the edge of his yard next time we wanted to go for a walk on his land.

Generally, strangers were not welcome in this rural backwater, where everybody knew everybody else and their vehicles. On exploratory trips to other points around the lake and parking the car somewhere, we were always relieved to come back and find it undamaged. More than once my tires were again flattened, or a mirror broken off. One day I actually watched through binoculars as a vandal stopped by my parked vehicle and bent down by the front wheels. As it turned out, he slashed one of the tires. After that, I made it a habit to explain to the landowner what I was going to do and parked my car on the same cow pasture every time. For economic reasons, I kept my white Volvo station wagon for twenty years. After the mileage counter reached the half million mark, I bought a second Volvo station wagon of the same colour.

Like all shallow water bodies in Alberta, Beaverhills Lake is frozen solid from early November to April, or even as late as May. In any season, birding trips to the lake often meant coping with muddy, dusty, or slippery roads. Just once, I was overconfident and got stuck in a mud hole. The farmer who had to uncouple his plough and come to the rescue cursed me to high heaven. Birdwatchers be damned! Another irate farmer rolled up his sleeves and wanted to "beat the shit" out of me, because he thought that I was a hunter, and he had a huge problem with some hunters who used his fence posts for target practice. Just in time, I told him that the stick I was carrying was not a gun but a telescope.

Over the years, a major environmental concern affecting access to the lake was its instability. Water levels rose and fell depending on annual precipitation and evaporation. Because of the lake's flat base, a drop of half a metre had a big impact on shoreline habitat, and heavy rain could inundate access routes. To me, the seasonal fluctuations and changing shorelines were of added interest. Repeat visits from year to year to the same sections of lake led to a growing appreciation of plant and habitat succession and its importance for the bird community.

Based on reports from long-time residents, periodic drought conditions during the 1930s and 1950s had left widening mudflats all around the shore, until one year when it rained all summer. "The lake rose four or five feet," a local resident said. "From April to October, it rained for three days, stopped for one day, and rained again for three days, all summer long."

In the spring of 1974, I saw a similar surge in water level, not after a rainy summer, but due to an exceptionally high runoff of winter snow. By late March, the drifts had accumulated to fence-top height, and when the melt was finally underway, the lake rose about one metre. County roads were cut off and inland fields flooded well away from the former shore.

High waters inundate and kill emergent vegetation, which explains why the west shore had been free of cattails and bulrushes in the mid-1960s, when I began my regular visits. And up to the 1980s, the sandy, wave-washed beaches along the south and east side of the lake were great for long walks. However, after the water level had remained quite stable for a decade or more, the formerly open littoral zone gradually became overgrown with a widening belt of bulrushes, cattails, and reed grass.

What will the lake look like in the future? A critical certainty is that this huge sheet of shallows is cyclic and at the mercy of the vagaries of climatic conditions. Lake levels are bound to go up and down from one extreme to the other, which is exactly the inherent value of this wetland ecosystem. The water level has to fluctuate so as to perpetuate its rich biodiversity. Periodic floods function to drown out emergent and encroaching vegetation. Decaying organic matter becomes a trophic bonanza for trillions of microbes and billions of midges and their larvae. In turn, these lifeforms constitute the food base for tens of thousands of birds that nest locally or stop over on the lake during their migrations to and from arctic regions.

CHAPTER 19
Conservation Controversies

Wetland conservation is deemed to be of increasing importance today for a variety of environmental reasons, but the overriding concern of the recent past had to do with the decline of North American waterfowl. Early European settlers took full advantage of unregulated and unrestricted duck hunting. Superimposed on their kill was the disappearance of duck breeding habitat. Everywhere, farmers were draining marshes and ponds to increase their productive acreage, until alarm bells went off in conservation circles. In the 1930s, to their everlasting credit, American waterfowlers got together and set up a new organization called Ducks Unlimited. Their stated mission was to reverse the decline of waterfowl by halting the destruction of duck nesting grounds. Canada followed suit in the 1940s. Reportedly, by that time well over half of former wetlands in the pothole prairies of central Alberta had already been lost.

In 1973, Ducks Unlimited Canada (DUC) set their sights on Beaverhills Lake. As I understood their intentions, they were going to compensate farmers for not ploughing up any more wetlands and marshes in the region. Like every other conservation-minded Albertan, I applauded that idea and thought that it would just be a matter of money. Word spread that DUC's pockets were bulging with donations from its membership and government grants. As it turned out, my expectations were naive. DUC had other plans. Instead of just saving existing wetland, they intended to actively create duck breeding habitat. To that end they had to tap into the same watershed as Beaverhills Lake. Apparently, no thought was given to the obvious point that any diversion of inflowing streams from the Beaver Hills and Elk Island National Park would come at a cost to Beaverhills Lake itself, and that their planned withdrawals might actually harm the lake.

The lake's most important feeder stream is Amisk Creek, which enters the southeast bay that used to be called A-Lake, later changed to Lister Lake. Much of this bay was quite shallow and the earliest part of the lake to fall dry during periods of drought. For that reason, Lister Lake was a great place for shorebirds during the migration seasons, and the traditional destination for birding excursions of the Edmonton Bird Club. For me, it was the turn-around point for long eastbound walks up the lake's south shore. In the summer of 1973, I got a nasty surprise when I arrived at Lister Lake, on seeing the destruction going on there.

A biologist driving a bulldozer had time for a chat and explained DUC's plans for the area. They were going to build a dam across the neck of Lister Lake and deepen part of the bay, using the bottom mud to construct islands, which should make excellent nesting habitat for waterbirds. Personally, he said, he had also wanted to clear out a lot of the surrounding brush by bulldozing the trees into windrows. "Wouldn't that be great for your cottontails and quail?" he mused. To his surprise and regret, Alberta Environment had not permitted him to go ahead, he said. Apparently, this man was from the southern United States, where rabbits and quail were popular game for hunters. The conversation came to an abrupt end when I said that there were neither cottontails nor quail around here.

Earlier that spring, DUC personnel had informed the Edmonton Bird Club of their plans to dam Lister Lake. When I objected that it would destroy the lake's most productive mudflat habitat for shorebirds, a federal biologist said that compensatory habitat would be created on the outside of the dam, which seemed to make sense. Quietly, I saw a positive side to a dam. It would bridge the narrow neck of the bay and connect the south and east shores of the lake. After the project was finished, the dam should allow me to cross the bay without getting my feet wet. Continuing my long walks for several kilometres up the east shore was an attractive prospect, because there were no farms or any other man-made structures for miles and miles up that tree-lined strip of rough pasture.

The dam was several hundred meters long and about three metres high. A depressed section of about ten metres wide was reinforced with a concrete curb to allow overflow water from Lister Lake to enter the main lake. A few willows were planted on the east end of the dam. All in all, it looked like a solid job, and DUC was ready to congratulate itself until Mother Nature blew a fuse, so to speak. The snow runoff in the spring of 1974 was exceptionally high, and the dam, which was constructed of sand, was completely washed out. The lake level rose by one metre, inundating county roads and agricultural fields well inland. To get to the remnants of the dam and Lister Lake, I had to wade long stretches of the trail through flooded poplar woods. All of that summer, with the water close to the top of my rubber boots, I scattered schools of sticklebacks and minnows. This was just one aspect of the lake's ecological response to high water.

Billions, if not trillions, of chironomid lake flies hatched from drowned vegetation, and their mating swarms hung over the east shore like a curtain of smoke. These harmless midges attracted masses of migrating ducks and shorebirds. Fish-eating species set up large breeding colonies, including pelicans, cormorants, night herons, gulls, and terns. There were hundreds, perhaps thousands of grebes in a variety of sizes and colours: eared grebes, horned grebes, red-necked grebes, western grebes, and pied-billed grebes. Even muskrats were catching fish, which seems rather unusual for a rodent that is supposed to be a vegetarian. Time and again, I watched rats come up from a dive with a brook stickleback or fathead minnow in their jaws and munch it down like a monkey eating a banana.

The dam was rebuilt the following year and reinforced with boulders. Unfortunately, DUC's projects had a negative and unforeseen side effect on the fish population. In the fall, when Lister Lake began to freeze, there were thousands upon thousands of sticklebacks and fathead minnows caught in the ice, unable to get over the weir. Apparently, they had sought deeper water, but their exodus to the main lake had been blocked by the dam. Unable to get over the weir, they froze into the ice. Reverse fish migrations on the northwest corner of the lake were similarly held back after DUC engineers placed high weirs in several inland marshes. Their overflow into Ross Creek, which drains Elk Island National Park, was blocked. During the spring runoff, thousands of fishes were vainly trying to ascend the steep cascade of incoming water. Surprisingly soon, or so it seemed to me, after the 1974 peak the water level dropped back to the former lakebed and remained rather stable until the mid-1980s. In those days, birdwatching and bird photography were gaining in popularity. While Beaverhills' fame spread nationally, the lake acquired a number of accolades. In 1982, the Canadian Nature Federation designated it as its very first National Nature Viewpoint. In 1987, the Alberta government declared it a Wetland for Tomorrow in the context of the North American Waterfowl Agreement. In the same year, the lake was added to the prestigious Ramsar Convention as a Wetland of International Importance. Its status was raised another notch in 1996, when it was added to the chain of Western Hemisphere Shorebird Reserves. One year later, BirdLife International ranked it as an Important Bird Area of Global Significance.

These designations came with the responsibility for wise stewardship on the part of the signatories. No matter how well-intended, though, they turned out to be ineffective. The tragedy was that government and private organizations were helpless when the lake continued to decline, due to drought, and the upstream water withdrawals were seen as negligible. After a short-lived comeback in the 1990s, the lake dropped alarmingly until the last remnant pool of water dried up completely in September of 2006.

During its dying days, I pleaded with representatives of various conservation groups, including DUC, the Canadian Wildlife Service, Alberta Environment, and Nature Canada. I wrote articles in the *Edmonton Journal*, the *Edmonton Nature News, Nature Alberta,* and *the Tofield Mercury,* and I gave PowerPoint presentations at meetings with the Provincial Water Branch, the Beaver Hills Initiative, and the Sherwood Park Fish and Game Association. Unfortunately, the audience ignored or shrugged off my explanation for the lake's decline, unwilling to place part of the blame on water diversions.

The facts were straightforward. There was no doubt that the cause of the severe drop in water level was related to a regional drought. But the upstream water impoundments were superimposed on low precipitation. The total amount withheld per year amounted to 1.5 million cubic metres of water annually, as calculated by a hydrologist who had been hired by the Water Branch of Alberta Environment in response to my concerns. According to my own simple calculations, this loss of inflow water would come down to just over one centimetre in the level of the main lake at its former size of 140 square kilometres. The difference may seem very minor. "Just a good day's rain," a government biologist said, and he was right. But since 1973, when DUC built its first dam, to be followed by 18 others in the upstream watershed, the deficit accumulated to 34 cm. Furthermore, as the lake shrank in size and became shallower, annual water losses increased proportionally due to the rising rate of evaporation.

My fact-based calculations were modest compared to an assessment by the DUC habitat manager for Alberta, who was quoted in the August 2007 issue of an American birdwatching magazine. He said that the annual impact of DUC's water control projects was very small, resulting in a drop of about one inch (2.5 cm) of water level in the lake. This was more than twice my own estimate and looked incriminating because at this rate, and over the 34 years since dam construction, the water losses could have accumulated to a total of 85 cm, close to the average depth of Beaverhills Lake, which was then roughly 90 cm. The same magazine article included an offhand opinion from an employee of the National Water Research Institute of Environment Canada. "In the drying-up of lakes, climatic changes that have lengthened summers and shortened winters appear to play a major role."

In the spring of 2007, one year after the lake's complete loss, a bigger than average snow run-off brought the lake back up to about half its former size. However, due to its shallowness, the evaporation rate stayed high and during the following summer the lake gradually shrank back, exposing a wide margin of mud.

What the lake would do from then on was not only of interest to birdwatchers and waterfowl hunters, but also to the farmers whose cattle grazed the shoreline pastures. The popular view of the conservation and birding communities was that the main reason of the lake's sad demise was low precipitation and excessive evaporation. Of course, there was no denying that the twenty-first century began with a serious drought. To better understand the dynamics, I looked at the official records for rain and snow recorded at Edmonton, available from Environment Canada. Their data for the total of annual precipitation per calendar year go back to 1883.

To restore the lake, some people suggested that all upstream irrigation permits should be cancelled. Another plan called for the construction of a pipeline to bring in water from the North Saskatchewan River. This idea was proposed in 1969 by forest ranger and fellow Dutchman Edo Nyland, who wrote a comprehensive article under the title 'This dying watershed.' His idea was enthusiastically considered in some quarters, but according to Edo, it ran aground on the opposition of landowners who did not want their shoreline properties flooded.

Concern about the future of the lake was shared by longtime birder Robert Lister, who remembered that a major reason for the lake's drop in level goes back to 1926, when a canal was dug between the town of Camrose and Miquelon Lake, the southernmost water body in the Cooking Lake chain. Robert also pointed out that one or more weirs had been built, many years ago, in Amisk Creek, the lake's main feeder stream from the south. These weirs are still in place and have in fact been augmented for the purpose of irrigating farmland. The Kallal meadows now are a popular hotspot for birdwatchers during the spring migration of shorebirds and ducks. Chatting with provincial livestock people, I learned that farmers have two reasons for wanting spring flooding on their hay meadows; that is, to stimulate the growth of grass, and to drown-out pocket gophers, so as to stop them from making holes and burrow mounds that impede and damage harvesting equipment.

In the dry '30s, livestock farmers along the north shore had joined hands to drill a windmill well to pump ground water up for thirsty cattle. During the deep drought of the 21st century, livestock owners were pumping water from Amisk Creek to fill their dugouts. A spokesman phoned me to say that he knew of about fifty farmers doing so. And at a stony point along the middle portion of the east shore, the Department of Agriculture had parked a tractor to pump water through a 12-inch pipeline to inland farms. Is it any wonder that the lake dried up in 2006?

A well-known parallel involving water diversions by farmers and horticulturists that led to the demise of an inland body of water concerns the Aral Sea in Russia. The decline was total, destroying the local fishery and all shipping. A less well-known case was the drying-up of Cheyenne Meadows in Kansas, a prairie wetland similar in size and biology to Beaverhills Lake. The cause of its near-total collapse was again water diversion by surrounding farming interests. In that case, though, Ducks Unlimited became the saviour and worked out a scheme that eventually led to the partial restoration of Cheyenne Meadows, which today is an important wetland again.

In my view, the surest way Beaverhills Lake could ever regain its former glory is through record high winter snow, comparable to the spring of 1974. But a monsoon summer as previously mentioned could have the same effect. That summer it would rain for three days, then dry up for one day, and rain again for three days. That pattern would be repeated all summer, resulting in a major rise in lake level.

Such drastic climatic fluctuations are unpredictable but again possible. Major weather-related changes have occurred in the region's known past. For instance, there were exceptionally high floods in 1899 and 1915, when the North Saskatchewan River rose 13 metres over normal. Historical photos show residential communities in Edmonton under a metre of water. In 1912, Beaverhills Lake was brimful to overflowing. Long-time Tofield Reeve John Warner relates how his parents, driving a horse-drawn wagon, had great difficulty finding the bridge that crossed Beaver Creek, the lake's outlet at the north end, which was inundated by the spring flood. The lake stayed high during the 1920s, when a steamboat plied its vast expanse of water, and local farmers caught wagonloads of pike and whitefish in the creeks connecting Beaverhills to Cooking Lake.

Could it happen again? Or are today's precipitation levels much below those of earlier years? To determine how much the Edmonton area receives in the form of *aqua pura*—this most precious and elemental natural resource—I researched past records, listed on Environment Canada's website and going back to 1883. Over time, the expanding metropolis has undoubtedly affected its own ambient temperature as well as urban precipitation, but the earliest records should be comparable to rural conditions in central Alberta. In 1961, a new meteorological station was constructed at the Edmonton International Airport

Of course, daily amounts of rain and snow can vary a great deal at localities only a few kilometres apart. There can also be a bit of uncertainty about past records due to the methods used to convert snow into water. As a rule of thumb, ten centimetres of the white stuff equals one centimetre (10 mm) in liquid form, but in actual fact the moisture content of snow varies, making visual estimates imprecise.

Nevertheless, the occasional small mistake is flattened out in the long series of data amassed by the professionals and volunteers working for Environment Canada. Prior to 2006, the year when Beaverhills Lake dried up completely, weather records for the Edmonton region go back 124 years. A comparison between the latest data and those obtained a century ago, in terms of annual precipitation and mean temperature, have not changed much if at all. My brother Marius, who is a mathematician, placed those 124 years in a bar graph. Over the years the vertical bars go up and down like a yoyo, but when he analyzed the statistical variation, he reported that the regression line was flat. Apparently, over the long term, there had been no significant change in precipitation levels. In fact, the data showed a very slight rise toward the end of the 1900s.

Canada's precipitation records for Edmonton from 1883 to 2006 add up to an annual mean of 454 mm. From year to year, the data differ significantly. The highest value amounts to 745 mm and the lowest to 207 mm. Both of these extremes were measured a century ago, respectively in 1900 and 1889. Apparently, the weather was just as capricious then as it is now.

The data also show that the precipitation levels around the turn of the last century were indeed on the low side. In fact, the second lowest annual total of only 267 mm fell in 2002. This is the year Albertans remember as the bad one, with withering crops south and east of Edmonton, rural pastures turning to dust, and sloughs drying up. Moreover, 2001 and 2003 also were below average.

Before concluding that those years were drier than ever, I placed the data in perspective by organizing all records into twelve blocks of ten years each. Statistically, the variation is now insignificant and all ten-year precipitation totals are close to the long-term average of 454 mm per annum. Furthermore, seven decades received more than 454 mm, and five a bit less. The highest amount of 517 mm dates from 1900–1909. But the previous decade, 1890–1899, had the lowest precipitation, with an annual mean of 427 mm.

The ten years before the lake's demise, 1997–2006, received a below-average of 436 mm per annum. However, this is more than in the 1890s and 1920s and only 3 mm less than during the 1960s. The conclusion is clear and unequivocal; the ten years prior to the lake's disappearance were comparatively dry but not exceptionally so.

Of course, there are three other factors that can worsen a drought, namely wind speed, temperature, and evaporation rates. Were the summers of the current century perhaps hotter than in the past? In view of the contemporary focus on global climate change, the topical question here is whether or not the climate of central Alberta has become warmer.

For an answer, I again looked at the 124 years of weather records on the Environment Canada website. They include the annual mean temperatures and the mean maximum temperatures. Following are the data for the most recent ten years prior to 2006, recorded at the Edmonton International Airport. The mean annual temperature was 2.7 degrees Celsius, and the mean maximum 9.1 degrees. This compares to 2.8 and 8.9 degrees as the average of the fifty earliest years that have complete records, beginning in 1890. The difference is minuscule, respectively just one-tenth and two-tenths of one degree. In other words, based on these official and unassailable data, the decade prior to 2006 was not warmer than a century ago. How to explain these surprising findings? First of all, these data just present the amount of rain and snow. They do not directly pertain to the lake's level, which is governed by two opposite factors. First, the inflow, and second, the outflow.

The above findings underscore my contention that there must have been additional reasons why Beaverhills Lake dried up completely in 2006, reasons related to the upstream water impoundments that were expanded in 1973 and superimposed on the years of drought. Furthermore, I had a sobering chat with an employee of a major resource company. He said that the oil and gas industry, quietly and unobtrusively, had been drilling into the aquifers underlying the entire chain of lakes draining the Beaver Hills. Their withdrawals came on top of those by other ground water users, including tree farms, golf courses, livestock farmers, and various private acreage owners.

Annual precipitation data recorded at the Edmonton International Airport continue to be fascinating. The decade following the lake's 2006 demise averaged 426 mm per year, well below the long-term mean of 454 mm. The first three years, 2007–2009, were actually very dry with a combined mean of 333 mm, but the next four years registered a value of 497 mm, which was beginning to look promising. The most recent data are also very good. Mean annual precipitation for 2016 was 497 mm, and in 2017 it was 486 mm, well above the long-term mean.

The winter of 2018–2019 is ongoing at the time of writing and, thus far, with a lot of snow. I am looking forward to the spring runoff in 2019. Already in May and June of 2018, the lake had come up to the same level as in 2007. I checked this out on the east shore of the lake, at a spot that used to be called Mundare Beach. There, a fence line runs straight east to west down into the lake. In May and June of 2018, the water had come up to where it was in 2007.

We should not get our hopes up too high, though. One glance from the county road south of the lake, overlooking the vast wetland basin to the north, suffices to confirm that the lake's current expanse is still nowhere near its ocean view of half a century ago. After a series of years with above-average precipitation, the lake may have partly regained its former size, but, obscured by emergent vegetation, it looks more like a big, shallow slough, rather than a sheet of water reaching to the horizon.

For birdwatchers, the lake's special attraction may have changed. Is there anyone now who walks miles and miles of shoreline on a regular basis? As noted by old-timer Bob Gehlert, in season you would never be out of earshot of the marbled godwit. Across the wide pastures, you were met and accompanied by one noisy breeding pair after another. The godwits are gone today.

Perhaps their absence is partly a question of habitat. Shoreline pastures used to be well grazed. Today, much of the range is overgrown with poplar and willow brush. Here and there, the thistles are shoulder-high.

During the years when the lake was on its way out, I maximized my time there. Bird-wise, the drought years had a golden afterglow. While the mudflats widened, I increased my visits to the east shore, where the last pool of shallow water attracted huge numbers of migratory shorebirds. On several days, my rough estimates exceeded 100,000 sandpipers of a variety of species. When the last pool had evaporated, the land became a desert, a wasteland of windblown dust and mineral salts, scoured of all life.

CHAPTER 20
To Graze or Not to Graze the Grass

A well-known maxim states that all meat is grass, and an ancient Chinese adage links grass with patience: 'In due time the grass will turn into milk.' Grass has had an important bearing on the kind of places where I have spent most of my time watching wildlife. Around Beaverhills Lake, the kind of habitat I liked best was a grassy shoreline. The shorter the grass, the better. The same goes for my old stamping grounds in Jasper National Park. The valley bottoms used to be free of shrubbery and the grass was short. I hurry to say that my attitude is not the same as the social imperative of homeowners to maintain a neatly short lawn around the house, be it a rural mansion or a city bungalow. My preference has to do with the chance of spotting wildlife.

In both habitats, around Beaverhills Lake and in Jasper Park's lower montane, short-grass meadows have become increasingly rare and seem to be shrinking in extent. The reasons for this have been and continue to be a fascinating subject for long-term observation, but I am beginning to understand the key factors involved.

At Beaverhills Lake, as related in the previous chapters, the first access point Irma and I explored in August of 1964 was from the west. An unmarked road allowance of about one kilometre led straight to the shore. Unless the track was too muddy or deeply rutted, we could drive all the way to the last fence. At that time, miles and miles of wide-open range around the lake were Crown land, leased to local livestock owners. During our first visit, when we climbed over the barbed wire and walked to the shore, a large herd of Herefords happened to be grazing some distance away. All along, the pasture was short-grazed and the water line was entirely free of bulrushes and sedges. As I understood later, the lake level had gone through a decades-long cycle of low water and had recently come back up to a high, with the result that all emergent vegetation had been flooded out. The muddy margin of the littoral zone was now perfect for shorebirds. It was the time of year when the return migration of sandpipers from their arctic breeding grounds had begun. Scanning the distant shore through binoculars, I was hoping to pick up a flock of waders towering up into the sky and careening back and forth in the agitated way they assume if a predator is sighted. As luck would have it, during that first visit we spotted a parasitic jaeger as well as a peregrine chasing the sandpipers. The unobstructed habitat along the lakeshore allowed me to follow both hunting sequences from start to finish, which is precisely the reason I prefer and look for open shorelines.

Exploring all around the vast lake, I became fond of a peninsula on the north end, which I called the windmill point. During the '30s, when the lake shrunk back alarmingly, local ranchers had drilled a well and set up a metal windmill. It was still there, riddled with bullet holes. If the wind picked up, the blades turned spasmodically with a sudden rattle and screech.

The wide-open windmill point was also favoured by cattle, perhaps because the wind kept mosquitoes at bay. The short grass was littered with lichen-encrusted stones left by the retreating glaciers of the Pleistocene. I had my favourite boulders to sit on or lean against, and I spent countless happy hours observing the shorebirds and waiting for peregrines to fall from the sky. On good days in mid-May, thousands of sandpipers, including hundreds of buff-breasted, came down to feast on lake flies that were covering the ground to get away from the wind.

One day I met the local rancher, who was checking up on his cows and calves. I asked him why the grass on this pasture was so nice and short. His answer was gruff and to the point: "By grazing the hell out of it."

Earlier that summer, I had been confused by the opinion of a university student, who was doing a vegetation study on the island across the water. There were no cattle there and he had a different view about grass. The vegetation on the point was not to his liking. By contrast, conditions on the island were pristine, he said.

Be that as it may, the crusty farmer had opened my eyes. I now understood a basic tenet of farming and wildland management. If you want to keep the grass free of weeds and bushes, herbivores can do the job, be they cows, bison, or elk. Of course, bovines can do much damage by overgrazing and trampling plant communities that birds need, either as a food resource or to nest in. Complaints about cattle destroying duck-breeding habitat came in from hunters and birders alike. In response, the Alberta government set to work erecting more fence lines to keep livestock away from the soft littoral mud. Whether their well-intended campaign had any positive side effects remains to be seen. Conservation measures that may work during a high-water cycle might prove to be worthless when the lake level drops, and vice versa.

During the 1970s and 1980s, the water levels remained rather stable, and emergent vegetation began to sprout and spread. Gradually and unobtrusively, the entire north, west, and south shores became rimmed with a wide belt of bulrush and cattails. This might be great for some birds, such as rails and blackbirds, but not necessarily for other species. Along much of the shore, lake levels dropped below the level preferred by ducks, which need water deep enough to submerge if the need arises. For instance, when a hawk comes too close for comfort. Except for teal, few ducks frequent wind-blown mudflats. But one or two centimetres of water is great for shorebirds.

As mentioned in the previous chapter, the snowmelt of 1974 was a whopper, which changed everything. The lake level rose by one metre and large sections of the surrounding pasture lands were inundated. In low spots the flood waters stayed long enough to kill the grass, and when the water subsided, the muddy ground was open to a snowstorm of poplar seeds blowing in from an upwind woodlot. In a surprisingly brief span of years, the swales grew dense groves of saplings. Other sections of the formerly open pasture near the windmill point became clogged with willows. The local rancher complained that he was losing too much pasture and tried to remedy the situation with a brush cutter pulled by his tractor. When the results were slower than expected, he resorted to spraying herbicides.

By the end of the twentieth century, environmental conditions went back to drought, and the lake level dropped alarmingly, with mudflats widening and reed beds drying up. Fresh mud does not remain bare for long, though. Seeds, dormant in the soil or blowing in from the surroundings, landed on fertile open ground. The vacant scar of new land sprouted a succession of colonizing plants. Marsh ragwort bloomed massively and went to seed early, to be replaced by foxtail barley. As the mud dried, the prominent forbs were many-flowered aster, oak-leaved goosefoot, and tall western dock. After two growing seasons, part of the former lakebed was transformed into a hip-high jungle of sedges, rushes, and reed grass. Less welcome were the clumps of shoulder-high Canada thistles. This noxious weed is incorrectly named and not native here. Like the common dandelion, it's an invasive pest accidentally introduced by European settlers.

In its dying days, Beaverhills Lake became an Eldorado for tens of thousands of shorebirds. A kilometre or so off the east shore lay a remnant pool of shallows that I approached from a point that used to be called the Mundare Beach. The water was ephemeral, expanding in spring and shrinking in fall. Each April I looked forward to seeing what the snowmelt would do and the changes it would bring. During the last decade of the lake's existence, from 2000 to 2009, I averaged 25 day-trips per year, and each time I walked four kilometres to a stony point overlooking the last remaining pool of water. I walked that stretch of shore a total of 178 times, returning by the same route. At my end point, a 40-centimetre-high boulder served as a water level marker. I sat there for hours to enjoy the view and the birds. On an additional 68 days I visited other parts of the lake to check for the presence of waders, geese, ducks, divers, and gulls. As a passionate raptor aficionado, I paid special attention to the falcons, hawks, and eagles hunting the waterbirds.

The road distance from my Edmonton home to the lake's east side was exactly 100 km one way. To conduct my ten-year survey, I drove a total of 52,800 km, while the price of gasoline went up and up. The money came out of my own pocket, but to my mind, those ten years of discovery were worth every penny spent.

Water is the wellspring of life. Conversely, its absence spells death. Over sixty years, I have witnessed the sad decline of Beaverhills Lake, a once huge and world-famous wetland, vibrant with the comings and goings of tens of thousands of birds. The lake went from a teeming avian treasury to a wasteland. As its level dropped, the first birds to go were the fish-eating and island-nesting species, including pelicans, cormorants, grebes, and terns. The collapse of reedbeds and marshes led to the departure of bitterns, night herons, and blackbirds. Nesting habitat also vanished for ducks, willets, and Wilson's phalaropes.

As mentioned in the previous chapters, annual precipitation has increased sufficiently to make a difference. In May of 2018 the water had risen to where it was in 2007. However, one environmental factor quite different from a decade ago is the fact that there were no cattle grazing on that section of shore. And the grass, sedges, and rushes were at their most luxuriant.

Following is a chronological list of my ten last years of bird surveys at the lake. The list was published in 2010 in *Nature Alberta* (40(1):22-28), and is reprinted here.

2000. May 1. On this year's first visit, I checked the Ducks Unlimited weir blocking the inlet of Amisk Creek. Winter snow had been below average and there was no inflow of melt water. Thousands of **Snow Geese** were bypassing the area and heading farther north. During the remainder of May, I walked various sections of the lake shore. Numbers and species of waders were not out of the ordinary, except on May 28, when I counted 18 **Red Knots**, more than I had seen in some years. Once quite common, these waders have declined everywhere. The fall season was again unremarkable, but on September 23 there were about one thousand **Black-bellied Plovers**, an unusually large number for this locality.

2001. After an unremarkable spring passage of geese and shorebirds, May 21 stood out in my diary with a sighting of 22 **Buff-breasted Sandpipers**. Some decades ago, this species could be counted by the hundreds. On August 31, I saw two **Upland Plovers**, a locally rare southern species that used to be a regular on the pastures along the north shore. In September, the number of **sandpipers** was again unexceptional. Tens of thousands of **Snow Geese** stayed into mid October.

2002. This year turned out to be the second driest ever since regional weather records began 120 years ago. With only 260 mm of annual precipitation, the lake retreated far from its former shores, leaving a wide belt of mudflats. By late May, whilst inland sloughs dried up, **shorebirds** concentrated at the lake and reached unprecedented numbers exceeding 50,000 and probably approaching double that estimate. This surpasses the total of 52,000 **shorebirds** recorded in May of 1995 when Ducks Unlimited crews, driving ATVs, conducted a census of the entire lake. Their report became the basis for a successful application to add the lake to the international list of Ramsar Wetlands. On May 27, 2002, about half of the thousands of **shorebirds** thronging the east shore were **Stilt Sandpipers** and **Sanderlings**, which are normally far less numerous than **Semipalmated, Least,** and **Pectoral Sandpipers. White-rumps** were present too but required a careful look to confirm their identification. Farther out on the water, dense flocks of **Red-necked Phalaropes** rose high into the sky at the approach of **Peregrines** and **Merlins**. On May 27 and again on May 29, I had very close views of a gang of seven **Parasitic Jaegers** hunting shorebirds. On September 8, out on the drying mudflats, there were 40 **Killdeer**. Also **American Avocets** were more numerous than normal (but still well below the huge numbers seen during the next two years).

2003. The month of May was again superlative for **shorebirds**. On the 18th, I carefully determined the mean number per linear metre of shore, and then extrapolated that figure to the circumference of the entire lake in its present much reduced size. Added to the huge flocks of **phalaropes** and **dowitchers** foraging far off-shore, my estimate worked out to at least 100,000 **shorebirds**. They stayed several days and attracted many migrating **Peregrines**. On May 22, I tallied 20 sightings. Often there were two or more falcons simultaneously stooping at the waders. Engaged in peregrine studies elsewhere, I did not visit the lake during the return migration of arctic shorebirds, which starts in early July. Other local birders saw masses of **sandpipers** in the East Bay. On August 2 and 10, Brian Genereux and Stan Gosche reported 1,500 **American Avocets**. My rough estimate of avocet numbers was one thousand on October 5, and there were still more than 700 on October 21. **Snow Geese**, using the lake as a daytime resting and staging site, stayed late into October and reached overwhelming numbers. Impossible to count or even estimate, their flocks might have contained in excess of 100,000 birds.

2004. As always, **Canada Geese** were back in early March, and already on April 2, thousands of **Snow Geese** were passing over the south side of the lake. On April 9, my impression of their number was again in the order of 100,000. The only way to obtain a realistic estimate of geese numbers of that magnitude is through aerial photography of roosting flocks. **White-fronted Geese** were present by the hundreds until the second week of May. **Ross Geese** stayed until May 16, when I saw about 500 lifting off from the east shore and flying inland to feed on stubble fields. Another interesting phenomenon this spring was the concentration of **Rough-legged Hawks** and **Northern Harriers**, evidently attracted by the local explosion of voles in the matted vegetation covering the former lake bottom. On the late afternoon of April 31, while scanning the area through binoculars, I counted 11 **Short-eared Owls** flying far and near. Later that spring and early summer, the owls performed their peculiar courting display. The migration of **shorebirds** began rather early. On May 10, I recorded tens of thousands of dowitchers all over the shallows and vast mudflats. It was quite a spectacle to see their flocks billowing up into the sky, alarmed by **Peregrines** or **Merlins**. On May 16 and 19, I again made an effort to calculate the total avian population of the lake by extrapolating the mean number of birds per linear metre to the entire extent of shoreline. And again, I reached a figure of around 100,000 **shorebirds**. The relative proportion of species was difficult to assess, but it seemed that the **Semipalmated Sandpiper** was the most numerous by far. Tens of thousands stayed until May 24, until they were suddenly gone the next day after a warm southerly wind had sprung up overnight.

2005. This was again an interesting year. Realizing the value of keeping score of the migrations at this vanishing Ramsar site, I increased my visits to a total of 41 days: 5 in April, 10 in May, 3 in June, 3 in July, 5 in August, 7 in September, 5 in October, and 1 in November. On April 2, there were hundreds of **Canada Geese** and thousands of **Snow Geese** along the south and west shores. Small flocks of sandpipers arrived in the first week of May and built up to a total of about 1,000 on May 8. By mid May, there were many thousands. On May 22, I count-estimated 50,000 **Semipalmated Sandpipers** along my 4 km of East Bay shore. On the 26th of May, the last of the northern migrants included some 100 **Black-bellied Plovers** and untold masses of **Red-necked Phalaropes**. In early evening of the same day, I counted 27 **ravens** flying by, perhaps on their way north or to a local roosting site.

Return migrations began early that year. On June 1, my walk along East Bay was enlivened by many small flocks of **Sanderlings**, easily totalling 2,000 birds. They were gone on June 16. On July 2, there were about 200 **Semipalmated Sandpipers** and three **Baird's** in addition to a hundred or so **Red-necked Phalaropes**. By July 9, scattered along the entire shore, there were many **Lesser Yellowlegs**, some 40 **Marbled Godwits**, and three **Hudsonians**. On July 26, I counted at least 500 **Hudsonian Godwits**. Others were too far away for certain identification. This record and the June sighting of 2,000 **Sanderlings** shows how the passage of some species could easily be missed during this time of year when few birdwatchers visit the lake. On August 2, there were still about 40 **Hudsonians**, but none on August 10. On the 19th, I spotted 3 **Black-necked Stilts**, always rare on the main lake. Another rarity for this time of year were 4 **Buff-breasted Sandpipers**. The most common wader was the **Long-billed Dowitcher**. Far and near, they numbered about a thousand. At the end of the month, many **Black Terns** had joined the clouds of **Franklin's** and **Bonaparte's Gulls** hawking lake flies over the water. By September 8, the peeps had greatly declined. During my usual walk along East Bay I saw 60 **Sanderling**, 200 **Baird's Sandpipers**, 20 **Semipalmated**, 10 **Pectoral**, and 2 **Least**. In the last week of September, there were still 700 **dowitchers**, 200 **Black-bellied Plovers**, 50 **Golden Plovers**, plus several hundred **White-fronted Geese** and a few dozen **Tundra Swans**. In earlier years, when the water was deeper, numerous migrating swans used the lake as a traditional staging site, dredging up the roots of the abundant Sago Pond Weeds, which have now practically gone. Predictably, tens of thousands of **Snow Geese** stayed well into October. On

November 1, the lake was frozen except for some holes kept open by the last of the geese. In late afternoon, as seen from the west shore, several thousand **Snow Geese** flew inland to feed on the stubble fields, which they shared with scattered flocks of **Snow Buntings**.

2006. As seen from the south end, the former lakebed looked like a vast wasteland stretching to the horizon. On April 11, half a dozen **Short-eared Owls** and **Northern Harriers** were winging to and fro over the matted vegetation. As is usual, shorebird migrations began during the first week of May and peaked during the third week. There were thousands of **Semipalmated** and **Baird's Sandpipers**, many hundreds of **Stilt Sandpipers**, and tens of thousands of **Red-necked Phalaropes**. On May 21, in awe of what I had seen that day, my notes included this phrase: **several hundred thousand shorebirds!** On May 24, I guesstimated the **phalaropes** alone at about 100,000. On one memorable day, when several other local birders were present, I saw six **Peregrines** in simultaneous pursuit of a **dowitcher**. It made a miraculous escape by plunging down into the middle of a group of swimming **ducks**, which kicked up water to ward off the persistent falcon. During June, as the East Bay shrank in size, **ducks** were concentrated into great rafts, consisting of 50% **shovelers**, 20% **teal**, 15% **mallards**, 10% **gadwall**, and 5% **pintails**. During two summer visits—on July 15 and 30—there was a scattering of the usual waders, including **yellowlegs, dowitchers, avocets, godwits,** and some **Stilt Sandpipers. Willets** had been scarce all year. A single **Whimbrel** made my day on July 30. By early August, the last remaining pool had become too shallow even for ducks. Unable to dive at a falcon's attack, they had flown away to deeper water. Here and there on the wet mud, a few **Baird's Sandpipers, Black-bellied Plovers,** and **Killdeer** were running about, snapping up flies. By the first of September, all water had dissipated, and the flats turned the colour of chalk. On windy days, dust devils swirled high into the sky and soda salts drifted low over the ground like winter snow.

2007. This year began with a surprisingly good snowmelt runoff from the lake's huge watershed in the Beaver Hills to the west. Both major inlet creeks—Amisk in the south and Ross in the north—kept running well into June. The Lister Lake weir was overflowing vigorously, releasing its surplus waters into the dry basin of what used to be the main lake. Flooded out of their shelters in the protective vegetation, **Meadow Voles** became vulnerable to predators. On April 14, scanning through binoculars from a point on the south shore, I counted at least 16 **Short-eared Owls** and 10 **Rough-legged Hawks,** in addition to many **ravens** and **harriers**, quartering the ground for prey. The life-giving waters rose to restore the lake to about one third of its former size. Walking my 4 km survey route, I was pleased to see that the marker stone was completely inundated. Meanwhile, dormant roots and seeds of bulrush and cattail began to sprout, and by mid August extensive stretches of the formerly open waterline became overgrown. Another noticeable change was the return of **sticklebacks, minnows,** and aquatic crustaceans, apparently flushed into the lake by the overflowing weirs inland. The fishes supplied a food base for **pelicans** and **grebes**, which had been absent for several years. Also attracted by the enriched habitat were a dozen or more B**lack-necked Stilts**, which established a nesting colony in the wet meadows south of Lister Lake. Another two pairs nested successfully on East Bay. By contrast, the 2007 spring passage of **shorebirds** was very poor. The explanation was simple. All dried-up sloughs in the region had been rejuvenated by snowmelt, and Beaverhills Lake was no longer the only available wetland for feeding. By the third week of May, flocks of **peep** and **plovers** along my route were no larger than a few dozen, or at most a couple of hundred, a far cry from the preceding years. Another change was the return of a few nesting **Wilson's Phalaropes** and **Marbled Godwits**, formerly common around the entire lake but absent during the drought years. Migrants on their way south began to make their appearance in mid-July, when I recorded several hundreds of **Lesser Yellowlegs** and **Hudsonian Godwits**. Two weeks later, on July 31, the **Hudsonians** were gone. In early August, numerous **sandpipers**, many of them **pectorals**, were foraging in wet grass. Along shore, I counted 13 **Willets** and 10 **Marbled Godwits**. The lakebed must have been rich in aquatic foods, such as the larvae—called bloodworms—of midges, for the buildup of **dowitchers** was spectacular. From September 9 to October 7, perhaps as many as ten thousand **dowitchers** were probing the shallows far and wide. As well, the lake was a place of plenty for fish-eating species. **Common** and **Forster's Terns** were hovering over the water, and some 200 **White Pelicans** collected on a gravel bar near the location of their former breeding colony. In addition, after a long absence, I saw a couple of **Western Grebes**. Three **Hooded Mergansers** represented the first specimens of this beautiful species I had ever seen on the main lake. As usual, **Franklin's, Bonaparte's,** and **Ring-billed Gulls** filled the sky, and on September 27, I spotted a **Sabine's Gull**, which was later photographed by Gerald Romanchuk.

Birds of prey were well represented. Throughout September, it was routine to see several **Peregrines** and **Merlins**, and in mid-September Richard Klauke reported a **Gyrfalcon**. I had seen this big falcon several days earlier but failed to identify it correctly because I seldom carry a telescope during my long walks. My previous earliest fall record for the **Gyrfalcon** was September 25. In most years, during summer and early fall, the odd **Prairie Falcon** shows up at the lake, where it hunts shorebirds. In this wetland habitat, Prairie Falcons are easily mistaken for Peregrines. Gerald Romanchuk obtained an excellent photo of a **Prairie Falcon** as it passed right overhead. On September 10, my diary entry reads: tens of thousands of **ducks** and **geese**. This wealth of waterfowl attracted many eagles. On September 30, Gerald and I counted 10 immature **Bald Eagles** roosting in the trees near the Mundare road. On that date, I also watched a **Golden Eagle** hunting ducks. In the meantime, the lake continued to drop and by October 7 my marker stone was entirely free from the water line. This means that the lake had lost about half a metre in level over the summer. On October 22, the last of the **shorebirds** included a dozen **Black-bellied Plovers**, their sad whistles haunting my walk over the ever-widening mudflats.

2008. This was another poor spring for runoff despite a fair amount of winter snow. Apparently, the melt water went straight into the parched and cracked ground. During the first two weeks of May, **geese** and **gulls** were common, and there were a couple of hundred **avocets** in East Bay. **Sandpipers** increased to several thousand on May 19 and 24, but the pelicans and other fish-loving birds had gone. During June and July, on the extensive flats of sand and grit, I was delighted to come across several **Piping Plovers**. On July 15, one pair was guarding four chicks. On that same date, there were many **Stilt Sandpipers** probing the shallows. During August the remaining pool of water continued to shrink, but the wet mud attracted good numbers of **peep** as well as a few **plovers** until August 29. On September 19, I saw no water at all. Like last year, **Black-bellied Plovers** were the last to hang around.

2009. Another very dry spring. In early May, a few migrants were attracted by the shallow pool of snowmelt and wet mud near the centre of the former east bay. On May 16, there was a fair range of species including 20 **Red-necked Phalaropes**, 2,000 **Semipalmated Sandpipers**, 50 **Semipalmated Plovers**, 10 **Stilt Sandpipers**, 2 **Baird's**, 3 **Sanderlings**, 3 **Black-bellied Plovers**, 20 **Golden Plovers**, 12 **dowitchers**, and one each of **Whimbrel**

and **Marbled Godwit**. This day became my last ever to walk the survey route. I decided that another visit, involving 200 km of driving, did not seem worthwhile. That spring the weather continued warm and windy without rain. At the lake, all birdlife would soon vanish into dry air.

CHAPTER 21
Bachelor Birds at Cooking Lake

After Beaverhills Lake had completely dried up, ending my seasonal bird surveys there, I switched over to Cooking Lake. Conveniently located just off Highway 14 east of Edmonton, it was only 40 km from my home, less than half of the 100 km drive to Beaverhills Lake's east shore. Starting in the spring of 2009, I began a bird survey at Cooking Lake, now in its twelfth year. The similarities and differences between the two locations proved to be interesting.

Around huge Beaverhills, the environs were wide open, and the vista from the height of land along the county roads was magnificent, whereas Cooking Lake breathes a more intimate atmosphere. Perhaps that is what gave rise to its cozy name *apiminawasu*, a Cree phrase that roughly translates into 'a place to cook our food'. A century ago, Cooking Lake was a favourite picnic site and recreation spot for Edmontonians. The water was clear and deep, there were sandy beaches, fish to catch, a sailboat club, and varied entertainment facilities at Coney Island. There was also a dance hall, and its biggest event was bachelor night. All of these amenities are gone now, and the lake has declined in size and popularity. The one facility remaining is the Cooking Lake airport, which is the oldest public airport currently operating in Canada, having opened in 1926. It functioned as the gateway to the North. Accessible to wheeled aircraft as well as ski-equipped and amphibious planes, it was the home base for adventurous bush pilots with famous names like Punch Dickens and Wop May, who provided a year-round link with remote northern communities.

The airport's services as a float plane base ended years ago, after the lake's drastic drop in water levels, but in June 2016, a 76-year-old pilot capsized his pontoon-equipped craft two kilometres from shore. The story goes that he had taken off for a flight to Smoky Lake when he noticed that he had left a side window open and decided to fly back to the base. As he was making the turn, one wing tip hit the water and the plane flipped upside down. The man wasn't seriously injured, but his rescue took a little over five hours. The fire department had come out earlier, but their airboat got stuck in the mud. In the end, a man in a canoe reached the downed plane. A few days later, while I was watching through binoculars from the south shore, a giant Cormorant helicopter arrived and hoisted the crippled craft from the water.

The biological characteristics of Cooking Lake were studied intermittently by the University of Alberta and Alberta Environment. In 1979, the lake's surface area was calculated at 36 square kilometres and the length of its wandering shoreline at 72 kilometres. Its deepest point was about three or four metres, but its average depth was much less. Between the mid-1960s and the 1980s, when I was focussed on Beaverhills, I seldom visited Cooking Lake because a wide margin of bulrushes and cattails obscured the view on the water and shorebird habitat was practically absent. However, after a series of years with below-average precipitation—which led to the drying up of Beaverhills Lake— Cooking Lake shrank back, too. The waterline withdrew several hundred metres away from the inland woods. The strip of former lakeshore that fell dry became a favourite racing track for ATVs and 4x4 trucks that tore up the soft ground, turning it into a rutted morass, pitiful to see. Their activity was probably illegal, but no one was there to protest.

Walking the former lakebed, trying to ignore the ATV-caused destruction, I noted that the succession of colonizing plants, healing the damaged land, was similar to what I had witnessed around Beaverhills. After a few years, the virgin soil sprouted a hip-high jungle of reed grass, sedges, rushes, and Canada thistles. Ironically, thanks again to the ATVs, I had a trail to follow through the dense vegetation and continued my walks up the east shore all the way to the narrows. Eventually, the authorities restricted vehicle access to the lakeshore by placing blocks of cement on the access points. By that time, I had shortened my bird survey to 3–4 km of the south shore, and I walked that stretch and the same way back once or twice a week from early April until freeze-up. The number and variety of shorebirds were greatest when the water was shallow, leaving wide mudflats. Conversely, mudflats were nonexistent when the lake had flooded into the littoral vegetation.

The American avocet, with its striking black and white plumage, was the dominant wader. Its food resource appeared to be abundant, because the avocets spent most of their day roosting. From time to time, they scooped up aquatic insects or crustaceans by swiping their long, upturned bill back and forth through the shallows. In deeper water, they foraged while swimming, and, surprisingly, they might even probe the bottom levels by up-ending, in the way ducks do, their tail pointing skyward.

I roughly estimated the summer avocet population at several hundred, and later in the season at between one and three thousand. With such large numbers present from spring to fall, one would expect that many avocets would lay eggs and produce young. Odd as it may seem, there did not seem to be much evidence of breeding.

Avocets are known to nest in loose colonies, preferably on islands that provide refuge from coyotes and foxes. Included in my survey route was an islet of about sixty metres long and roughly the same distance from shore, with an outlier of stones. In 2015, I noted that avocets were nesting on the islet and decided to spend more time there the following spring. To minimize disturbance of the birds, I did not access the islet and sat down on a low footstool or a convenient field stone on the main shore, armed with binoculars, rarely bothering with the telescope.

In 2016, the lake was free of ice by April 3, and one week later I spotted the first avocets of the season. During May, the population of the islet grew to about 50, and by early June there were several hundred, perhaps even as many as 500. A precise count was difficult to obtain because an unknown number of avocets could have been sitting out of view behind boulders or vegetation. Others were obscured by flocks of gulls that used the islet as a daytime roosting site.

On June 26, I spotted the first three avocet chicks, walking in shallow water near the islet. And on June 30, there were five chicks, chaperoned by adult birds. On July 2, three family groups included a total of seven chicks. In addition, I came across two loudly protesting pairs with chicks some distance farther along the main shore. Precocious from the moment they struggle free of the egg, avocet chicks are capable of picking up food items for themselves. They tend to wander at will, and their parents are known to lead them well away from the nesting colony.

Breeding populations of avocets can be expected to contain a few unmated floaters, but such a large number of non-nesters as at Cooking Lake has, to my knowledge, not been reported before. German ornithologists, who colour-banded European avocets in an eleven-year study, concluded that their birds did not breed until they were two to five years of age. Dutch researchers recently found an oystercatcher that was banded 46 years ago. If large shorebirds enjoy such a long lifespan, there might not be an evolutionary imperative for avocets to produce offspring year after year. Most of Cooking Lake's avocets were apparently content to sit out their summer in idleness on the lake's productive shallows.

Whether or not there is a disparate sex ratio among avocets remains unknown but seems unlikely in view of what has become known about ducks. So-called rape flights of mallards and shovelers—gangs of males in hot pursuit of a single female—are a common sight in spring and create the impression that there are many more males than females in the population. However, the sex ratio of newly hatched ducklings is 50-50. A possible shortage of females later in the season is explained by circumstances. The hen does all of the brooding and may be more vulnerable to predation and accidents. In my observations of peregrines and gyrfalcons in pursuit of flocks of flying ducks, I have often noted that the falcons selected a female. The reason seems simple. The duck is smaller and more easily carried and subdued than a drake.

As to peregrine predation on avocets, the amazing truth is that these eye-catching, spindly-shanked waders seem untouchable and invulnerable. In all of my many years of watching falcons in avocet country, I have yet to see a single capture. Furthermore, neither at Beaverhills nor at Cooking Lake have I ever found a prey remains, a feather stain or a plucked carcass of an avocet, although flocks rise early at the approach of a falcon. In fact, I make it a habit of keeping my eyes on a roosting or feeding flock and wait for their alarm reactions. A peregrine may make a swift pass, but seldom a serious effort at catching one. The startling black-and-white plumage of avocets creates a disruptive pattern that may dazzle the predator, and the flushing of a dense flock is an explosive event that may confuse and discourage any raptor. A single avocet could present a different kind of target. One day, when I was watching at a peregrine nest on the Red Deer River, I saw two avocets fly by, the only ones I have ever seen there. Ten minutes later, the female peregrine came back to the nest cliff, an avocet dangling from her claws.

At Cooking Lake, the only serious looking attack on an avocet involved a large, immature gyrfalcon. She had driven an avocet down into a few centimetres of water, but each time the falcon swooped, the avocet jumped up and spread its wings. After a dozen or more futile swoops, the falcon gave up.

Another common open-country bird that graces the inland lakes of Alberta is the Franklin's gull. With its black head, red bill and red legs, it is the prettiest of the gulls. In breeding plumage, the white chest of the adult takes on a pink hue. They nest in noisy colonies in the reedbeds of large wetlands such as at Whitford Lake, about 50 km north of Beaverhills Lake. But there is no current record of their nesting at Cooking Lake. This is all the more puzzling because these gulls are super common from spring to late summer, and there is no lack of food. What could be the reason for the large number of bachelor birds among the Cooking Lake avocets and the gulls?

Like avocets, Franklin's gulls feed heavily on chironomid midges, also called lake flies. As mentioned in a previous chapter, these flies superficially resemble mosquitoes, but they do not sting. Their eggs are laid in water and develop into worm-like larvae that eventually metamorphose into the flying insect. Hatching in incredible numbers, lake flies form dense mating swarms that hang like a smoke screen over the shoreline vegetation when the wind is down. Scientists report that the vast majority of these swarming insects are males. So, what are their chances for a successful mating? The number of bachelors in the bug population may be similarly high as in the avocets or perhaps even higher by comparison.

While the gulls are experts at catching lake flies in the air and picking them up from the water's surface, avocets zero in on the larvae. Developing in four stages, some larvae attach themselves to the lake bottom, others burrow into the mud or are suspended in the water column. The largest larvae are a few centimetres long and red in colour, which is why they are called bloodworms.

Researchers from the University of Alberta and the provincial environment department, who studied Cooking Lake's zooplankton, found the water slightly saline and hyper eutrophic, which means rich in nutrients that promote excessive growth of algae and other vegetation, but less suitable for animal life in need of oxygen. As detailed in the comprehensive *Atlas of Alberta Lakes*, published by UofA in 1990, the **wet weight** of the benthic invertebrates was expressed in milligrams of biomass per litre of water and per square metre of bottom. Chironomid midge larvae represented 92% of the phytoplankton biomass, but they were not counted individually, which prevents comparisons with other lakes where the results were given as the number of midge larvae per square metre of lake bottom and as a percentage of the biomass in **dry weight**.

A very thorough study of a shallow lake in the Netherlands came up with 2,000–3,000 bloodworms per square metre. By comparison, the number of chironomid larvae in Cheyenne Meadows, a large prairie wetland in Kansas, was calculated at fifty bloodworms per square inch, which works out to roughly six per cm2. The number of bloodworms per square metre of lake bottom at Cheyenne Meadows varied from 6,000 to 65,082.

The abundance of bloodworms apparently varies temporally as well as spatially, depending on environmental factors. Besides shorebirds and gulls, ducks also feed voraciously on midge larvae, and so do fishes. At Cooking Lake, dabbling ducks are common all summer long, but fishes, even minnows and sticklebacks, were frozen out after the lake's water levels dropped to the current lows.

In 2016, a prominent additional food resource for the gulls were *ephydriday* flies. This was a new discovery for me. About half the size of a house fly, their common name is shore fly (brine fly in Britain). Locally super abundant along the water line, these flies feed on biofilm, the thin residue of microscopic algae and bacteria that stays behind and coats the mudflats when the water retreats.

I saw the gulls use a novel and very effective method of catching the flies. Walking along the waterline in group formation, like an advancing army, their beaks partly open, the gulls snapped up flies that flushed just ahead. This pedestrian foraging method of Franklin's gulls has, to my knowledge, not been described before in the scientific literature.

Another odd, and very numerous, insect of wet places is the minuscule, 2 mm springtail (*commembola*). Massed tightly together in puddles of water left behind by the retreating lake, a collection of springtails looks like an oil spill polluting the beach. If you examined it closely, you might be surprised to see that those black smears consist of hundreds, if not thousands, of tiny insects. When you try to touch them, these funny critters flex their folding tail and jump away like fleas.

A serious peril for waterbirds of all kinds is avian botulism. At Beaverhills, I have seen the horrible toll of this disease when shallow waters warm and the poison spreads, crippling and killing hundreds, if not thousands, of ducks. In some summers their carcasses littered miles of shore.

In the late summer of 2004 and again in 2015, while walking my birding route along the south and east shores of Cooking Lake, I came across a dozen or so flightless shorebirds that I suspected of being botulism victims, weakly flapping their wings. There were several dowitchers and lesser yellowlegs, as well as semipalmated and Baird's sandpipers. Affected by the neurotoxin of botulism, birds lose control of their muscles and are unable to stand or hold up their heads.

Scavengers and raptors that feed on sick waterbirds are struck by secondary poisoning. In 2014, I found one dying and two dead harriers, and in the fall of 2015, I picked up the dried remains of a peregrine that had died the year before. The previous summer I had actually watched this falcon retrieve a large prey from the grass, an item that I suspected was a dead or dying duck. The peregrine skeleton had numbered bands on both legs and was identified by Gordon Court as having fledged from a nest box on an Edmonton area industrial plant. In August 2015, Gord also had an unbanded young falcon sent to him that had been found on the shore of Cooking Lake by a birder, who took the cripple to the Wildlife Society. There, it was given water and clean food, and it soon perked up. After its recovery, the peregrine ended up with an Alberta falconer, to be flown for the season and released next spring.

Evidently, some birds that are affected by avian botulism can recover. Long ago, I found a flightless short-eared owl at Beaverhills Lake and took it home. After feeding it several laboratory mice, I tethered the bird to an axe and left it overnight on some newspapers spread on the kitchen floor. Next morning, the owl had white-washed the place and appeared to be fit and feisty enough for release back at the lake.

Birds of prey, especially the young and inexperienced, tend to catch what comes easiest. At Cooking Lake I saw merlins scare up thousands of sandpipers that flushed well ahead. But the odd one did not rise in time, or at all. The merlin turned back to collect these easy pickings, which might well have been affected by botulism. In some cases the 'lucky' merlin was immediately pursued and robbed by a peregrine. Of course, the peregrine is exposed to the same peril, in accordance with nature's rule, which states that a predator's function is to weed out the weakest members of prey species. Checking the issue of botulism on Google, I read of two crippled peregrines, suspected of having been affected by the disease, that were picked up by birdwatchers in Idaho. Both falcons eventually recovered through the efforts of the local wildlife rehabilitation society and were successfully released in October of 2013.

After the demise of Beaverhills Lake a decade or so ago, Cooking Lake has become a popular wetland destination for Edmonton birders. During the spring of 2014 the water was right up to the shoreline vegetation, but the level began dropping during summer, resulting in a belt of mudflats along a shallow section of the southeast shore. By east winds, the water retreated half a kilometre or more. During late July and August of 2014, the mud attracted a few hundred sandpipers and a thousand or more avocets. In the dry summer of 2015, the mudflats grew even wider and extended for several kilometres along the east shore. In both years, from July to October, I spent a lot of hours watching foraging flocks of shorebirds, hoping to see them react to attacking falcons.

While the best place to watch migrating peregrines in action used to be Beaverhills Lake, I always kept an eye out for them at Cooking Lake, especially in May and September. Some sequences turned out to be quite noteworthy.

On September 29, 2009, several migrating falcons passed by close enough to identify them as either grey-blue adults or brownish young of the year. One smallish male gave a fascinating demonstration of the problems immature peregrines encounter in learning their trade. One late afternoon, I found him resting on a shoreline stone, and I watched him through binoculars for more than an hour until he finally took wing. He flew over the lake to meet flocks of ducks that promptly dropped out of the way and splashed into the water. After several failed passes, he returned to the shore at great speed to overtake a pair of shovelers. When one of them hit the water, the falcon quickly circled back and began a series of swoops at the swimming duck, which each time kicked up a spray of water. Attracted by the action, three large gulls alighted nearby and one of them began to viciously peck and stab the duck until it stopped moving. Ignoring the gull, the falcon tried again and again to retrieve the floating prey, hovering over it with dangling claws. He twice landed on a nearby stone for a brief rest, then resumed his attempts. The drama ended with the arrival of a bald eagle, who picked up the dead duck in one easy pass. The frustrated peregrine retreated to another stone a few hundred metres away.

Sitting on a shoreline stone myself, I kept the falcon in the glasses. After some time, he again flew out over the lake and swooped at ducks rising from the shallows, but all of them dropped right back into deeper water. The falcon then climbed with furious wingbeats to overtake a Ring-billed Gull and seize it from below. Holding on, he fluttered steeply down. Unable to carry his prey to dry land, he released the gull again just above the water. Regaining altitude, the falcon then left and headed for the opposite shore of the lake. Far away, he descended like a meteor and vanished from view. Such long-distance attacks are more typical of adult peregrines than young of the year.

On May 26, my last spring visit of 2010, with a cool east wind blowing, there were several thousand red-necked phalaropes scattered over the wide expanse of the lake's northeast bay. When a flock flushed from the surface, I aimed the binoculars just in time to see them overtaken by an adult peregrine, which seized its prey at once and carried it back to shore. Later that afternoon, another falcon, a dark immature, launched half a dozen attacks far out over the water, stooping at the rising phalaropes, each time missing the target. Giving up, the falcon flew away and soared high, drifting downwind over the lake and dwindling to a tiny speck in the glasses. Eventually, after many minutes, he came back upwind, his wings set and passing high overhead like a black trident. I was hoping that he would make his next attack in good view, but he flew on, gradually descending and boosting his speed with a burst of wingbeats until he dropped out of sight far away.

During the fall of 2011, falcons were less common than the previous years, but I happened to see something I had never seen before. An adult peregrine, which I had watched for an hour or so, took off from a shoreline stone and climbed far and high over the lake to intercept a lone bird. Pursuing it on a downward course back to the land, the falcon had time for three or four swoops, narrowly missing its target. To my surprise, that dodgy bird turned out to be a magpie. Upon reaching the shore, it managed to drop into the safety of bushes. This was indeed the first time ever I had seen a peregrine hunt this wily corvid. Obviously, part of the fun of watching wildlife is that after half a century in the field, you may still see something new.

A major surprise of another dimension developed in 2020, my most recent season at the lake. The snow melt runoff amounted to some 15 centimetres, further boosting last year's rising level. Soon after the ice went out, the first avocets arrived, but they did not stay. And in great contrast to previous years, throughout April and May, I saw no more than two or three avocets at the lake. Many spring visits of 2020 came and went without sighting a single one. Other shorebirds were similarly scarce. The reason seemed clear. There were no mudflats this spring, no habitat suitable for shorebirds at all.

Equally surprising, at least until the end of May 2020, was the complete absence of Franklin's Gulls, which, like avocets, used to number in the hundreds or thousands during the preceding decade. In 2020, the only gulls to nest on the lake were the large California gulls. Their traditional island had been reduced in size by the rising waters, which may have been the reason several dozen breeding pairs moved to the tiny islet formerly used by nesting avocets. One regular representative of the lake's avian community that had stayed at the same level was a pair of Canada geese, the brooding bird half-hidden in the islet weeds.

Walking the muddy shore and trails around Cooking Lake, I always kept an eye out for tracks of mammals. Coyotes, deer, and moose were quite common in the area, but there were a few surprises. One day I identified the spidery signature of a raccoon, very rare in this part of the province. Also unusual were the pads of a large black bear. It occurred to me that scavenging bears could perform a beneficial task by cleaning up the cadavers of ducks during an outbreak of botulism, and in that way prevent the spread of the spores into the soil.

Another singular recording was of a female elk, which came running out of the trees at full tilt, as if she had been pursued by a pack of wolves. After a few steps, she sank into the black mud and fell over on her side. Gulping a quick drink, she extricated herself again, muddy all over, and ran back into the woods, the only 'black' elk I have ever seen.

Although red foxes may locally be common, even numerous, their spoor was hard to find around the lake. In loose sand the difference between the print of a coyote or a fox can be obscure. Just once, in a thin layer of fresh snow, I was happy to ascertain with certainty that the sign I had found was that of my old friend Reynard. In past winters I had spent a lot of time following foxes, trying to unravel their interactions with their arch rival, the coyote. In other books I have included details on how to identify the fox's footprint with certainty by the narrow ridge of callous across the heel pad, which is lacking in other canids, dogs as well as coyotes. What excited me greatly was coming across the tracks of a large wolf on the lakeshore. Habitual wanderers, wolves may turn up anywhere in west central Alberta, particularly on the east side of Cooking Lake, which is less than 20 kilometres from the Blackfoot grazing reserve. There, a pack of wolves had taken up residence until they were destroyed by government agents setting out poison baits.

More recently, I again tracked a wolf-like canid near the lake's narrows, where it had run into the water on a spot where I had earlier seen a beaver, a singular sighting of this rodent at Cooking Lake. Differentiating between a large dog and a wolf is tricky and often not possible. Generally, a wolf's footprint is oval-shaped, whereas dog pads are rounder. A secondary consideration in deciding what you are looking at is the presence or absence of human sign in the immediate area and the same timeframe.

Ironically, what eventually stopped me for a while from visiting the lake's south shore was an unpleasant experience with the wolf's relative and mankind's so-called best friend. In the fall of 2018, I suffered a direct attack by three medium-sized dogs. They came at me barking and at full tilt. One of them sprang up at me, threw me off-balance and bit my thigh. I had to visit a medical clinic and received a tetanus shot. Later, I met the woman who owned these aggressive mongrels. She apologized profusely and said that she had not known that Cooking Lake was a popular birding spot. Henceforth, she intended to go elsewhere, which took a big load off my mind.

As to meeting special people, during that pivotal year I ran into a fellow birdwatcher whom I knew from his student days. Now an executive with an oil company, he was aware of and appreciative of my concerns about the lakes in central Alberta. When I told him that the current level of Cooking Lake was still about two metres below what it once was a few decades ago, he casually said, "You should know how much our industry has affected the ground water in these parts."

What the future holds for Cooking Lake and other water bodies in central Alberta remains to be seen.

In the past, the mountain sides near old Jasper House were bald due to frequent fires set by aboriginal people to keep their hunting grounds open.   Jasper House 1872 – Public Archives of Canada

Today, these same slopes are forested and the valley bottom is overgrown with mixed woods. The bushes in the lower photo are wolf willow (aka silver berry) which are choking formerly open grassland.

CHAPTER 22
The Not-So-Natural History of Jasper

The prehistoric human population of Canada, having lived here for thousands of years, did not leave a written history, which makes the travelogues of early European explorers all the more interesting. The first white man to reach western Alberta and saw what he called 'the shining mountains' was Anthony Henday. The year was 1754, a half century before the celebrated Lewis and Clark expedition arrived at the foot of the Rocky Mountains on the American side of the border. Travelling overland, Canada's Alexander Mackenzie reached the Pacific coast in 1793, also ahead of Lewis and Clark, who reached their goal in 1806.

From then on, other geographic discoveries followed each other at a brisk rate, stimulated by competition, not just internationally, but between the English and the French. Their bone of contention had to do with setting up exclusive trade links with the inhabitants of the inland wilderness, the native peoples, today called the First Nations. Whereas the Spaniards exploring South America were driven by their greed for gold, the most valuable treasures of Canada were the skins of fur-bearing animals. French voyageurs employed by the North West Company started from Montreal. English fur scouts were sent out by the Hudson's Bay Company from their maritime base on the bay of that name. All explorers relied on native guides, and their mode of travel was by birchbark canoe.

On their way to the Pacific coast, European explorers crossed Alberta's mountain barrier via the Howse pass, west of today's Rocky Mountain House. In 1810, David Thompson had to forego the Howse Pass because of the presence of a hostile native band. Instead, he made a detour of several hundred kilometres to the Athabasca Pass, in today's Jasper National Park. In the dead of winter he became the first white man to travel through Jasper's lower main valley. The Athabasca pass subsequently became the common route to the west coast for the fur brigades. Today, the busy traffic corridor from Jasper to the west uses the Yellowhead Pass, but the modern highway from Rocky Mountain House to the mountains is named after David Thompson.

When I began my long-term wildlife observations in the Devona district of Jasper Park, I wondered what the earliest European travellers had seen in the way of animals in this strategic valley, and how their sightings would compare to what I was seeing today. Driven by a deeply felt curiosity I searched the literature, starting with the diaries of David Thompson, who was not only a great geographer but also an astute naturalist. To obtain information on the practices of the fur trading emporiums, I relied heavily on the fact-filled research of Alberta's own historian, James MacGregor. The following information on the fur trade is gleaned from his 1974 book *Overland by the Yellowhead*.

The first white explorers to reach the Jasper region were employees of the North West Company. Starting out from Québec in the early 1800s, they found their way across the Precambrian wilderness of Ontario to Manitoba via an interlocking system of lakes and portages. Crossing huge Lake Winnipeg, they ascended the North Saskatchewan River all the way to Fort Edmonton. There, they faced a critically important choice of how to proceed. There are two main rivers rising in Alberta, both fed by Rocky Mountain glaciers, the Saskatchewan and the Athabasca River. The south arm of the Saskatchewan flows by Rocky Mountain House, but after that route to the Pacific coast had been abandoned, fur company voyageurs used the Athabasca River. To switch over from the Saskatchewan route to the Athabasca, the travellers had to leave their canoes at Fort Edmonton and journey overland to another fur trading post called Fort Assiniboine. To get there, the company made horses available for the transport of goods. The 110 km trip took three or four days, but the going could be difficult during the wet season, because the trail crossed swampy depressions in which the heavily loaded pack horses might get mired in mud up to their saddle. At Fort Assiniboine, which was situated on the south bank of the Athabasca River, the trade goods and provisions were again transferred to wooden canoes for the next stage of this incredibly long and arduous journey across the continent. In admiration of the hardy fur traders, historian James MacGregor reminds us that their enterprise was more lucrative for its European investors than the much-written-about spice commerce with the Orient. Nevertheless, the fur business may seem frivolous today, for its most valuable product was the skins of beaver, used in the manufacture of gentlemen's top hats.

Continuing their journey west of Fort Assiniboine, the fur brigades worked their way upriver until they got within sight of the mountain barrier.

Near today's Hinton, the men camped on the banks of Brule Lake at a windowless shelter called the hunter's shack. Here, the company kept horses that had been brought in from Fort Edmonton. In 1813, a new post was built a dozen kilometres upriver, near the confluence of the Athabasca with the Snake Indian River. Around this time the historians first mention a company interpreter named Jasper Hawse, who was the year-round manager of the newly built post, which later became known as Jasper's House. His first name was subsequently conveyed to the National Park.

In the meantime, the rivalry and hostilities between the two fur emporiums increased. Outright war was prevented in 1921 when clearer heads prevailed, and the two competitors amalgamated. Henceforth, all trade between the Europeans and fur trapping natives was supervised by the Hudson's Bay Company. Quite apart from them, an unknown number of independent Metis trappers and traders, the so-called freemen, arrived from eastern Canada. In addition, venturesome Indigenous groups canoed up the Saskatchewan River. Displaced from the east, they had obtained metal knives, axes, and rifles from the Europeans. In 1798, David Thompson mentioned the arrival at Fort Edmonton of 250 Iroquois, Algonquins, Ojibwas, and Nipissing. Some headed north to trapping grounds in the Slave River region. Others turned south and settled along the eastern slopes of the mountains. Understandably, their incursion into territories already occupied by resident native people was bound to lead to trouble. Historic reports are replete with bloody clashes between Indigenous groups. The Battle River in central Alberta was named on account of the enmity between the Blackfoot Nation and the woodland Cree.

When I began my wildlife observations at Devona in the lower Athabasca Valley, my winter tent was a twenty-minute walk from the original site of old Jasper House. It was burned to ashes long ago, but the stones of the fireplace are still in evidence, and the site has been dug up repeatedly by archaeologists.

For information on historic wildlife populations, I wrote to the Winnipeg headquarters of the Hudson's Bay Company, and after explaining the reason for my request, I asked for the earliest records in their files on Jasper House. In response, I received the handwritten notes from one of the early post masters, transferred to microfilm, which I then viewed at the research facilities of the Alberta Provincial Museum.

In 1829-1830, Jasper House was manned by a Scot named Michael Klyne. According to an early visitor, his place was "a miserable concern of rough logs," and Klyne himself was described as "a jolly old fellow with a large family." As was common for company men, he lived with a native woman, and when his time in the service was done, he returned to the old country, leaving his children and their mother behind. In later years, Jasper House may have been rebuilt, for another visitor commented that it looked like a Swiss chalet and that it contained three scrupulously clean apartments, one for the factor and his family, the other two for staff and visitors.

Klyne's very readable diaries paint a grim picture of wildlife conditions in the valley. During winter, his full-time Metis hunter made extensive forays into the surrounding country but often returned with nothing, sometimes without having seen a single track. Additional proof that game was scarce can be inferred from Klyne's frequent references to hungry Indians, who came to the post to barter beaver skins. By early March, 1830, three families of Shuswaps arrived at the post. "They are starving all the time," he writes.

On March 25, a Shuswap arrived "almost dead of starving. I gave him a little meat for himself and a little to take to his family. I cannot give him much. I have little myself. In the evening my hunter arrived. Saw nothing."

On April 10, a Shuswap woman showed up at Klyne's post with three children. "A few days past, two other children and her husband had died of hunger." Two weeks later, during the night, the Shuswap woman departed, leaving two of her children at Jasper House. Klyne described the tragedy in very few words. "I sent after her to come for her children but no-one could find her track."

The above leaves no doubt as to the original inhabitants of the lower Athabasca Valley, although some historians called the local tribe by a different name, such as Snaring, Snake, or Carrier Indians. Paul Kane, who visited old Jasper House in 1845, spelled the Shuswap name as Shoo-Schawp. In his 1925 book *Wanderings of an artist among the Indians of North America*, he wrote that a band of Shuswaps was entrapped by a hostile tribe who invited them "to sit down and smoke the pipe of peace, but before they had time to smoke, their treacherous hosts seized their arms and murdered them all."

The brutal treatment of the resident Shuswap by invading tribes was mentioned by several other early European visitors to Jasper House. Historian James MacGregor reviewed the records and wrote that the Shuswap men were tricked into coming unarmed to a much larger camp of their long-term Assiniboine enemies under the pretext of making peace. When they were seated, the Shuswap were shot. The Assiniboine then rushed to the Shuswap camp and killed everyone there, although some managed to escape, and three girls were taken prisoner. Apparently, it was their practice to capture young women and adopt them as slaves. Worried about what the Hudson's Bay Company might think of their cowardly act, the Assiniboines fled downriver to the company fort of that name. There, the three captives eventually regained their freedom, although historical records differ somewhat as to whether they were bought out by a European visitor or that he just helped them escape. Given a knife and a fire-making kit, the girls fled during the night. Two of them were never heard from again, but one managed to survive in the wilds until she was recaptured by an Indigenous hunter, who took her to Jasper House. There, she was eventually reunited with one or more survivors of her own community and language. Historians mention that the Indigenous women led a very hard life and had to do all of the hard work in camp. Suicide was a last way out.

Like all other fur-trading posts in Canada's prairie provinces, the main food supply of Jasper House was pemmican, made from pounded bison meat and fat, sometimes enriched with Saskatoon berries. During the fur trading epoch, the number of bison on the plains east of the mountains was still amazing, as noted by all contemporary travellers. Riding horses, their progress was sometimes blocked by massive herds. Canoe parties reported that in some years miles of shoreline were piled high with the washed-up carcasses of bison that had broken through the ice in winter and drowned while crossing the river in their seasonal migrations.

The number of bison killed by the fur traders and their employees seems shocking by today's standards. Metis hunters shot and butchered hundreds of bison to prepare pemmican for the voyageurs. It was packed in bags made of bison hides. Each traveller was allotted eight pounds (3.6 kg) of meat a day. The appetite of the fort's residents was also demanding, and the number of visitors could be high. For instance, Fort George was inhabited by 70 men, 60 women, and numerous children. The population of Fort Edmonton was on the same order of magnitude, and Paul Kane wrote that there also were 200 to 300 dogs.

Within the protection of a six-metre-high palisade of upright timbers, company forts enclosed a dozen or more buildings, including an icehouse for the storage of meat. A square excavation in the ground was big enough to contain several hundred bison carcasses, with the heads and legs cut off. The bottom of the hole was neatly cemented with big blocks of river ice, and the top was insulated with a thick layer of straw.

For the mass capture of bison, the plains peoples constructed buffalo pounds at strategic locations and drove the fleeing herds into a corral, its opening widened with a winged funnel. Hundreds of bison could be caught by this ancient method. Panicked and milling about, the animals were then killed. In southern Alberta, native people banded together to stampede bison across a precipice, forcing the fleeing animals to jump to their death. The arrival of Europeans altered the balance between humans and bison. The introduction of the repeating rifle made it possible to kill more easily, while the invention of new tanning methods drove up the monetary value of bison skins. Commercial hunters, prospectors, and early settlers joined in the slaughter, while south of the border, exterminating bison was promoted as a means of controlling the Indigenous population and forcing an end to their nomadic way of life. The impact of all this began to show by the late 1800s. The last of the great bison herds were gone by 1885.

The former lords of the plains were often starving and hit hard by contagious diseases brought in by the Europeans. Entire villages succumbed to smallpox. Historian James MacGregor wrote that by the 1870s, the native people of this area had been reduced to a fraction of their former numbers.

From 1835 to 1850, the man in charge of Jasper House was Colin Fraser, a colourful piper from Scotland, who dazzled the locals with his bagpipe lament. Part of his task was to guard two or three hundred horses the company kept at Jasper House for use by the fur brigades. Colin and the next postmaster, Henry Moberly, loved hunting and made extensive horse trips along the so-called pitching trails in the foothill forests. On one pack trip, accompanied by many Indigenous and Metis hunters, they shot some seventy moose in addition to caribou, bighorn sheep, and mountain goats. Elk were notably absent in their report. The explanation has to do with the fact that elk are more vulnerable to overhunting than moose. Elk are herd animals and like to graze on open hillsides and montane meadows. By contrast, moose are loners and isolate themselves in the forest. The absence of deer is harder to explain. Bighorn sheep, despite their open habitat, are less vulnerable to hunters because they frequent high elevations throughout the mountains. In 1859, company man Henry Moberly hunted sheep with dogs, and in 1859, when the cyclic population of snowshoe hares was at or just past its cyclic peak, he treed and shot many lynxes.

As to the shooters' preferences, they were not fussy. Birds —even owls and eagles—were bagged and went into the pot. Added to their menu were whitefish and trout netted in the lakes. The group might stay two or three weeks at a location until the vicinity was hunted out.

Historian James MacGregor mentions that Indigenous hunters made concerted efforts to drive all large animals in front of them along the Bosche Range, which starts due west from Jasper House and runs all the way to Munn Creek, a tributary of the Wildhay River. The ridge ends in a steep escarpment. Yelling and shooting their guns, the hunters caused the frightened animals to panic and forced them to jump to their death down the cliffs. At the base of the ridge, women and old men would be waiting to slit the animals' throats. The meat was cut up and dried for transport back to Jasper House.

With that kind of hunting pressure, it's little wonder that the wildlife inventory of Alberta went into a tailspin. In the words of a senior government biologist, the large mammal population of the province reached its lowest ebb at the turn of the nineteenth century. Extremely cold winters were a contributing factor. Finally, when the concept of conservation began to spread, hunting was restricted and outlawed in the national parks of Banff and Jasper.

According to a French saying, the more things change, the more they stay the same. Today, more than a century after the establishment of Jasper National Park, its natural history and wildlife are again at the mercy of human travellers who use the park's lower Athabasca Valley as a transportation corridor on their way to and from the west coast. And again, the victims are its animals.

One day during the early fall of 2019, I was checking out the south shore of Jasper Lake, as always looking for tracks. Some fresh wolf sign led me to the edge of the trees, when a large black wolf suddenly sprang up out of the lower bushes, practically at my feet. Next instant, the animal streaked across the open shore flats, splashed through a shallow arm of the Rocky River and vanished into the woods on the opposite side. Having seen numerous wolves during my 55 years of field observations in the park, it was obvious to me that there was something wrong with this animal. Its back was hunched and it kept its body low to the ground, as if one or both of its hind legs were broken.

On the way home, I stopped off at the Pocahontas station near the park's east gate. The warden was at home. A few days ago, a travelling tourist had rung his doorbell to report that he had just hit a wolf running across the highway right in front of his car. The warden had gone out to look for the poor animal but he had found no sign of it in the roadside woods.

"This road is a killer," he said. "And it's getting busier all the time, especially with transport trucks. On their way to the west coast, they do not stop for the night. Some time ago, a truck hit a herd of elk and killed six of them. The guy did not even report it to us." During his many years of residence at the Pocahontas station, the warden had been called out all too often to pull dead or wounded animals off the pavement.

Since 1980, Jasper staff have kept track of wildlife mortalities on the Yellowhead Highway, which transects the park. As of 2018, the toll of dead elk had risen to 1,140. During the same period, the number of wolves killed on the highway was 79. Another 580 elk and 31 wolves were hit on the Canadian National Railway line, which parallels the highway and takes up a wide slash of the critically important Athabasca Valley. Over time, the traffic corridor passing through Jasper Park will become even busier, and the future toll of dead wildlife is certain to rise. Based on Alberta Transportation records, the number of vehicles passing the park's east gate has grown from an annual mean of 2,180 per day in 1980 to 4,900 in 2018. In an average year, 1.7 million vehicles drive through the lower Athabasca Valley, the park's critically important wintering habitat for elk and other animals. Trucks and cars often exceed the posted speed limit of 70 to 90 km/h. In tandem with the rise in Yellowhead traffic, the frequency of passing trains has also increased.

Faced with a similarly catastrophic traffic situation, Banff National Park, south of and adjacent to Jasper, started to take a hard look at methods for mitigating wildlife fatalities in 1992. Today, the four-lane Trans Canada Highway west of Banff is fenced off, and over its 82 km to the provincial border with British Columbia there are six overpasses and 38 underpasses for the safe crossing of wildlife.

"The decision to go to fencing," says Dr. Clifford White, retired manager of Ecosystem Research in Banff Park, "was made after losses for several species of animals had exceeded 20 percent of their estimated population in the Bow River Valley. For example, it was 20 percent for elk, 30 percent for moose, and over 30 percent for wolves and grizzly bears."

Tourist traffic through the congested traffic corridors of the Rocky Mountain National Parks is boosted by provincial advertising campaigns. My old friend Paul Ditters, a graphic designer who used to work for an Edmonton agency holding the lucrative Travel Alberta contract, reports that Dutch newspapers and magazines are plastered with ads promoting the glories of Canada's Rocky Mountain Parks.

How would a nature-oriented tourist actually react to the sight of highway fences in a national park, you wonder? In the spring of 2019, I was visited by two Dutch widows, who had rented a camper truck in Toronto and driven all the way to Victoria. In awe of the landscapes and the scenery, they were surprised by the crowded roads in western Canada and particularly disappointed by the divided and fenced highway in Banff. "Who wants to see an endless column of cars, trucks, and tourist buses in Canada's premier nature preserve?"

Unquestionably, the future of Jasper's road-kill situation is bound to follow the example set years ago in Banff. No doubt, Parks Canada authorities in Ottawa are monitoring the kill statistics and have set a time limit for taking measures that seem inevitable to mitigate the current problems.

Hopefully, and surely, it will lead to improved security for elk and other animals, while at the same time, fencing would remove the traveller's worry about animal collisions on the highway. An added positive would be the feeling that something has finally been done to lower the damage we are doing by our mechanized intrusion into one of Canada's most majestic natural monuments.

CHAPTER 23
Perspectives

Sixty years ago, when a citizen of Holland—one of the smallest and most densely populated countries in the world—wanted to immigrate to the second largest country on the planet, he or she was carefully vetted. In 1959, I started out by applying for and filling out government emigration papers, followed by a maddeningly long wait for a personal interview at the Canadian Embassy in The Hague. Once there, successful applicants were selected on the basis of their education, occupation, language skills, attitude, and financial position. After a physical examination by a medical doctor, I was sent home again for another agonizingly long wait.

In those days, migration was a win-win for both Holland and Canada. To reduce the rate of its population growth, Holland was happy to let its young people leave. Conversely, Canada wanted to add to its thinly spread workforce, and in contrast to today's policies, new immigrants did not have to pay any fees for admission. Quite the contrary; the Netherlands and Canada sent you on your way with a financial incentive to cover the cost of travel and a few days of accommodation. However, Canada was quite particular as to your destination. Asked where I would like to settle, I had unhesitatingly chosen Vancouver, because it's there that two attractive habitats meet: ocean coast and mountains. However, official permission to go there was refused, because British Columbia's unemployment rate was considered too high. However, the embassy official was willing to send me as far west as booming Calgary. Once there, I was free to take the bus and travel on at my own initiative and cost.

The three-day rail journey from Montreal to Calgary was made extra enjoyable by a comfortable seat in the passenger dome of the Canadian Pacific. Watching the forests and lakes of Québec and Ontario gliding by, I was thinking of pristine wilderness with wolves and bears, a dream for which I had left my native country. However, the closer the train got to my destination, the more the landscape went through an increasingly monotonous metamorphosis from boreal forest to farm fields as far as the eye could see, pockmarked with reedy sloughs and sectioned by barbed-wire fences.

Promotional literature for Alberta, acquired before my departure, included spectacular photos of the Rocky Mountains with wild rivers and waterfalls. But as the train rolled on westward, mile after mile, that kind of scenery was sadly missing, and by the time the outskirts of Calgary came into view, I had given up all hope. Rows of free-standing wooden bungalows, painted pink, yellow, light green or white, stood on freshly bulldozed mounds of raw earth. Not a tree in sight.

Why, oh why, had I decided to leave home only to end up in this barren place? Frankly, I did not think that I was going to stay here more than a month, long enough for a look around before returning home, not as a failed emigrant, but as one who had given it an honest try. That one-month stay became a summer season, which was tentatively extended and eventually grew into sixty years.

Before leaving Holland, I recalled that a fellow Dutchman, a former colleague at a publishing company where both of us had been employed, had also emigrated to Canada, and he too had been sent to Calgary. When I wrote to his overseas address, Jan Buur promptly replied to say that he would be happy to welcome me. All I had to do, upon arrival at the Calgary train station, was to locate a pay phone and call his residence. His wife would then alert him at his current place of work. On the long-awaited day in July 1959, Jan showed up in his big American car, and after a lively greeting, he drove me to his home on the east side of town.

Although I had never met his wife, she was kind enough to make room for me in their modest house, even though she already had two guests from Holland, Jan's brother and their mother. In the next few days, Jan kindly advised and helped me with finding a rental accommodation of my own. A day after my arrival, he took me to the printing shop where he worked and introduced me to the art director. The same day, on the merits of my portfolio, I was offered a job in my own trade, as a graphic designer. My salary, as it turned out, was about half the usual rate.

"How lucky can you get," Jan commented, a big smile on his face. "When I started there, I was told that I could sweep the floor and clean the toilets."

Very pleased and relieved to get my feet on the ground, I now could concentrate on what had brought me here in the first place, the pursuit of unspoilt nature, the hope of finding birds and mammals that had become rare or extinct in my country of birth.

198

The Buurs lived in an older part of town, across from a golf course and within easy walking distance from the Bow River Valley. At that time, golf had not yet become popular in the Netherlands, and when I came across a little white ball that looked like a bird's egg, lying on the shorn grass, I picked it up for a closer look. Alerted by an outburst of shouting from a group of people farther back down the meadow, I dropped the ball and hurried to the nearest wood. Struggling through the trees, I emerged in the clear on an open riverbank several metres above a fast-flowing stream. With the evening sun in a clear sky, I stood admiring the glorious scenery, until my reverie was suddenly shattered by a very loud explosion, as if someone had thrown a brick that had just missed me and splashed into the water. Had I been followed by an angry golfer? Or had I perhaps trespassed on private property?

I do not quite remember how and when it dawned upon me that the startling splash had been made by a beaver, slapping its muscular tail on the surface of the water as a warning to others of its kind. Swimming silently, just its nose and eyes above water, that beaver had remained hidden from my view. But with its super sense of smell, it had no doubt picked up my sweaty BO drifting down over the river.

Apart from a few towering evergreens, most of the trees in this valley were poplars; some huge, others just saplings. Here and there, I noted a few slender birches and alder. Later I learned that the number of tree species in Alberta is very much less than in other regions of the Americas, depending on how far south the glaciers had descended during the last ice age. For instance, the list of Ontario's native trees and shrubs is over 120, compared to about 18 in Alberta. The explanation is that some ten thousand years ago, a mere instant in geological time, most of Alberta had been buried under a mile of ice. After the big melt, only a few hardy species had managed to put down roots this far north.

The astonishing realization was that these trees were old-growth and that none had been planted by people, quite different from Holland where practically all woods had to be reseeded and cultivated after the original forests had been cut down for fuel or building material. Looking up at the huge poplars around me, with their rough bark and lofty crown of wind-rattled leaves, I was awed.

There was another discovery in store for me that magic evening. Upon a close look at the stumps of aspen saplings that had recently been cut near the riverbank, I noted that the surface of the wood was gouged by the marks of teeth. And slowly, unbelieving at first, I had to come to the exciting realization that the beaver, one of the animals I had hoped to find in the wilderness, was actually living in the middle of the big city.

Since then I have spent a lot of time along small tributaries of the Bow River, intrigued by the way this industrious rodent managed to avoid its many enemies and survive the long winter. Near my hometown, the village of Beverwijk is named after the beaver, which in the dim past must have been common in all wetlands of Europe as well as in North America. How marvellous was it that I had found this fabled furbearer, with the scientific name of *Castor Canadensis*, on my first nature outing in the country of my choice.

As I read later, two centuries ago the beaver had played a pivotal role in European exploration of Canada. Beaver pelts became the gold standard of the forest, and men's top hats, made of beaver fur, were all the rage in the fashion capitals of Europe. In 1811, the intrepid Scot David Thompson, a fur scout for the Hudson's Bay Company, became the first European to cross the Rocky Mountains overland to reach the company's western trading post of Fort Vancouver. While he and his French competitors had largely been motivated by the demands of commerce, my meek venture into Canada had nothing to do with monetary politics.

During my youth in war-ravished Holland, books and other information sources about nature had been scarce, a far cry from today's rich kaleidoscope of articles, photos, films, and television. Public schools were often closed, and my formal education was cut short to a minimum of secondary learning. After the war and a few years at a college, where I was taught English, French, German, and Latin, as well as my own tongue, I concentrated on what would become the dominant language of the western world. Striving to become a wordsmith in English was a process I greatly enjoyed. Today I take a fierce pride in being my own editor, whereas other writers have to depend on a battery of professionals. In my scientific publications I simply report what I have seen, while giving credit to other researchers. For better or worse, I have often invited one or two co-authors, people who saw some of what I had seen. Adding their name and position lent credibility to my information, although it might backfire if my co-authors later changed the order of names and placed theirs first. A recent case was particularly puzzling, concerning one of my proudest reports, titled "Elk and Wolves in Jasper National Park from Historical Times to 1992." For that technical paper I had invited a Jasper Park warden and an Alberta carnivore biologist as co-authors. That joint publication was recently listed in a self-published book by the biologist, who had switched the rankings and placed himself first, while I was demoted to second place. Only the cream of scientists are fair in citing others, or so it seems to me. I am not sure what is more irritating, to see one's publications and insights ignored, or stolen and copied. After a number of such unpleasant experiences, I came to agree with the opinion of famous geneticist Dr. David Suzuki, who in one of his older newspaper columns wrote about the myth that scientists are objective and open to new ideas. He blamed their lack of integrity on an inability to rise above their humanity.

One of the joys of immigrating to Canada was the openness of its society. In 1964, soon after Irma and I had moved to Edmonton, we joined the local bird club and learned that the core of that group consisted of university people, and that they were approachable. One of the friendly professors I met was the late Otto Hohn, an immigrant from Switzerland, who was a medical doctor as well as a birdwatcher. When he heard that I was very much interested in peregrines, he asked whether I was familiar with a paper by Gustaf Rudebeck. I had never heard of him. To my astonishment, at the following bird club meeting, Otto handed me a photocopy of that publication. It was the first science paper I had ever read, and it opened my eyes to what could be done by just watching hawks in the field. Rudebeck was a Swedish ornithologist who looked at the hunting habits of falcons and other raptors in the early 1940s. While Sweden remained neutral during the WWI1 inferno that engulfed the world, Rudebeck was quietly recording the migrations of northern birds at Falsterbo, the southern tip of Scandinavia, which later became a famous mecca for birdwatchers. In his paper, he described the hunting methods of peregrines and what they were seen to catch. His list of observations amounted to eighteen kills, which impressed me very much. Little did I know then that I, after sixty years of watching, would beat him numerically by a factor of about thirty.

Rudebeck's unique publication added value to what I had begun in Holland before emigrating. Each fall when fieldfares and other thrushes came down from the north, I waited in the cover of bushes for the hawks that shadowed the migrants. In those early days peregrines had become increasingly rare, but the sparrow hawk, a medium-sized accipiter, was still quite common. Like Rudebeck, I kept notes of the number of kills I saw, the hunting methods used, and their success rate.

After the peregrine's exciting comeback to Europe and North America, this celebrated raptor has become the most studied bird species ever. In

2007 my growing list of publications drew the attention of a professor at the University of Wageningen in the Netherlands, who invited me to write a doctoral dissertation on the hunting tactics of peregrines and other falcons. On February 18, 2009, at the age of 75, I was honoured as the oldest PhD ever to graduate from that illustrious institution.

As explained in the introduction to this book, my decision to immigrate to Canada had much to do with a fervent desire to observe wild wolves. That iconic apex predator has since become the most studied mammal in the world. In 1983–1992, I served as the editor, principal writer, and graphic designer of the quarterly *WolfNews*, published by the Canadian Wolf Defenders and funded by World Wildlife Fund Canada. In its ten years of publication, I wrote hundreds of newsworthy articles, notes, and reviews pertaining to wolf conservation, management, and research. The eight-page magazine was well illustrated, printed on glossy paper, and mailed to subscribers and supporters throughout the world. By the time I withdrew from that self-imposed task, the wolf wars seemed to have come to a temporary stalemate. On the cover of the last issue, I summed up the attitudes of the main debaters involved. The lament of one big-game hunter and wildlife manager was thus: "We kill thousands of moose, deer and elk in hunting season each year. It's ridiculous that we are not allowed to kill a few hundred wolves."

A government wolf scientist kept sitting on the fence and said: "Wolf control to increase ungulates is perfectly acceptable. However, it has become socially unacceptable." Many other wolf scientists wanted to continue their more and more sophisticated research. The following laconic quote is from an experienced American wolf researcher: "One radio-collared wolf from Alaska dispersed and mated with a radio-collared wolf from the Yukon. Unfortunately, they did not have radio-collared pups."

Interestingly, wolves, dispersing from Germany, have in recent years showed up in the Netherlands, creating havoc in agricultural regions by killing domestic sheep, although the predators are welcomed by the majority of city people. In 2018, two or more wolves had settled down in the woodlands of the Veluwe and produced pups.

Great changes have taken place in other areas, too. In the 1950s and 1960s, when I left the country, peregrines had been brought close to extinction in western Europe. After the end of the pesticide era, they spread into Holland, and their 2019 breeding population is around 200 pairs. Also the sea eagle, of which I as a boy could only dream, is now a year-round resident. As of 2019, the count of tree nests built by the white-tailed eagle has increased to nineteen.

In various aspects of nature management, the Dutch have been innovative and industrious. Fenced reserves with dense populations of deer, formerly confined between highways, are today interconnected by overpasses and underpasses. To keep grasslands open and free of woody brush, ecologists have introduced exotic cattle. However, their idealistic try at creating a so-called 'new wilderness' has gone spectacularly overboard. After the former Zuiderzee had been drained in stages and turned into an agricultural polder, the wettest corner that would not fall dry completely was designated as a National Park and called the Oostvaardersplassen. This reedy wetland of 56 square kilometres was fenced and stocked with hoofed mammals, including Konic horses, Heck cattle, and red deer. The idea was that the herds could be left alone and would be controlled and limited in number by their food supply. In the absence of hunting by humans and large predators, the herbivores increased to an astonishing density. By 2012, there were 3,300 red deer, 1,200 horses, and several hundred Heck cattle. There was no shortage of natural forage during the growing season, but during winter the meadows were grazed into the ground and the woods destroyed. To the dismay of farmers and city people alike, the animals starved and succumbed in droves. After years of expert meetings and despite huge protest demonstrations by the general public, park biologists boasted about their unique experiment and continued to sell the park internationally as 'the Serengeti of the North.' In 2018, forced by escalating demands and controversy, several thousand deer were shot and most horses removed. Eventually, the park's managers were forced to concede that their notion of 'rewilding' the place had failed. The way I see it, their embarrassing disaster had sprung from a genuine desire to create a wilderness ecosystem unspoilt by human activities, a dream I can identify with, a dream that inspired me to leave Holland and immigrate to Canada.

CHAPTER 24
Companions and Credits

S ome of the most memorable wildlife experiences came my way when I was camping solo in the backcountry of Jasper, but the reason I often went alone was that I could not always find someone to come along. My most trusted hiking buddy was Peter DeMulder. Born in Belgium, he had immigrated to Canada with his British wife in the same year as Irma and I. We met at Beaverhills Lake. He was a keen birdwatcher and very interested in wild country, but except for road trips to the mountain parks and driving the Alaska Highway, he had not done any camping. He gladly accepted my invitation to join me on a backcountry hike to Willow Creek. As narrated in Chapter 4, we also made several bicycle trips into the Willmore Wilderness until we were stopped by the mixed blessings of summer: rain, mud, heat, mosquitoes, and the fear of meeting another grizzly bear with cubs. Peter jumped at my suggestion for a winter bivouac, and in short order we purchased a heavy canvas winter tent and a light metal woodstove, an idea I had thought of for years but had never acted upon.

As manager of a busy medical lab, Peter had to plan the timing of our trips well in advance, no matter what the weather forecast might be. He loved driving and never charged me a cent for gas, but he always insisted on leaving at 6 a.m. On our first trip, in the dead of winter, we parked the car on the side of the road within view of Jasper Lake. We loaded the tent and other camping gear on a toboggan and took turns dragging it through knee-deep snow while the other guy broke a trail on snowshoes. Upon reaching the base of the Devona lookout hill, on the banks of the frozen Snake Indian River, Peter exclaimed that he had never in his life been so tired. The day was short, though, and we got to work at once, clearing a patch of ground among the trees and cutting pine saplings for tent poles. Blocks of wood served as basic furniture, and our sleeping bags were spread on a thick mattress of fragrant spruce boughs.

Near dusk, we were ready for the big moment of lighting the wood stove. Within minutes, the temperature inside the tent rose to tropical values.

With no shortage of fuel or clean snow to melt for water, we were happy and comfortable. That night the outside thermometer dropped close to minus 30, but the morning was calm and clear, and we immensely enjoyed a brilliant winter day.

Upon leaving, we dismantled the tent and cached it in the woods. At each subsequent arrival, over many winters, Peter delighted in setting up camp, always finding some new way to increase our comfort. While there, we enjoyed encounters with various wildlife, including wolves, cougars, foxes, pine martens, bighorn sheep, deer, and elk. Birds were few. Peter was always pleased to call in a boreal chickadee or spot a black-backed woodpecker.

As the raven flies, our camp was no more than five kilometres or so from the main highway transecting Jasper Park, but vehicle access to our spot was restricted. By mid October, the narrow Celestine Road into the district was closed to the public and often blocked by drifting snow. To reach our campsite, we preferred to canoe across the Athabasca River or cross the ice after Jasper Lake had frozen over. Both of these approaches could be hazardous, dodging ice floes in the turbulent river or carefully choosing our way around open leads in its outlet. For safety on the partly frozen lake, I had devised a pair of skis consisting of long two by fours with a leather strap to fit our boots. Peter never bothered with these awkward contraptions and just started walking, testing the ice with a small stick and picking his way across. All I had to do was follow his tracks. This is when I began calling him Mister Intrepid. Years later, looking back on our ice crossings, Peter shuddered at the risks we had run. The way I see it, we must have had a guardian angel perched on our shoulders in those days.

On two occasions, though, recognizing the critical condition of the rotting lake ice and extensive overflow, I refused to agree to his foolhardy plan of crossing the lake, and I insisted on walking the extra twelve kilometres or so around the lake to Snaring. That decision may well have saved our lives.

I am not quite sure when Peter and I stopped making winter trips to the mountains. One day, after tracking the local wolf pack, we sat down in the late winter sun on the banks of a frozen beaver pond. I had just made a small fire of dry spruce twigs to melt a pot of snow for tea, a ritual Peter loved, when he suddenly placed a hand on his chest and said: "I am in trouble …"

Evidently, his heart problem was acting up. I quickly doused the fire and prepared to leave. We silently threaded our way back through the woods and across the hillsides, taking an hour or more to reach the warden cabin where we were staying for the night. Upon arrival, without a word, and after having taken his medication, Peter retired to his bed, while I rekindled the stove. After a long silence, he roused, and I softly asked how he was doing. "I am all right," was all he said.

To this day, when I climb the familiar escarpment behind our former campsite and scan the vast hinterland of mountains and river flats, I marvel at the memory of the many secluded beauty spots Peter and I discovered and revisited, with him as my ever-cheerful companion.

Sometime during the early 1980s, at a meeting of the Canadian Wolf Defenders, I met Brian Genereux. A mountain hiker himself, he quickly warmed to my stories about Jasper and soon proved to be a most reliable and helpful companion. We never cancelled a planned trip over the 38 years of our association. Although wolves were of major interest to us, Brian did not care for their predatory habits and turned away when he thought that they had made a kill. In the cabin, he wouldn't even squash a fly or mosquito, and instead took the trouble of catching these insects in his hands or a towel and releasing them through the open door. When mice were overrunning the cabin, I did not tell him that I was setting traps. Taking the life of any living creature was bad karma, he said.

As I got older and spent part of the afternoon at rest, Brian left the cabin on his own, walking the routes we had done together over the years. One day, when he had been out since midday and had not returned at dusk, I became deeply worried, and will never forget the immense relief when his silhouette finally darkened the cabin trail.

On several trips to Willow Creek and Devona, I had the pleasure of being accompanied by Irma and son Richard. My youngest brother Cornelis, on a holiday visit from Holland, happened to pick an unusually eventful couple of days. A professional engineer who had worked on major projects in England and the Middle East, he was a man of many hobbies, including nature study. A backcountry hike into the wilds of Jasper National Park with his emigrant brother was a dream come true. On an August afternoon in 1970, we canoed across Rock Lake and worked our way up Rock Creek as far as we could. We then stashed the canoe in the bushes, carried our packs up the Willow Creek trail and set up the tent on a beauty spot in the meadows. During the evening of the second day, the sky clouded over, but I soothed my brother's weather worries: "It doesn't rain much here if the wind is from the west." As darkness fell, the downpour began and did not stop overnight. At daybreak, while the rain was still pounding the canvas, I said: "We've got to get out of here before the road turns into a quagmire." We struck the tent and packed up. Fording Rock Creek was a challenge that we just managed without falling over in the raging torrent that reached to our middle. In our hurry to launch the canoe, we almost upset the craft in mid-stream. Fortunately, the parked car started and we managed to get up the muddy hill to reach the Rock Lake campground. But we needn't have hurried. "You won't get far," a man said. "The bridge is washed out."

Forced to stay at Rock Lake for several days, we soon ran out of food. But when the sky cleared a helicopter came in. "We've had six inches of rain," the forestry officer said. "All four bridges between here and Hinton are washed out. We are rebuilding the road. You guys need any help or food?" The following day he returned with some backcountry staples: five pounds of flour and a huge bag of wheat puffs.

Several years after I began my wolf investigations in Willow Creek, I met Ludwig Carbyn, who embarked on a doctoral wolf study project for the University of Toronto. We teamed up in the field and talked up a storm about our shared interest. Lu introduced me to the contemporary literature on wolves, which consisted of a few insightful reports, quite in contrast with today's flood of new and often repetitious studies. Provincial carnivore manager John Gunson opened my eyes to the published diaries of early European naturalists who ventured west as far as the Rocky Mountains. Of particular interest was the narrative of David Thompson, who is believed to be the first white man to travel through the Athabasca valley in today's Jasper National Park.

Over the years, I occasionally invited a companion on trips to Willow Creek or Devona, including Alan Ballash, Ludo Bogaert, Paul Ditters, Jan de Haan, David Henry, Cedric Hitchon, Arne Jonasson, Gordon Kerr, Kees Kunst, Ron Slagter, and Jim Wolford. Our camping comfort greatly increased when chief warden Duane West permitted me to use the Devona cabin. Special thanks are due to park wardens Wes Bradford and Greg Slatter for logistics support in the field and sharing their wildlife sightings. Greg came to my rescue after a near-tornado had picked up my canoe and deposited it upside down on the other side of the river. He and I cooperated on a paper for the Canadian Field-Naturalist (2009. 123:236-239), which illustrates how elk movements are influenced by their fear of wolves. Greg's part of the research included telemetry data on a radio-collared elk herd that fled back and forth between Devona and Rocky River, which I correlated with wolf presence.

My 1981 and 2006 interim reports on wildlife sightings at Devona were statistically analyzed by my mathematician brother Marius. Contemporary elk population data for this book were supplied by park biologist Mark Bradley, based on his annual road-side and aerial elk surveys in all of Jasper. He also reported the grim figures for wildlife fatalities in the park's transportation corridor. Provincial biologist Jeff Kneteman shared his 2018 aerial survey of Jasper National Park's bighorn population.

Self-employed as a commercial artist and an independent wildlife researcher since 1965, my long-term field studies of migrating peregrines at Beaverhills lake were conducted under a volunteer contract with the Alberta Fish & Wildlife Division, supervised by research director William Wishart. The arrangement included the standard remuneration for car mileage and meal expenses. My field observations of peregrines wintering on Vancouver Island were made affordable after Edo Nyland kindly invited me to stay at his huge house for several weeks each year from 1980 to 1994. My long-term peregrine and dunlin studies at Boundary Bay on the Pacific coast were part-funded by Dr. Ron Ydenberg of Vancouver's Simon Fraser University. He also sponsored three research periods of several weeks each at the Bay of Fundy in New Brunswick. Generous funding for my last three winters at Boundary Bay came through Dr. Mark Drever of CWS Delta. With the main focus on dunlins and peregrines we were particularly interested in parasitic interference from the ubiquitous bald eagles. Three periods of observations on the hunting habits of peregrines wintering on the Frisian coast of the Netherlands were made possible by Dutch Nature Reserve guardian Albert Ferwerda. In Canada, the late Dr. Wayne Nelson gave me a free ride to watch the big peregrines of Haida Gwaii.

From 1983 to 1992, I was editor, writer, and graphic designer of the illustrated quarterly WolfNews, published and paid for by the Canadian Wolf Defenders and World Wildlife Fund Canada. In writing this book, as well as for all of my earlier titles, I have been my own editor. Son Richard frequently helped out with computer problems and he sharply proofread the text of the current book. The final version also gained from a copy edit by Hancock House.

For the photographs that illustrate this and earlier books, I am indebted to Dr. Gordon Court, Don Delaney, Robert Gehlert, Brian Genereux, John Gunson, David Hancock, Dr. David Henry, Kay Hodges, Martijn de Jonge, Jane Lidle, Gerald Romanchuk, Monte Sloan, Mike Tabak, Jan Uilhoorn, Hank Wong, and the Public Archives of Canada.

The digital camera and the computer are wonderful technical tools that make publishing a lot easier than it used to be, but the tough part still is selling a book. World-famous Canadian author Margaret Atwood is fond of telling her readers that finding a publisher was a long and very frustrating process that made her feel ready to go back to sucking her thumb. When she finally found a Toronto publisher, he sent her on a promotional tour through the city's streets as a scantily clad Lady Godiva riding a white horse.

A published nature writer in my native country at the age of seventeen, it was a giant step for me to leave and begin again in Canada. Apart from the essential switch of language, my problem was the same as Margaret's: finding a publisher for my first book, which featured a full colour collection of my wildlife paintings. It was printed by a company in Saskatchewan. Another very productive and early contact began with biologist David Hancock of Vancouver. As to the current book, the 60-year title is my own choice, but the catchy predation phrase is David's. He also suggested a change in chapter sequence. Instead of beginning with my 1959 first arrival in Canada, he wanted to start my narrative with a first-hand observation of a prey-and-predators event, which was a better idea. I owe him a debt of thanks for the consistently reliable way his firm has kept abreast of sales and royalties over the years. I hope Hancock House will stay in business for many more years of productive cooperation.

EPILOGUE
Sixty Years of Change

My first visit to Jasper was sixty years ago. As a new immigrant from the Netherlands, I had already been to Banff National Park. So, by the time I got to Jasper I was prepared for the majesty of the Rockies. Approaching from Edmonton, the view of the front ranges was just as impressive and abrupt as the drive from Calgary to Banff. I read somewhere that central Alberta's mountain front is the most spectacular section of the continent-long chain of cordillera.

As of today, the highway through Jasper National Park (JNP) has not changed very much at all. It is still the same two-lane road, although it has been repaved and modernized a bit here and there, but unlike the twinned highway in today's Banff, the Yellowhead Highway transecting JNP is not fenced and there are no overpasses or underpasses to facilitate wildlife crossings. Compared with past years, Jasper's traffic volume has greatly increased and is now surpassing 1.6 million vehicles per year. The road's annual toll of wildlife has also risen.

Park staff have religiously recorded all traffic kills. From 1980 to 2018, elk fatalities amounted to 988 on the roads and 514 on the rails, for a total of 1,502 dead elk. Over the same time span, there were 524 highway casualties of bighorn sheep and an additional 398 were killed by the trains, adding up to 922 dead sheep in JNP.

These losses are all the more serious compared to the declining overall population. In 2016, the wardens' roadside survey in the main valley was down to a shocking low of 94 elk, compared with 700 in 1995. This represents a decrease of 87% over 21 years. The 2018 aerial survey of elk in all major valleys of the park was 318. This level of decline may seem unbelievable if you recall that official elk estimates for 1945 and 1970, respectively, were 3,000 and 2,000–2,500! What could be the principal cause of such a dramatic drop?

As to sheep numbers, biologist Jeff Kneteman of Alberta Environment kindly supplied the results of his 2018 aerial survey of all sheep ranges in

JNP. Similar surveys were flown in 1987, and the comparative data indicate an overall decline of 61%. The exact figures are 1,382 sheep sighted in 1987 and 842 in 2018.

In 1992, I gave a presentation at the Second North American Symposium on Wolves organized by the University of Alberta and the Canadian Circumpolar Institute. The title of my slide talk was: "Elk and Wolves in Jasper National Park, Alberta, from Historical Times to 1992." In 1995, I published a paper under the same title, co-authored by JNP wildlife warden Wes Bradford and Alberta's carnivore manager, John Gunson.

Here, for added perspective on the current and ongoing population fluctuations, I am reviewing some salient aspects of JNP's wildlife history. By the time of the park's establishment in 1907, Alberta's elk had been extirpated. They were reintroduced to the park in 1922, with 88 animals imported from Yellowstone. Due to complete protection and the absence of predators, the elk multiplied to 3,000 in 1945. These huge herds were overgrazing their winter range and competing with bighorn sheep. To reduce elk numbers, park wardens culled 250 elk per year. During that same time span, the return of wolves was viewed with misgiving. They were shot on sight, their dens and pups destroyed.

By the 1970s, the park's elk population had declined to 2,000–2,500. A major turning point arrived in 1974 with a very severe winter. By the end of March, snow was still one metre deep around Jasper town. Elk were starving. Furthermore, wolves had come back with a vengeance, so to speak. Between 1975 and the mid-1980s, elk estimates declined and stabilized at approximately 1,000.

The above declines were paralleled by my 1965–1985 data for the Willow Creek valley. By the end of the 1970s, elk were practically gone, and there is little doubt that the return of the wolves had been a crucial factor, particularly after the severe winter of 1974. Superimposed on these natural causes was heavy elk hunting pressure by humans on the provincial boundary at Rock Lake.

Although hunting was not a problem inside the park, elk declines were also major at Devona. In my 1981–2001 interim report to the park superintendent, I wrote that the mean size of the largest elk herds seen each winter was 49, and there was no statistically significant change over those twenty years. The largest group of mature elk bulls recorded during that period varied from nine to 22, with an annual mean of 16. Five years later, my 2006 interim report placed the annual mean of the Devona cow herds at 38, down from 49 in the previous tally. Between 2010 and 2017, the regression line dropped from 38 to 28, and bull groups seen from the lookout hill were down to five.

In March 2017, after the park's elk herd had declined to a remnant of earlier numbers, their traditional wintering grounds on the Devona flats were obstructed by a two-metre-high artificial berm along the Snake Indian River. Several hundred metres long, the berm was made of huge plastic bags filled with stones and gravel. This abominable and unnatural dike was built by railway crews to protect the CNR tracks lower down from river overflows. During that winter, the main channel had become blocked and diverted by an ice dam. Apparently, the berm will remain in place until a permanent solution is found to protect the CNR rails from floodwater when and if a similar problem might arise in future. In my 38 winters of experience at Devona, the 2017 river overflow was the worst I had ever seen. The plastic dike effectively discouraged me from continuing my visits to the Devona flats. During my last two-day trip in October 2018, I saw just one lone elk cow near the railway and a single bugling bull by the east end of Jasper Lake.

A review of historical information also adds perspective to the decline of the Devona population of bighorn sheep. The differences are dramatic. In March of 1969, during one of my earliest hikes to the Ram Pasture, I had taken a Kodak colour slide of a compact band of 25 mature bighorns on their traditional wintering grounds, a grassy bluff above the north end of Jasper Lake. This rare photo is reproduced and included in my interim reports. Most if not all of those 25 rams were full-curl. We may never see such a large gathering of the big boys again.

As detailed in my 2006 report the ram band declined from an annual mean of 18 members in 1981–2001 to 11 in 2001–2006. Since then, the group has collapsed to four in 2011. Earlier that winter, six rams were reportedly killed by the train, possibly while they were nibbling on grain spilled from leaking rail cars. In 2012, I recorded three rams, and none in 2014, 2015, and 2016.

A mixed band of sheep, consisting of ewes, yearlings, lambs, and sometimes one or two mature rams, traditionally used the sun-warmed slopes above the Snake Indian canyon. These sheep also suffered a statistically significant decline. As detailed in my interim reports, the largest band size varied between 21 and 77 members, with an annual mean of 40 in 1981–2001.

Between 2001 and 2006, the mean dropped to 26. The downturn persisted and could have nothing to do with the trains. The end phase was a near-total collapse. My last sheep counts obtained in October 2015 and March 2016 produced only 10 and 13 sheep, respectively. None were seen on the canyon in September 2016, March 2017, September 2017, and October 2018.

My interim reports and a paper published in the 2009 *Canadian Field-Naturalist* (123:236-239) include a discussion of the possible causes of the sheep decline, such as predation and a four-year drought. In 1993, the Ram Pasture was overgrown with Russian thistle, commonly known as tumbleweed, an invasive and drought-resistant weed accidentally imported from eastern Europe. This unpalatable and prickly annual spreads its seeds when native ranges are overgrazed. Fortunately, after elk and sheep numbers on the Ram Pasture collapsed, the range recovered and the thistles were again crowded out by native vegetation. The key to that recovery was low grazing pressure and ample rain. The summer of 2017 was the wettest on record.

The interplay of precipitation and large herds of hoofed mammals is fascinating to observe over the long term, and there is much to be said about that, but at this point I like to backtrack to the start of my sixty years of experience in Jasper National Park.

In retrospect, landscape disturbance in the lower Athabasca Valley had already begun by the time of the park's establishment in 1907. Then, two rival railway companies were battling it out over their planned route from Edmonton to Vancouver. Construction of the Yellowhead Highway was next. The road transected the park and crossed the western boundary into British Columbia via the Yellowhead Pass. In addition, there is the controversial oil pipeline. Sixty years ago, at the time of my first visit to Jasper, draglines and bulldozers were at work on a buried route from Alberta to Vancouver. More recently, the line's capacity has doubled and is again under review for more work. The pipeline corridor passes right through my long-term study area at Devona. During past stages of work, I was told to stay out of their way. Sadly, the latest round of track widening led to the destruction of the traditional Devona wolf denning site. In the winter of 2018–2019, the pipeline corridor became the trajectory for another invasive construction project, an overhead power line from Hinton to Jasper town.

Notwithstanding all of this disturbance in the lower Athabasca Valley, very little has actually changed in the backcountry. To their everlasting credit, JNP authorities have managed to keep out people on ATVs, snowmobiles, and four-wheel drive trucks, who practically are free to damage Alberta's foothill forests and provincial parks. Park Canada's managers and the Jasper Environmental Association, under the inspired leadership of Jill Seaton, its long-term and very committed president, have had to counteract recurring challenges from stakeholders inside and outside the park.

Things could have been much worse, though. For instance, during my first exploratory visit of Jasper's north boundary region, the provincial forestry officer stationed at Rock Lake mentioned that he and some like-minded colleagues were advocating for a new road to be pushed through the Snake Indian valley, all the way down to Jasper Park's main valley and the Yellowhead Highway. "It would give people a nice circular route for a scenic drive," the officer thought. During that same time period, spokesmen for Jasper town's business community were pressing their political masters in Ottawa with another great idea for opening up Jasper's tourism potential: a road from Maligne Lake up the Skyline Trail and across the alpine heights, back down to the main valley. Who knows how close these plans actually came to their realization?

Support for these schemes was not only coming from outsiders, but here and there also from inside the park. I remember visiting the Willow Creek park warden, who at that time was stationed year-round in his lonely cabin. He was mad at head office for not allowing his friends to come visit him in winter on their skidoos. In the meantime, snowmobile travel has been allowed into the Tonquin Valley for the benefit of those who run the tourist cabins. The packed trail gives wolves easy access to the high country where caribou used to isolate themselves, protected by undisturbed deep snow. In Banff National Park, outspoken wolf biologist Paul Paquet reported that wolf packs even take advantage of ski trails.

Suggestions and demands for opening up the mountain national parks were regularly voiced by Alberta's politicians. I recall public statements from that quarter to the effect that the province should take over the management of the national parks, because Travel Alberta could do a much better job of boosting the tourism potential of Jasper and Banff, and after all, these parks were on provincial lands. A critical case in point, long ago, was a proposal to hold the next winter Olympics in Banff, an idea that was narrowly defeated by public protest.

In the meantime, what has happened to Jasper's wolf population? As reported in previous chapters, there is no good news. Along park boundaries, trappers are maintaining permanent bait stations that are surrounded by steel snares.

And in the foothills north of Jasper Park, provincial crews continue to shoot wolves from helicopters with the excuse of saving the last of the woodland caribou from their predators. These professional biologists should be ashamed for having gone back to the dastardly methods of the past, the placing of strychnine poison baits that are indiscriminately destroying not only wolves but also wolverines, foxes, martens, weasels, ravens, and eagles.

As to the wolves of JNP's main valley, while they are protected from trappers and hunters, their major problem is traffic. From 1980 to 2018, official records include 76 road kills and 29 train kills, amounting to 105 dead wolves over the 31-year period, for a mean of 3.4 dead wolves per annum. As of 2019, the known wolf population of the Athabasca Valley has reached a new low. There was only one pack—consisting of three adults and two pups—ranging from the town site to Jasper Lake. In March 2019, one of the adults was killed by a transport truck. The wolves were feeding on the remains of an elk that had been killed on the road.

In 2017, Parks Canada surprised everyone by allowing a group of First Nations people to hunt in Jasper. The tribe receiving the permit was the Shuswap, currently residing in British Columbia. Their chief claimed that their ancestral hunting grounds once included the Jasper region. The permit was for one week in November, and a group of young band members were directed to walk the Celestine Road, which would then be closed to the public. Armed with modern rifles, they ended up shooting three bull elk, two bighorn rams, and one white-tailed deer, close to the maximum number of animals they were allowed to kill. Whether hunting by First Nations groups will become a new policy for some national parks remains to be seen. Rumour has it that other First Nations bands are clamouring for their turn.

As detailed in previous chapters, the diaries of Michel Klyne, who was the postmaster at old Jasper House in 1829–1834, prove that the earliest known inhabitants of the lower Athabasca valley indeed belonged to the Shuswap people. With their stone-age weapons, they were outgunned by newcomers from eastern Canada, the Assiniboines and Iroquois, who had already obtained guns, metal knives and axes from European traders. Historian James MacGregor describes the Iroquois as venturesome hunters, who explored every valley and watershed in the wide surroundings. Henry Moberly, who managed Jasper House around 1858, was a passionate hunter himself and often teamed up with groups of Indigenous people on extensive expeditions with a long train of pack horses. Starting from Devona, the hunters made concerted efforts, taking several days, to drive all hoofed mammals ahead of them along the Bosche Range, which is sandwiched between the Wildhay, Moosehorn and Snake Indian Rivers. In those days, this range and all other sun-facing slopes were practically devoid of trees, as can be seen on the rare photo taken in 1872, picturing Roche Ronde, northwest of Jasper House. Riding along the open ridge and making as much noise as they could, shouting and shooting their guns, the hunters drove the animals before them all the way to the canyon above Munn Creek. There, the panicked animals were forced to jump or fall down to their death. Today, trying to drive hoofed mammals along the same route would be futile, because after a century of fire protection, the Bosche Range and all other neighbouring slopes have become overgrown with trees. The reason those mountainsides were bare in the 1850s is no secret. The "old people" knew how to manage their environment. To them, it was important to keep trees down. Scouting for game, they wanted to be able to see far ahead, and they had an instinctive affinity for open ground where they could feel safe from ambush, and conversely, spot enemies in time. Furthermore, sun and wind kept snow cover down on open ground.

The natural plant succession on meadow habitats, given the right climatic conditions, is from grasses and forbs to bushes and trees. The main reason I stopped going to Willow Creek was that the formerly semi-open montane habitat had increasingly grown up to willows and bog birch. Due to the collapse of the elk population, and after outfitter horses had been banned, aspen trees had begun to sprout dense copses of saplings that blocked the trails and obscured the view ahead. Hiking the Willow Creek trail, I felt increasingly insecure and worried about suddenly coming face to face with bears.

The obvious method of restoring open ground is to burn the brush. By setting 'prescribed' fires, park staff had already made several attempts to clear the Willow Creek trail. The bushes readily burned, but by next growing season the roots sent up multiple shoots, fertilized by ashes. As reported in other chapters, by the mid 1980s, I abandoned Willow Creek and changed over to the park's main Athabasca Valley.

There, prescribed fires set by park staff had successfully created large openings between the town and the east gate. I was hoping for a major burn on the Devona flats, because much of the meadows had been taken over by wolf willows. However, to set fires this far down the Athabasca Valley would be risky, because the predominantly westerly winds might push the flames out of control and onto provincial and private lands beyond the park. The fire crews restricted their activities to the eastern flank of the lower Athabasca Valley, opposite Devona. Spot fires were safely set there and burned themselves out, until one day the flames became unstoppable and engulfed all of the Rocky River drainage, finally dying down 40 km up the heavily wooded mountain valley. Some wardens privately admitted that burning the conifers was a good thing anyway. The fire had rejuvenated and opened up the closed forest. The park office later sent out a press release to the effect that the Rocky River inferno had resulted in a fire guard that might eventually help protect the town of Hinton in the event of a runaway wildfire blowing out of control again during a period of drought and blustery winds.

In the past, before Jasper Park's establishment in 1907, the foothills and front ranges had been routinely set ablaze by First Nations people. As mentioned, they had their own reasons for doing so, including the improvement and maintenance of grassland habitat for big game, such as elk and bison, and to create a dead zone between potentially hostile peoples. The Indigenous residents probably did not worry much about the path the flames might take.

An early witness to the historical conditions was David Thompson, purportedly the first European to travel through the Athabasca Valley. In his 1811 journal, Thompson wrote that his journey across the foothills towards Jasper was often impeded by downed and smouldering trees. In his words, the forests were in a constant state of conflagration, due to wildfires repeatedly set by Indigenous people.

A century and a half ago, the early European settlers of the Alberta plains took a leaf from the native peoples and started fires to clear the land for agriculture. The plains between Calgary and Red Deer were kept treeless, and the parkland woods east of Edmonton, including today's Elk Island National Park, were burned year after year. When the fires died down over the winter season, they were ignited again the following spring. Such land-clearing methods of the early settlers are part and parcel of the historical literature on the province's past.

Of particular concern to me are the ongoing habitat changes around Cooking Lake. The former lake bottom that fell dry after the water level dropped around the turn of the last century has become overgrown with weeds and brush. The new land is several hundred metres wide. A few years ago, the reedy vegetation was hip-high. Locally, willows and aspen saplings are closing ranks, blocking the view of the water. Here, too, a natural method to control the brush would be by burning. The other proven method is heavy grazing. But there are no cows along the entire south and east shores of Cooking Lake. A third method of eradicating bushes and noxious weeds is with herbicides. No matter how convenient and effective their use may be for a variety of landowners, these chemicals have serious side effects on insects and birds. Repeated applications on agricultural crops have turned most of central Alberta into a dead zone. Open-country sparrows are practically gone. So are sharp-tailed grouse, a hardy native species capable of surviving the deepest snow because in winter they feed on the buds of poplars. Herbicide use is particularly deadly for the chicks of grouse and partridges because the supposedly harmless chemicals destroy the insects on which young birds depend. A new group of insecticides, called neonicotinoids, is used to treat agricultural seeds before planting. Subsequently, their residues drain into wetlands, with harmful impacts on insects and the food base for birds.

Herbicides were used in Jasper Park to kill a dense growth of canola plants that sprouted along the train tracks from seeds spilled by leaking rail cars. A more widespread problem is the natural succession of trees and bushes on formerly open grasslands. At Devona, masses of spruce seedlings are invading the montane meadows below the lookout hill, and mature conifers are growing taller, obscuring the flats. Often, when I walk the old track to the Snake Indian, I think back to a day, long ago, when I spotted three wolves walking by the river, in plain view and oblivious of me. Nowadays, at that same location any passing animals would be obscured by a wall of willows. Across the flats, I used to follow a well-trodden elk trail that was often padded down by wolves. Today, the route is overgrown and hard to find. Stumbling along, dwarfed by the bushes, I have to slap branches out of my face every step of the way.

What the park's future will be like remains to be seen. But it's good to remember the past.

Using huge plastic bags filled with stones, CNR crews erected a two-metre high dike along the Snake Indian River to protect the adjacent railway from occasional river overflows caused by ice dams

Photo Brian Genereux

The south-facing slope of the Snake Indian Canyon is part of the traditional winter range for a band of big-horn sheep.

PUBLICATIONS

Dick Dekker is the author of nine illustrated books about nature, 46 papers in refereed biological journals, 120 articles and notes in regional and local periodicals, 29 articles in national magazines, 11 technical reports, 26 articles and book reviews in newspapers, and four scripts for television specials. From 1983 to 1992, he was the editor and principal writer of the illustrated quarterly *WolfNews*, published by the Canadian Wolf Defenders and funded by World Wildlife Fund Canada.

Canadian Field-Naturalist

1969. 83:64–66. A Plea for Federal Protection of the Peregrine Falcon.

1972. 86:307. The Need for Complete Protection of the Peregrine Falcon.

1979. 93:296–302. Characteristics of Peregrine Falcons Migrating through Central Alberta.

1979. 93:68–69. With R. Lister, T. Thormin, D.V. Weseloh, and L.M. Weseloh. Black-necked Stilts Nesting near Edmonton, Alberta.

1980. 94:371–382. Hunting Success Rates, Foraging Habits and Prey Selection of Peregrine Falcons migrating through Central Alberta.

1982. 96:477–478. Occurrence and Foraging Habits of Prairie Falcons at Beaverhills Lake, Alberta.

1983. 97:303–306. Denning and Foraging Habits of Red Foxes and their Interaction with Coyotes in Central Alberta, 1972–1981.

1985. 99:90–93. Responses of Wolves to Simulated Howling on a Homesite during Fall and Winter in Jasper National Park, Alberta.

1985. 99:383–385. Hunting Behaviour of Golden Eagles Migrating in Southwestern Alberta.

1986. 100:272–273. Coyote Preys on Two Bighorn Lambs in Jasper National Park, Alberta.

1986. 100:550–553. Wolf Numbers and Colour Phases in Jasper National Park, Alberta, 1965–1984.

1989. 103:261–264. Population Fluctuations and Spatial Relationships among Wolves, Coyotes, and Red Foxes in Jasper National Park, Alberta.

1998. 112:709–710. Pack size and colour morphs of one wolf pack in Jasper National Park,1979–1998.

1998. 112:694–697. Over-ocean flocking by Dunlins and the effect of raptor predation at Boundary Bay, British Columbia.

2001. 115:395–401. With J. Lange. Hunting methods and success rates of Gyrfalcons and Prairie Falcons preying on feral pigeons (Rock Doves) in Edmonton, Alberta.

2009. 123:157–164. Declines of Bighorn Sheep, *Ovis canadensis*, on deteriorating winter range in Jasper National Park, Alberta, 1981-2010.

2009. 123:236–239. With G. Slatter. Wolf avoidance behaviour by American Elk, *Cervus elaphus*, in Jasper National Park, Alberta.

2015. 129:159–164. With M.C. Drever. Kleptoparasitism by Bald Eagles (*Haliaeetus leucocephalus*) as a factor in reducing Peregrine Falcon (*Falco peregrinus*) predation on Dunlin (*Calidris alpina*) wintering in British Columbia.

Journal of Wildlife Management
1987. 51:156–159. Peregrine Falcon Predation on Ducks in Alberta and British Columbia.

Canadian Journal of Zoology
1988. 66:925–928. Peregrine Falcon and Merlin Predation on Small Shorebirds and Passerines in Alberta.

2013. 91:25–29. High-tide flight by wintering Dunlins (*Calidris alpina*): a weather-dependent trade-off between energy loss and predation risk.

Journal of Raptor Research
1984. 18:92–97. Spring and Fall Migrations of Peregrine Falcons in Central Alberta, 1979–1983, with Comparisons to 1969–1978.

1995. 29:26–29. Prey Capture by Peregrine Falcons Wintering on Southern Vancouver Island, British Columbia.

1997. 31:381–383. With L. Bogaert. Over-ocean hunting by Peregrine Falcons in British Columbia.

2003. 37:91–97. Peregrine Falcon predation on Dunlins and ducks and kleptoparasitic interference from Bald Eagles at Boundary Bay, British Columbia.

2003. 37:161–163. With G. Court. Gyrfalcon predation on Mallards and the interaction of Bald Eagles wintering in central Alberta.

2005. 39:386–395. With R. Taylor. A change in foraging success and cooperative hunting by a breeding pair of Peregrine Falcons and their fledglings.

2006. 40:255–263. With R. Corrigan. Population fluctuations and agonistic interactions of Peregrine Falcons and Prairie Falcons in central Alberta, 1960–2006.

2016. 50: 363–369. With M. Drever. Interactions of Peregrine Falcons (*Falco peregrinus*) and Dunlin (*Calidris alpina*) wintering in British Columbia, 1994–2015.

The Condor
2004. 106:415–419. With R.C. Ydenberg. Raptor predation on wintering Dunlins in relation to the tidal cycle.

2012. 114:290–294. With D., M. Out, M. Tabak, and R. Ydenberg. The effect of kleptoparasitic Bald Eagles and Gyrfalcons on the kill rate of Peregrine Falcons hunting Dunlins in British Columbia.

Waterbirds
2011. 34(2):195–202. With I. Dekker, D. Christie, and R. Ydenberg. Do staging Semipalmated Sandpipers spend the high-tide period in flight over the ocean to avoid falcon attacks along shore?

Northwestern Naturalist
2018. 99:93–100. With M.C. Drever. Mule Deer, White-tailed Deer, and Wolves in Jasper National Park, Alberta, 35 years of sightings 1981–2016.

2020. (Submitted). Road and Rail Fatalities of Elk, Bighorn Sheep, and Gray Wolves in Jasper National Park, Alberta, 1980–2018.

Journal of Heredity
2014. 105:457–465. Hedrick, P.W., D.R. Stahler, and D. Dekker. Heterozygote Advantage in a Finite Population: Black Color in Wolves.

Natural Areas Journal
2014. 34:346–352. July Issue. The effect of water diversions and drought in the drying-up of Beaverhills Lake, a 140 km2 Ramsar Wetland in central Alberta.

Blue Jay (Saskatchewan)
1967. 25:175–176. Disappearance of the Peregrine Falcon as a Breeding Bird in a River Valley in Alberta.

1968. 26:16–17. Autumn Records of Parasitic Jaegers in Central Alberta.

1970. 28:20–24. Migrations of Diurnal Birds of Prey in the Rocky Mountain Foothills West of Cochrane, Alberta.

1972. 28:256. Merlin Captures Bat.

1973. 31:43–44. Red Foxes Make a Comeback after 30 Years.

1976. 34:151. Fish-catching Muskrat.

1979. 37:221–222. Long-tailed Jaeger Preys on Lesser Yellowlegs.

1984. 42:199–205. Migrations and Foraging Habits of Bald Eagles in East-central Alberta, 1964–1983.

1993. 51:179–180. Tree-climbing by Long-tailed Weasel: An Anti-predator Strategy?

2002. 60:115–116. Defensive behaviours of Long-tailed Weasels.

2005. 64: 115–117. Book review 'The Gyrfalcon.'

Alberta Naturalist
1976. 6:65–67. Mortality Rates of Red Fox Pups, and Causes of Death of Adult Foxes in Central Alberta.

1976. 6:73–75. First Sight Record of Western Sandpiper at Beaverhills Lake, with a Note on the Field marks of the Least Sandpiper.

1976. 6:184–185. Muskrat, Marbled Godwit, and Willet Feeding on Sticklebacks at Beaverhills Lake.

1977. 7:1–5. Field Identification of Peregrines, Prairie Falcons, and Gyr Falcons in South and Central Alberta.

1982. 12:1–5. An Introduction to Beaverhills Lake.

1983. 13:103. Gyrfalcon Sightings at Beaverhills Lake, AB. 1964–1983.

1983. 13:43–45. The Bald Eagle — Hunter or Scavenger?

1983. 13:89–90. A Wilderness Meeting — Wolf Pack Approaches Human Howlers.

1984. 14:48–49. Prairie Falcon Sightings in the Rocky Mountains of Alberta.

1984. 14:54–55. Golden Eagles at Beaverhills Lake.

1984; 14:98. Ancient Murrelet at Beaverhills Lake.

1985. 15:1–4. Jaegers at Beaverhills Lake, Alberta.

1985. 15:49–54. Elk Population Fluctuations and their Probable Causes in the Snake

Indian Valley of Jasper National Park; 1970–1985.

1986. 16:1–3. With G. Ericson. Releases of Peregrine Falcons in Southern and Central Alberta, 1976–1985.

1986. 16:65–67. Evaluation of Wolf-Ungulate Predation near Nordegg, Alberta (review of scientific report).

1986. 16:67–68. "Dogged" Pursuits of Deer by Lone Wolves.

1987. 17:173. International Wetland Status for Beaverhills Lake.

1989. 19:141–142. Otters Return to Jasper National Park.

1991. 21:84–88. Interview with carnivore manager John Gunson.

1992. 22(2):20. Book Review: Gray Wolf — Red Wolf.

1992. 22(4):10–11. Review: Alberta Releases Wolf Management Plan.

1993. 23(1):4–5. Historical and Contemporary Populations of Wolves and Elk in Jasper National Park.

1993. 23(3):53–56. Valley of the Falcons.

1994. 24(1):16–18. The Canid Equation.

1994. 24(2):35. Why do Long-tailed Weasels climb trees? And why have they become so rare?

1994. 24(3):54–57. Massive aerial survey of moose in northern Alberta.

Nature Alberta

2004. 34(3):10–12. Beaverhills Lake in the drought years 2001–2004.

2005. 35(3):14. Alberta sighting of an Ivory Gull — Long ago but vividly remembered.

2005. 35(4):10–13. The water crisis at Beaverhills Lake.

2006. 36(1):17–18. Sandpiper researchers discover new use for snot.

2006: 36(3):10–15. Wolf Wars: The Woodland Caribou issues in Alberta.

2007. 36(4):12–13. Historical perspective on Alberta's current wolf war.

2008. 37(4):26–30. Will Beaverhills Lake ever regain its former greatness? 124 years of Edmonton weather data show little or no difference in annual precipitation and temperatures.

2008. 37(4):42–43. Eagles, California Condors, and lead (poisoning).

2009. 39(2):22–24. Wolves black and grey: How grey is the gray wolf?

2009. 39(2):24–26. Black wolves and climate change.

2009. 39(3):11. Peregrine catches Hudsonian Godwit.

2009. 39(3):43. Herring Gull actively hunting ducks.

2010. 39(4):28–29. How to cope with the fearless coyote?

2010. 39(4):35–36. First Bald Eagle nest in River City downed by summer storm.

2010. 40(1):22–28. The ten last years of birding at Beaverhills Lake.

2010. 40(1):4. Coyote densities.

2010. 40(2):22–26. Woodland Caribou in Jasper National Park.

2010. 40(3):3–4. Coyotes, Foxes, and Long–tailed Weasels.

2011. 40(4):26–30. Birding highlights at Cooking Lake in 2009 and 2010.

2011. 40(4):31–32. Young Peregrines learning their trade at Cooking Lake.

2014. 44(1):25–26. Half a century ago searching for wolves in western Alberta was frustrating until routine poison controls were halted.

2014. 44(1):27. Finding wolves in central Alberta is rare, and their foot-prints can be difficult to tell from those of a dog.

2014 44(2):2–3. Editorial. Starling murmurations a misnomer.

2014. 44(3):42–43. Black Coyotes or Coydogs?

2014. 44(3):45–46. Grey Wolves, Black Wolves, Red Wolves, and Black Coyotes.

2016. 46(1):12–14. The Wolves of Jasper National Park

2016. 46(1):14. The case for a no-trapping buffer zone at Rock Lake.

2016. 46(2):20–25. Bugs and Birds at Cooking Lake.

2017. 46(4):20–24. Deer in Jasper National Park.

2017. 47(2):22–27. From Jasper to Yellowstone — Prescribed Indian fires, and wildfires.

2017. 47(3):22–25. The Supreme Predator — Hunting Habits of Peregrine Falcons migrating through central Alberta. Part 1.

2017. 46(4):20–24. Deer in Jasper National Park.

2017. 47(4):37–39. The Supreme Predator — Hunting Habits of Peregrine Falcons migrating through central Alberta. Part 2.

2018. 48(1):31–33. The Supreme Predator — Shorebirds and Peregrines. Part 3.

2018. 48(2):29–33. The Supreme Predator — Watcher at the Nest Site. Part 4.

2018. 48(2):5–6. The water level of Beaverhills Lake in 2017.

2018. 47(4):6. First Nation Band to hunt in Jasper National Park.

Edmonton Naturalist

1972. 1(2):7. Fall Migration of Ravens at Beaverhills Lake.

1972. 1(3):5–6. A Gyrfalcon at Cooking Lake.

1975. 3(5):6. Egret at Beaverhills Lake.

1975. 3(5):7–8. Red Foxes in Central Alberta.

1975. 3(10):9–10. Some Observations of Fall Migration of Geese at Beaverhills Lake, 1964–1975.

1975. 3(8):5–6. Snowy Plover and other Uncommon Shorebirds at Beaverhills Lake.

1975. 3(10):11–14. Fluctuations in Occurrence and Nesting of Shorebirds, Gulls, Geese, Herons, Pelicans and Cormorants at Beaverhills Lake as a Possible Result of Recent High Water Levels.

1976. 4:105–107. To Graze or not to Graze the Pastures at Beaverhills Lake.

1976. 4:230. Merlin and Mink Attacking Swallows.

1977. 5:144. Avocets and Habitat.

1977. 5:148. Chestnut-collared Longspurs at Beaverhills Lake.

1977. 5:149. Smith's Longspurs at Beaverhills Lake.

1977. 5:152–153. Beaverhills Lake — The Naturalist Guide to Alberta.

1979. 3:3 pages. Notes from Beaverhills.

1995. 23(2):23–31. Wolf articles and book review.

1995. 23(3):31–34. Watching Peregrines.

1998. 26(1):6–7. Twenty years of wolf watching in Jasper National Park.

1998. 26(2):10–11. Caspian terns, ospreys and peregrines at Wabamun.

1998. 26(3):9. Wabamun update.

1999. 27(1):10–11. With J. Lange. The downtown falcon versus pigeon show.

1999. 27(1):15–16. The great spectacle at Boundary Bay, B.C. — Peregrines and Dunlins.

2001. 29(1):11–13. The perplexing Christmas falcon.

2001. 29(1):22–23. The confusing large falcons.

2001. 29(2):7–8. Great whooper, small blooper.

2001. 29(2):22–25. The big slough near Tofield — Down and out?

Edmonton NatureNews

2004. 1(2):1. Picking a club logo.

2004. 1(2):16–19. Is Beaverhills Lake drying up completely?

2004. 1(3):1–2. Editorial. How to fill these pages.

2004. 1(3):3–6. Wolves abound in Jasper's Athabasca valley.

2004. 1(3):9–10. The saga of the satellite gyr.

2005. 2(1):2–3. Editorial. How (not) to fill these pages.

2005. 2(1):4. Editor's response. The caribou and gyrfalcon questions.

2005. 2(1):8–14. Lament for a dying lake: Probing deeper than the superficial.

2005. 2(1):17–18. The year of the short-ear.

2005. 2(1):19–21. Rare mammals in central Alberta: The elusive fisher and the not-so-rare raccoon.

2005. 2(2):7–8. Is the bald eagle nesting in river city?

2005. 2(2):12–13. Secret go the cats.

The Parkland Naturalist

2010: Autumn–Winter issue:14–16. Birding Highlights at Cooking Lake in 2009 and 2010.

2012. January–March issue: 18–19. The First Bald Eagles Nest in the City.

2012. April–June Issue: 20. Watching Peregrines at Cooking Lake.

2012. April–June Issue; page 21. The eagles are back, but ...

2012. July–September Issue, page 8. After losing their own two young, Edmonton's pair of Bald Eagles successfully fledged an orphan.

2013. October–November, page 13. After fledging two young of their own, a pair of nesting Swainson's Hawks adopted three orphans.

2013. January–April Issue, page 14. Four years of bird surveys along the changing shores of Cooking Lake, 2009–2012.

2013. January–April, pages 15–16. A comparison between Cooking Lake now and Beaverhills Lake then, before the latter's sad demise.

2013. May–August, page 16. Half a century ago searching for wolves in western Alberta was frustrating until poison controls were halted.

2013. May–August, page 17. Finding wolf sign in central Alberta is rare, and their footprints can be difficult to tell from those of a large dog.

2013. October–December, page 8. Last summer, the Edmonton pair of breeding Bald Eagles fledged two young from their riverside nest.

2015. May–August, Page 18: Black coyotes or coydogs? Grey wolves, black wolves, red wolves, and black coyotes. Page 19: Eagle update.

2016. October–December. The 2016 fall migration of shorebirds at Cooking Lake.

2017. Birding at Cooking Lake – Why are the avocets not producing any chicks this year?

2018. January–April, pages 18–19. Bill Bryson. A short history of nearly everything.

2018. May–August, pages 12–13. Spring migration of shorebirds, 2018.
2018. September–December 14–15. Cooking Lake Summer and Fall 2018.
2019. May–August 12–13. Buff-breasted Sandpipers in central Alberta.
2019. September–December. Pages 12–13. Cooking Lake, Avocets, Gulls, and Habitat.
2020. January–April. Pages 12–14. Beaverhills Lake, Past and Present.

Pica (Calgary)
1995. (4):14–19. Peregrine watching.
1996. 16(1):9–14. The Canid Equation.

Discovery Magazine (Vancouver)
1998. 27(1):35–37. Peregrines and Dunlins – The great spectacle at Boundary Bay.
2005. 34:20–22. Sandpiper researchers reveal new use for snot.

Thorkit Environment Magazine (Online)
2017. The wolves of Jasper National Park in the Canadian Rocky Mountains are snared on the park boundaries.
2017. Record wildfires and climate warming – Are most wildfires started by arsonists?
2017. The permafrost under the arctic tundra is thawing, causing huge problems locally and accelerating climate warming globally.
2017. Your job may be slowly killing you.
2017. Wolves return to Europe – A success story with growing repercussions.
2017. Insects and birds decline in Germany.

Technical reports
2001. Report for Environment Canada commissioned by the Superintendent of Jasper National Park: With W. Bradford, and other JNP park wardens Two Decades of Wildlife Investigations at Devona, Jasper National Park, 1981–2001. 51 pages plus appendices.
2006. Wildlife Investigations at Devona, JNP, for the winters of 2001–2006, with comparisons to 1981–2001. In cooperation with JNP Wardens Wes Bradford and Greg Slatter. (30 pp)
2007. Report for the Centre of Wildlife Ecology at Simon Fraser University: Roosting behaviour of wintering Dunlins on the North coast of Friesland. With special reference to predation risk by Peregrine Falcons and with comparisons to the pacific coast of Canada. (6 pp).
2009. Report for the Centre of Wildlife Ecology at Simon Fraser University under contract to Dr. Ronald Ydenberg: High-tide behaviour of migratory sandpipers in the upper Bay of Fundy, New Brunswick, with special reference to Peregrine predation. Preliminary field study conducted in August 1–7, 2009. (4 pp).
2011. Report for the Centre of Wildlife Ecology at Simon Fraser University: Interaction of Dunlins and avian predators at Boundary Bay, British Columbia, January 16–30, 2011. (8 pp).

2012. Report for the Centre of Wildlife Ecology at Simon Fraser University: Dunlin high-tide behaviour in relation to weather conditions and predation risk at Boundary Bay, BC, January 8–22, 2012. (6 pp).

2012. Report for the Centre of Ecology at Simon Fraser University. With Irma Dekker. Semipalmated Sandpipers and Peregrine Falcons at Mary's Point, New Brunswick. August 13–22, 2012. (6 pp).

2013. Report for Hemmera and Port Metro Vancouver. Roberts Bank Terminal 2 – Technical Data Report; Coastal Waterbirds – Assessment of changes of predation risk to shorebirds.

Magazine articles

1977. Nature Canada 6(4):2–5. The Peregrine – Master of the Air?

1982. Nature Canada Magazine 11(3):17–21. This Lake is for the Birds.

1983. Park News 19(3):10–12. The Wolves of Jasper National Park.

1987. Nature Canada 16(1):9. Veterans of a Thousand Hunts (merlins).

1987. Nature Canada 16(4):5–7. Helicopter Gun Ships Again?

1988. Park News 23(4):26–29. The Not-So-Natural History of Jasper Park.

1990. Nature Canada Magazine 19(3):29–33. Hit & Myths? A long-time observer takes a look at the hunting techniques of the peregrine falcon.

1991. Nature Canada Magazine 20(2):8–9. Coyote Fodder? A perspective on Swift Fox releases in Canada.

1991. Nature Canada Magazine 20(3):10–11. Grey Ghosts: A perspective on the Wolf-Caribou controversy.

1994. Nature Canada Magazine 23(2):19–20. The canid equation – The ancient rivalry between members of the wild dog clan has pitted foxes against coyotes on the prairies.

1994. Nature Canada Magazine 23(4):6. Vox Populi column: Is it time to curb native hunting?

1996. Nature Canada Magazine 25(1):7. Letters: Unduly negative. Perspective on the transfer of wolves from Canada to Yellowstone.

1991. Borealis 2(3):48. Banff and Jasper Elk Moving into Town.

1992. Borealis 3(3):46–47. Will Wolves for Yellowstone Come from Canada's National Parks?

1983–1992. WolfNews; Volumes 1–10; in total 240 pages, featuring articles, interviews and reports on wolves, wolf control, and wolf management in North America and Europe. Reviews of scientific papers and books on wolves.

1996. International Wolf Magazine 6(3):7–10. Do wolves think?

1996. International Wolf Magazine 6(4):6–10. Predator or Prey?

1998. International Wolf 8(2):6–9. Rocky Mountain Rendezvous.

1999. International Wolf Magazine 9(3):3–6. Is "Gray" Wolf a Misnomer?

2002. Canadian Geographic. Sep–Oct issue, page 20. Golden Eagle interview.

2003. Canadian Geographic. Nov–Dec issue. Yellowstone letter.

2006. Canadian Geographic. Mar–Apr issue, pages 56–62. Feature article: Dance of the Dunlins.

2007. Wild Lands Advocate. June Issue 15:3: Article pages 23–25. The Woodland Caribou Controversy.

2007. WildLands Advocate. June Issue 15:3: Article page 26. B.C.'s Woodland Caribou Recovery Plan calls for even more drastic measures than Alberta's current campaign.

2007. WildLands Advocate. October issue. Article pages 16–20. Alberta's War on Wolves – Then and Now.

2008. WildLands Advocate. June. Letters. Eagle Eyes and Wolves.

2008. WildLands Advocate. August issue. Letters page 29. Paying Paul, Robbing Peter (Beaverhills Lake and Ducks Unlimited).

2009. WildLands Advocate. December issue. Article page 14. Will Alberta's black wolves benefit from climate change?

2011. Bird Watching Magazine. December issue, pages 18–23. Ultimate Falcon (Gyrfalcon).

Newspaper articles, notes, and letters

1960. Calgary Herald (undated clipping). A Place for Wolves.

1960. Calgary Herald (undated clipping). Prairie Falcons (shot at nest).

1964. Edmonton Journal, November 12. Dissent Column: Is wolf control wrongly handled?

1966. Edmonton Journal, May 29. Dissent Column: National Parks should not be playgrounds.

1979. Edmonton Journal, October 13. Book review: Elk Island Park – The park year from a naturalist's eyes.

1987. Edmonton Journal, May 3. Amazing Alberta column: Prey and predators in a fragile balance.

1987. Edmonton Journal, May 31. Amazing Alberta column: Do peregrines like city prey?

1987. Edmonton Journal, June 3. Amazing Alberta column: A winter exposure to Jasper's beauty.

1987. Edmonton Journal, November 12. Feature article: The good old days? Not for wildlife!

1991. Edmonton Journal, August 4. Book review: Wildlife tales reveal his passion.

1991. Edmonton Journal, November 24. Book review: Books to dispel our fear of the "Meta Incognita".

1991. Edmonton Journal, December 22. Book review: Book fails to reveal vital details of wilderness tragedy.

1995. Edmonton Journal, June 6, page A11. Guest Column: Crying wolf over transfer to USA.

2004. Edmonton Journal, July 19. Guest Column: Dams threaten Beaverhills Lake wetlands.

2005. Edmonton Journal, October 5. Ideas Section. The slow death of a world-class wetlands area.

2005. Edmonton Journal, November 7, 2005. Letters. Elk ranchers need some guidance.

2005. Tofield Mercury, October 4 and 11. Parts 1 and 2: Beaverhills Lake then and now.

2006. Edmonton Journal, January 7. Ideas section. Jasper Park's wolves losing fear of humans.

2006. Edmonton Journal, May 31. Ideas section. Industry, not wolves, is biggest threat to caribou.

2007. Edmonton Journal, March 19. Some farms ill-equipped for raising deer or elk.

2007. Edmonton Journal. August 27. Opinion Page. Ingestion of lead threatens waterfowl and birds of prey.

2007. Edmonton Journal. September 30. Letters Page. 124 years of local weather data don't support global warming.

2009. Edmonton Journal. July 18. Letters. Lake water levels go up and down – The recent decline of Cooking Lake.

2009. Edmonton Journal. August 7. Letters. A rare casualty from summer storm – First successful nest of the Bald Eagle in River City blown down.

2009. Edmonton Journal. September 21. Opinion. Taming of the Wolf – Re: Wolves first tamed for their meat. And: Black wolves have evolutionary edge over their grey cousins: Black wolves and climate change.

2009. Edmonton Journal. November 9. Guest Column. Humans, as predators, have duty to control (fearless) coyotes.

2010. Edmonton Journal. February 8. Guest column. Create a woodland caribou sanctuary – Giving the animals a secluded refuge would mean Alberta could end the need for wolf controls.

2010. Edmonton Journal. December 5. Opinion. The reasons for war in Afghanistan: Industry benefits.

2011. Edmonton Journal. February 27. Sunday Reader Section, pages E1, E4 and 5. Standing their ground. Bighorn Sheep in Jasper National Park.

2011. Edmonton Journal. July 31. Opinion. Mosquito control hurts good bugs.

2011. Edmonton Journal. November 16. Opinion. Alberta's "big bad wolves" mere scapegoats.

2011. Edmonton Journal. December 15. Measurements don't mix. (Recent change in Alberta's liquor laws affecting impaired drivers).

2012. Edmonton Journal. March 2. Caribou decline not all that dire.

2015. Edmonton Journal. January 14. Ideas Page. Mass wolf cull an Alberta travesty. Initiative is ineffective and indiscriminate.

2015. Edmonton Journal. May 19. Ideas Section. Famous wetland is a sea of thistles.

2017. Edmonton Journal. July 6. Eagle-eyed rescuers deserve thanks. (One of four young bald eagles survives after their nest along the river nature trail was blown down.)

2018. Edmonton Journal. May 15. Too many signs distract motorists.

2018. Edmonton Journal, October 27. Strathcona County nature trails going to the dogs.

Television scripts

1996. Bison Beyond the Great River. Half-hour special. Karvonen Films.

1996. Wolves and Wapiti. Half-hour TV special. Karvonen Films.

1996. Under Jagged Peaks. Half-hour TV special. Karvonen Films.

1997. Mountain Splendour. One-hour TV special. Karvonen Films with the National Film Board of Canada.

Contributions to multi-author publications

1962. Silent paws and shining eyes. Pages 19–27 in: "Rubaboo—Stories for Young Canada." W.J. Gage Limited, Toronto; 209 pages.

1980. Beaverhill Lake. Pages 183–186 in: "A Nature Guide to Alberta". Hurtig Publishers, Edmonton.

1991. Song of the North—Rocky Mountain Rendezvous. Pages 62–73 in: "Buffalo Berries and Saskatoons. Stories and poetry from western Canada by Dutch Canadians." Editor H. Ruger. Netherlandic Press, Windsor, Ontario; 99 pages.

1992. Nature's Way—Elk, Wolves and Habitat. Pages 144–147 in: "Alberta's Parks—Our Legacy". Editor Donna Von Hauff. Alberta Recreation, Parks and Wildlife Foundation; 216 pages.

1996. With W. Bradford, and J. Gunson. Elk and wolves in Jasper National Park, Alberta, from historical times to 1992. Pages 85–94 in: "Ecology and Conservation of Wolves in a Changing World". Canadian Circumpolar Institute, Edmonton.

Dutch language publications

1951–1964. Two books, three nature guides, 29 articles in national magazines and newspapers, circa 150 illustrated stories about nature in youth weeklies.

1990–2010. Two books about nature in Canada and 19 articles in De Takkeling on falcon field studies in Canada and the Netherlands.

Other Titles by the Author

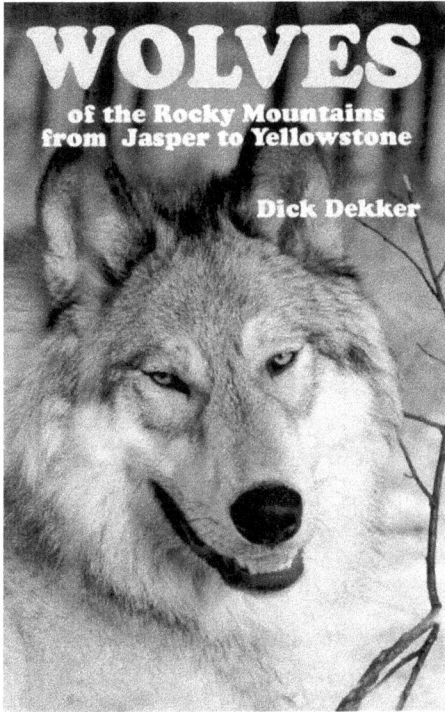

Wolves of the Rocky Mountains - from Jasper to Yellowstone
ISBN- 978-0-88839-916-3
1997, 208pp, 5.5 x 8.5

" *Dick Dekker's book chronicles his many years of watching wolves in the wilds of Jasper National Park, but it is also an unbiased insight into the science and politics of ever-controversial wolf management Dick's balanced perspective comes from his many years of observation, a directorship in the Canadian Wolf Defenders, participation in scientific wolf conferences, and from publishing his own wolf information. In this book he has woven a comprehensive story that needs to be told. It is the story of wolves in the Canadian wilderness, of their survival in the lean years prior to the 1970s, and of their ultimate triumph as the source population for the dramatic reintroduction to Yellowstone." -- John R. Gunson

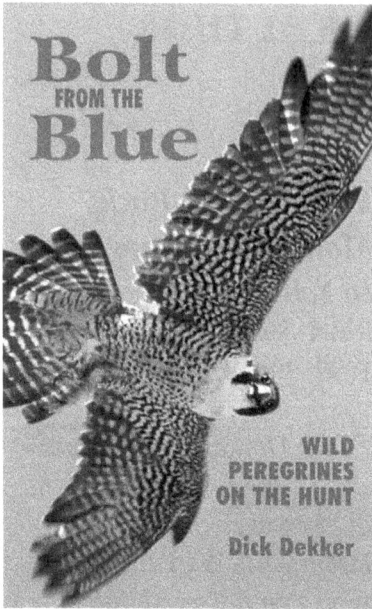

Bolt from the Blue - wild peregrines on the hunt
ISBN- 978-0-88839-434-7
1999, 192pp, 5.5 x 8.5

" Watching for migrating peregrines with Dick seemed, at first, about as inspiring as watching paint dry. After a few hours in the field it became very apparent to me that he is a man possessed of incredible patience -- the ultimate watcher. Dick positioned his car about a quarter mile from the lake (and consequently about the same distance from most of the bird life in the area) and repetitiously searched the sky and surrounding landscape with binoculars, for hour upon hour. Under these conditions, I rapidly lost interest in scanning empty skies, so it was no surprise that Dick saw the first peregrine of the day." -- Gordon Court, PhD

Hunting Tactics of Peregrines and other Falcons
ISBN- 978-0-88839-683-9
1997, 240pp, 5.5 x 8.5

" An outstanding scientific achievement, unprecedented really. This book, by a self-taught naturalist working mostly alone, reveals how careful and sustained field observations can yield fundamental scientific insights into how a predator interacts and influences its prey. Following in the best tradition of the great natural historians from Aristotle to Niko Tinbergen, Dick Dekker's work, spanning 48 years and based on 4,000 hunts and 460 kills by wild peregrines, has no parallel in the history of studies on birds of prey. -- Tom Cade, PhD

INDEX

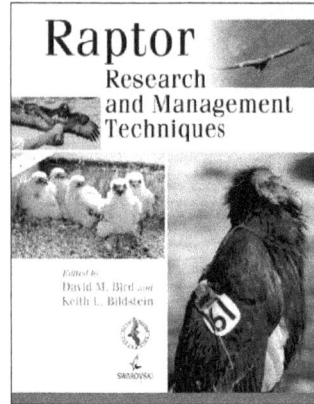

Behavior of the Golden Eagle: an illustrated ethogram
David Ellis, 2017
ISBN 978-0-88839-078-3 Trade SC
102pp, 88 illustrations, 8½ x 11

Enter the Realm of the Golden Eagle
David Ellis, 2013
ISBN 978-0-88839-704-1 Trade HC
496pp, 329 photos, 8½ x 11

Raptor Research & Management
David Bird & Keith Bildstein 2007
ISBN 978-0-88839-639-6 Trade SC
464pp, 66 photos, 8½ x 11

North Amer. Ducks, Geese & Swans
Frank Todd, 2018
ISBN 978-0-88839-093-6 Trade SC
208pp, 5000+ photos, 6½ x 9½

Wildlife of Southern Forests
James Dickson, 2017
ISBN 978-0-88839-017-2 Trade SC
480pp, 251 photos, 8½ x 11

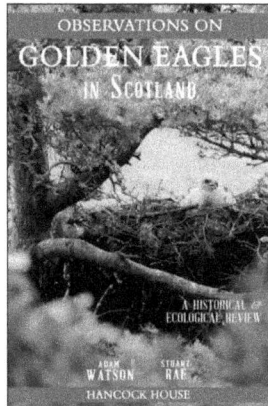

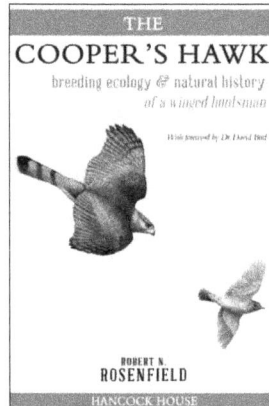

Golden Eagles in Scotland
Adam Watson & Stuart Rae, 2019
ISBN 978-0-88839-030-1 Trade SC
146pp, 116 photos, 6 x 9

The Cooper's Hawk
Robert Rosenfield, 2018
ISBN 978-0-88839-082-0
Trade SC
164pp, 73+ photos, 6 x 9

HANCOCK HOUSE PUBLISHER
19313 Zero Avenue, Surrey, B.C. Canada V3Z 9R
#104-4550 Birch Bay-Lynden Rd, Blaine, WA, U.S.A. 98230-943
(800) 938-1114   Fax (800) 983-226
www.hancockhouse.com   sales@hancockhouse.cor

www.ingramcontent.com/pod-product-compliance
Lightning Source LLC
Chambersburg PA
CBHW061726270326
41928CB00011B/2134